WEST ACADEMIC PUBLISHING'S LAW SCHOOL ADVISORY BOARD

MUSIC LAW
IN A NUTSHELL®

MARY LAFRANCE
IGT Professor of Intellectual Property Law
William S. Boyd School of Law
University of Nevada, Las Vegas

WEST ACADEMIC

860 Blue Gentian Road, Suite 350
Eagan, MN 55121
1-877-888-1330

Published in the United States of America

ISBN: 978-1-68328-673-8

OUTLINE

TABLE OF CASES XI

Chapter 1. Introduction 1

Chapter 2. Making Music Your Business 7

§ 2.1 Introduction 7
§ 2.2 Managers 7
§ 2.3 Booking Agents 13
§ 2.4 Producers 14
§ 2.5 Publishers 17
§ 2.6 Distributors 17
§ 2.7 Choice of Entity 20
§ 2.8 Special Considerations for Musical Groups 25
§ 2.9 Labor Organizations 26
§ 2.10 Insurance 30

Chapter 3. Copyright Law 33

§ 3.1 Introduction 33
§ 3.2 What Works Are Protected? 34
§ 3.3 Copyrights in Music and Sound Recordings 37
§ 3.4 Securing Copyright Protection: When Does Copyright Begin? 41
§ 3.5 Copyright Notice and Registration 44
§ 3.6 Who Owns the Copyright? 48
A. General Rule 48
B. Works Made for Hire 50
§ 3.7 Assignments 56
§ 3.8 Licenses 59

§ 3.9 How Long Does Copyright Last? 62
A. Works Created in 1978 or Later 62
B. Works Copyrighted Before 1978 64
C. Sound Recordings 68
D. Foreign Works 69
E. Works Created but Not Federally Copyrighted as of January 1, 1978 70
§ 3.10 Termination Rights 71
A. In General 71
B. Which Grants Can Be Terminated, and When 76
1. Post-1977 Grants 76
2. Pre-1978 Grants 77
3. "Gap" Grants 80
§ 3.11 Ownership Under Foreign Law 81
§ 3.12 Exclusive Rights of Copyright Owners ... 82
§ 3.13 Infringement 88
A. In General 88
B. Elements of Infringement Liability 88
C. Subconscious Copying 99
D. De Minimis Copying 99
E. Generative Artificial Intelligence 104
F. Secondary Liability 106
1. Contributory Liability 106
2. Vicarious Liability 109
§ 3.14 No Extraterritorial Reach 111
§ 3.15 Exceptions and Limitations 111
A. First Sale 112

B. Fair Use 113
1. Purpose and Character of the Use 115
2. Nature of the Copyrighted Work 117
3. Amount and Substantiality of the Portion Used 118
4. Effect on the Market for the Copyrighted Work 119
C. Other Exceptions and Limitations of Special Relevance to Music 120
1. Limitations Specific to Sound Recordings 121
2. Limitations Specific to Musical Works 122
D. Audio Home Recording Act 127
§ 3.16 Websites Hosting User-Provided Content 128
§ 3.17 Infringement Proceedings and Remedies 133
§ 3.18 Use of Music and Sound Recordings in Political Campaigns 135

Chapter 4. Publishing 141
§ 4.1 Publishing Basics 141
§ 4.2 Major Sources of Licensing Revenue 142
A. Public Performance Licenses 142
B. Mechanical Licenses 143
C. Synchronization Licenses 144
D. Electrical Transcription Licenses 145
E. Other Sources of Licensing Revenue 146

§ 4.3 The Songwriter's Publishing Options.... 146
A. Traditional Publishers.................... 146
B. Self-Publishing................................ 149
§ 4.4 Publishing Agreements 152
A. Copyright Grant.............................. 152
B. Writer's Compensation 154
1. Writer's Advance 155
2. Nondramatic Public Performance Royalties............ 156
3. Print Publication Royalties 157
4. Other Royalties 158
C. Publisher's Right to Revise the Work 158
D. Restrictions on Publisher's Exploitation Rights......................... 159
§ 4.5 International Subpublishing.................. 159

Chapter 5. Mechanical Licenses 161
§ 5.1 In General 161
§ 5.2 Compulsory Mechanical License 164
A. Substantive Rules........................... 166
B. Procedures...................................... 169
C. The Mechanical Licensing Collective 174

Chapter 6. Performance Rights in Musical Works 185
§ 6.1 Introduction 185
§ 6.2 Performing Rights Organizations.......... 188
A. Fractional Licensing 193
B. Allocating Fees................................ 193
C. Antitrust Scrutiny 194

D. Foreign Public Performance Royalties 200

Chapter 7. Performance Rights in Sound Recordings 203
§ 7.1 Limited Scope 203
§ 7.2 Streaming of Sound Recordings 205
§ 7.3 Interactive and Noninteractive Services Distinguished 207
§ 7.4 Interactive Streaming Licenses 211
§ 7.5 Non-Interactive Streaming Licenses 213
§ 7.6 Ephemeral Recordings 219

Chapter 8. Trademarks 221
§ 8.1 Introduction 221
§ 8.2 What Is a Trademark? 222
§ 8.3 Establishing Trademark Rights 226
A. Common Law Protection 226
B. Federal Registration 228
C. Trademark Protection Abroad 234
§ 8.4 Names of Musical Groups 236
§ 8.5 Unauthorized Use of Trademarks 239
A. Infringement and Dilution Claims 239
B. Trademark Claims Against Creative Works 241
1. No Likelihood of Confusion 245
2. First Amendment Protection 248
§ 8.6 Cybersquatting 252
§ 8.7 Truth in Music Laws 254
§ 8.8 Licensing and Merchandise 256

Chapter 9. Name, Likeness, and Voice Protections ... 257
§ 9.1 The Impact of Unauthorized Appropriation ... 257
§ 9.2 Rights of Privacy and Publicity ... 259
A. Scope of Protection ... 259
B. Postmortem Rights ... 260
§ 9.3 Licenses and Assignments ... 261
§ 9.4 First Amendment Considerations ... 263
§ 9.5 Artificial Intelligence ... 269
§ 9.6 Federal Anti-Bootlegging Statute ... 273
§ 9.7 Trademark and Unfair Competition Laws ... 274
§ 9.8 Cybersquatting ... 276

Chapter 10. Recording Contracts ... 279
§ 10.1 Approaching the Negotiation ... 279
§ 10.2 Term and Exclusivity ... 280
§ 10.3 Artist Commitment and Creative Control ... 282
§ 10.4 Artist Compensation ... 283
A. Advance ... 283
B. Royalties ... 286
1. Record Sales ... 287
2. Streaming ... 288
3. Master Use Licenses ... 289
4. Tour Support ... 289
§ 10.5 Controlled Compositions ... 290
§ 10.6 360 Deals ... 291
§ 10.7 Ownership of Masters ... 292
§ 10.8 Re-Recording Prohibitions ... 295
§ 10.9 Accountings and Audits ... 296
§ 10.10 Name and Likeness ... 297

§ 10.11 Key Person 298
§ 10.12 Termination 299

Chapter 11. Contracts with Minors 301
§ 11.1 Right to Disaffirm 301
§ 11.2 Limitations on Right 302
§ 11.3 Parental Guarantees 305
§ 11.4 Working Conditions 306

INDEX 307

TABLE OF CASES

References are to Pages

A&M Records, Inc. v. Napster, Inc., 110
Aalhmuhammed v. Lee, 49
Abitron Austria GmbH v. Hetronic Int'l, Inc., 235
ABKCO Music, Inc. v. Harrisongs Music, Ltd., 99
Adams v. Tabor-Smith, 305
American Dairy Queen Corp. v. New Line Productions, Inc., 251
American Society of Composers, Authors and Publishers, United States v., 197
American Society of Composers, Authors and Publishers, United States v. (In re Fox Broadcasting), 197
American Society of Composers, Authors and Publishers, United States v. (In re Turner Broadcasting), 197
AMF Inc. v. Sleekcraft Boats, 239
Andersen v. Stability AI Ltd, 105
Andy Warhol Foundation for the Visual Arts, Inc. v. Goldsmith, 117
Arista Records, LLC v. Launch Media, Inc., 207
Arnstein v. Porter, 98
ASCAP v. Pataki, 200
Atlanta Opera, Inc., 27
Bell v. Streetwise Records, Ltd., 9, 238, 302
Berg v. Traylor, 305
Bi-Rite Enterprises, Inc. v. Bruce Miner Co., 258
Boosey & Hawkes Music Publishers, Ltd. v. Walt Disney Co., 111
Bridgeport Music, Inc. v. Dimension Films, 103
Broadcast Music, Inc., United States v., 193
Brown v. Electronic Arts, Inc., 276
Buffalo Broadcasting Co., Inc. v. ASCAP, 190
Campbell v. Acuff-Rose Music, Inc., 116
Capitol Records, LLC v. ReDigi, Inc., 113
Caterpillar, Inc. v. Walt Disney Co., 244, 246
CBS, Inc. v. Liederman, 240
Cellco Partnership, In re, 197
Childress v. Taylor, 49

Comedy III Productions, Inc. v. Gary Saderup, Inc., 267
Community for Creative Non-Violence v. Reid, 50
Concord Music Group, Inc. v. Anthropic PBC, 104
Dallas Cowboys Cheerleaders, Inc. v. Pussycat Cinema, Ltd., 247
DC Comics v. Kryptonite Corp., 224, 232, 239
DC Comics, Inc. v. Powers, 224
Doe v. TCI Cablevision, 269
E.S.S. Entertainment 2000, Inc. v. Rock Star Videos, Inc., 250
Effects, Inc. v. Cohen, 61
Elsmere Music, Inc. v. National Broadcasting Co., 100
ETW Corp. v. Jireh Publishing, Inc., 250
F.B.T. Productions LLC v. Aftermath Records, 286
Famous Music Corp. v. Bay State Harness Racing and Breeding Ass'n, 109
Feist Publications v. Rural Telephone Service, 35
Fifty-Six hope Road Music Ltd. v. UMG Recordings, Inc., 55
Fisher v. Dees, 99
Fonovisa, Inc. v. Cherry Auction, Inc., 110
Foxworthy v. Custom Tees, Inc., 225, 240
Frank Music Corp. v. Metro-Goldwyn-Mayer, Inc., 187
Gershwin Publishing Corp. v. Columbia Artists Mgt., Inc., 106, 109
Global Music Rights, LLC v. Radio Music License Comm., 200
Google, LLC v. Oracle America, Inc., 118
Grant v. Trump, 135, 138
Gray v. Hudson, 94
Great Entertainment Merchandise, Inc. v. VN Merchandise, Inc., 23
Griffin v. Sheeran, 93, 95
HEC Enters., Ltd. v. Deep Purple, Inc., 237
Homevestors v. Warner Bros. Discovery, Inc., 251
Hormel Foods Corp. v. Jim Henson, 246
Horror, Inc. v. Miller, 50
Ideal Toy Corp. v. Fab-Lu Ltd., 89
Isaac Hayes Enterprises, LLC v. Trump, 137
Jack Daniels Props. v. VIP Prods. LLC, 248
Jean v. Bug Music, Inc., 93, 102
Kevin R. Foster, United States v., 13

Kingsmen v. K-Tel Int'l, Ltd., 237
Kirby v. Sega of America, 267
L.L. Bean, Inc. v. Drake Publishers, Inc., 243
Lancaster Symphony Orchestra v. NLRB, 27
Lehrman et al. v. Lovo, Inc., 260, 269, 270
Lerohl v. Friends of Minnesota Sinfonia, 27
Les Ballets Trockadero de Monte Carlo, Inc. v. Trevino, 235
Lil' Joe Wein Music, Inc. v. Jackson, 102
Louis Vuitton Malletier S.A. v. Warner Bros. Ent't, Inc., 250
Main Line Pictures, Inc. v. Basinger, 24
Malmsteen v. Berdon, 13
Martha Graham School & Dance Foundation v. Martha Graham Center of Contemporary Dance, Inc., 54
Martignon, United States v., 274
Matal v. Tam, 228
Mattel v. Walking Mountain Productions, 252
Mattel, Inc. v. MCA Records, Inc., 242, 243
MCA Records, Inc. v. Newton-John, 300
McDonald v. West, 93
Mechanical Licensing Collective v. Pandora Media LLC, 182
Meredith Corp. v. SESAC LLC, 199
Metro-Goldwyn-Mayer Studios, Inc. v. Grokster, Ltd., 109
MGA Entertainment, Inc. v. Harris, 223, 251
Midler v. Ford Motor Co., 260
Mills Music, Inc. v. Snyder, 74
Moghadam, United States v., 274
Motschenbacher v. R.J. Reynolds Tobacco Co., 259
Mutual of Omaha Ins. Co. v. Novak, 251
NCAA Student-Athlete Name & Likeness Licensing Litigation, In re, 276
Newton v. Diamond, 103
No Doubt v. Activision Publishing, Inc., 268
Oddo v. Ries, 61
Pandora Media, Inc., In re, 198
Parks v. LaFace Records, 249
Petrella v. Metro-Goldwyn-Mayer, Inc., 133
Polygram Int'l Pub., Inc. v. Nevada/TIG, Inc., 109
Presley, Estate of v. Russen, 265
Raden v. Laurie, 305

Radio Music License Comm. v. Global Music Rights, LLC, 199
Radio Music License Comm. v. SESAC, Inc., 199
Recorded Artists Actors Performers Ltd v. Phonographic Performance (Ireland) Ltd, 204
Recording Industry Ass'n of America v. Diamond Multimedia Systems, 128
Reznor v. J. Artist Management, Inc., 10
Rick v. Buchansky, 238
Ringgold v. Black Entertainment Television, Inc., 100
Robi v. Reed, 237
Rogers v. Grimaldi, 249
RSR Art, LLC v. Bob Ross, Inc., 262
Saregama India Ltd. v. Mosley, 102
Shaffer Smith, 2424, LLC v. Foster, 13
Shapiro Bernstein and Co. v. H.L. Green Co., 110
Singer Mgt. Consultants v. Milgram, 255
Skidmore v. Led Zeppelin, 93, 95, 98
Sony Corp. v. Universal City Studios, Inc., 107, 119
Stouffer v. National Geographic Partners, LLC, 251
Structured Asset Sales, LLC v. Sheeran, 95
Sullivan v. CBS Corp., 247
Swirsky v. Carey, 93
Thaler v. Perlmutter, 36
Three Boys Music Corp. v. Bolton, 93, 99
Tisi v. Patrick, 93
Twentieth Century Fox Television v. Empire Distribution, Inc., 250
Ulloa v. Universal Music and Video Distribution Group, 49
UMG Recordings, Inc. v. Shelter Capital Partners LLC, 132
UMG Recordings, Inc. v. Suno, 104
UMG Recordings, Inc. v. Uncharted Labs, Inc., 105
University of Alabama Board of Trustees v. New Life Art, Inc., 250
Viacom Int'l, Inc. v. YouTube, Inc., 131
Vidal v. Elster, 230
VMG Salsoul, LLC v. Ciccone, 89, 102
Waite v. UMG Recordings, Inc., 22, 55
Waits v. Frito-Lay, Inc., 260, 275
Walt Disney Productions v. Air Pirates, 118

White v. Samsung Elecs. America, Inc., 259
Williams v. Gaye, 95, 99
Winter v. DC Comics, 267
Woods v. Bourne Co., 74
Zacchini v. Scripps-Howard Broadcasting Co., 265

MUSIC LAW
IN A NUTSHELL®

CHAPTER 1

INTRODUCTION

Creating and performing music takes talent and hard work. Creative artists rarely have the time, resources, or inclination to consider legal matters. Their main concern is getting their music to the public, and perhaps even making a living at it. Too often, legal problems can sneak up on them unawares.

A music career will be more enjoyable, and potentially more rewarding, if the artist has at least a general familiarity with the legal concepts that are most relevant to the profession. From the start of the creative process to pursuing its potential financial rewards, each stage of the artist's journey involves decisions that may have long-term legal consequences. Yet the artist may be unaware that, simply by taking a particular action, he or she is making such a decision. In many cases, the act of creation itself triggers important legal consequences—especially when collaboration is involved.

There are also valuable legal rights that attach to the artist who creates or performs, whether or not the artist is aware of them at the time. Sometimes the artist can expand these legal protections by taking a few simple actions. Copyrights and trademarks are prime examples. Understanding these rights, how they arise, and how to enhance and enforce them, enables the artist to protect the fruits of his or her creative efforts.

Any artist whose work finds an audience will be asked to sign contracts of many kinds. This can begin quite early in the artist's career—sometimes while the artist is still a minor. The contracts may involve managers, agents, publishers, producers, distributors, venues, and perhaps record labels or tour promoters. Sometimes the contracts are quite lengthy, and their language may be difficult to understand. A contract may appear to be a standard form, needing only the artist's signature. Despite this appearance, many (if not most) of the contract's terms are negotiable—if the artist knows what to ask for. Therefore, step one is understanding the contract's terms, and how they will affect the artist's career, both in the immediate future and potentially much longer. Obtaining the advice of someone trustworthy and knowledgeable, such as an attorney with experience in music law, will be enormously valuable. Having a general understanding of the relevant legal concepts can help artists to ask the right questions, and get the most value from their legal advisors.

Fundamentally, music law involves the intersection between two major legal systems—federal copyright law, which protects creative works, and contract law, which governs the agreements that artists make in rendering their personal services as creators and performers, and in monetizing the intellectual property they create—musical compositions and recordings. During the artist's career, however, other legal regimes may become important, such as the laws that protect an artist's name, voice, likeness, and trademarks against unauthorized use by others. For some performers, labor law may be relevant as well.

This short introduction to music law is an overview of the legal issues that can and do arise in the music industry. It is designed to be helpful to non-lawyers, such as musicians and students learning about the music business, as well as to lawyers who are thinking about offering their services to clients in the music industry.

Most of the legal authorities discussed in each chapter are available for free online; therefore, the reader does not need access to a specialized legal database. While it can be helpful to look up some of these legal sources to get a deeper appreciation of the issues and concepts they illustrate, this text is intended to be fully understandable on its own.

Throughout this book, the term "artist" is used broadly to cover both songwriters and performers. Where a particular legal issue pertains to artists only in their capacity as performers, or only in their capacity as songwriters, the text will make that clear.

Chapter 2 introduces a few of the considerations that an artist may need to address at the early stage of a music career. Chapter 3 explains the fundamental concepts of copyright law as they apply to music and sound recordings. Chapter 4 explores the world of music publishing and the key provisions of a typical publishing agreement. Chapter 5 covers mechanical licenses—the licenses that generate royalties for songwriters and publishers when musical compositions are turned into sound recordings that are offered for sale and/or streaming. Chapter 6 explains the rights of songwriters and their publishers to collect royalties for the performance of musical compositions in public places, on radio and television, and on streaming platforms. Chapter 7 is also about public performance rights, but specifically the much narrower performance rights that attach to sound recordings as opposed to musical compositions. Chapter 8 introduces trademark law as it applies to band names and other types of branding in the music industry. Chapter 9 examines the laws that protect an artist against the unauthorized use of his or her name, likeness, and voice, including replicas created by artificial intelligence. Chapter 10 explores the complex provisions of recording contracts under which performers make multi-year commitments to deliver recordings to record labels in exchange for a share of the revenues generated by the recordings. Finally, Chapter 11 addresses the special considerations that arise when artists enter contracts while they are still minors.

Reading this book will not make anyone a legal expert. It should, however, help artists and those who work with them to recognize where legal issues may arise, and to understand when they should seek the advice of an experienced attorney.

While legal services can be expensive, artists may have access to some free or low-cost services through law school clinics, pro bono sections of local bar associations, or specialized arts-oriented legal organizations that exist in several states to offer free classes and referral services. Examples of the latter are Washington Area Lawyers for the Arts (WALA), California Lawyers for the Arts (CLA), and Volunteer Lawyers for the Arts (VLA) in New York. With many experienced attorneys willing to offer a helping hand, it never hurts to ask.

CHAPTER 2

MAKING MUSIC YOUR BUSINESS

§ 2.1 INTRODUCTION

Anyone choosing music as a profession should recognize that it is a business as well as an art form. Starting a business requires choosing a form of business—sole proprietorship, corporation, or partnership. It also requires choosing the professionals who will help to make the business succeed—for example, agents, managers, producers, publishers, and distributors. Musical performers who will work primarily in orchestras or as session musicians should also consider whether it is in their best interest to join a union.

This chapter provides a brief overview of the array of decisions that a music professional may face in launching a career.

§ 2.2 MANAGERS

Because musicians rarely have the experience, skills, time, and/or inclination to handle the business aspects of their careers while also pursuing their craft, they rely on *personal managers* to fill this role. Personal managers may serve as professional advisors, strategists, negotiators, and promoters.

Younger musicians may be tempted to give this job to a friend or family member. In some cases, this may work out. However, because of the importance of this role, a musician should select a personal manager primarily based on that person's experience, reputation, skills, and integrity. Unethical or inexperienced personal managers (and business managers, as discussed below) can have a devastating impact on an artist's career and finances.

Skilled managers can evaluate and provide advice on opportunities for live performance as well as publishing, recording, and merchandising deals. They can help to negotiate deals, arrange publicity, set budgets, set up and manage social media accounts, and select record producers, additional band members, and members of the musician's support team. When a musician goes on tour, the personal manager works with the tour manager as well as the concert promoter and/or booking agent with respect to tour dates, venue selection and preparation, security, lodging, transportation, and any other needs of the artist and support team. With ticketing practices (such as dynamic pricing and ticket resales) becoming increasingly complex, controversial, and frequently subject to legal regulation, clear communication between the personal manager and the concert promoter, ticketing agent, and/or venue operators with regard to ticketing policies is vital in order to protect the artist's relationship with fans. With international tours, the personal manager can make travel and security arrangements for the artist and his or her support team, and can work with immigration attorneys to navigate foreign visa requirements.

Because the role of a personal manager is not dictated by law, and is not governed by any industry standards, the artist's agreement with his or her manager should spell out the manager's responsibilities and authority in as much detail as possible. The more specific the agreement, the easier it will be to determine whether the manager has fulfilled his or her duties or whether there are grounds for termination. If the manager will have authority to enter contracts that are binding on the artist, to make or accept payments for the artist, or to make financial decisions on the artist's behalf, it is essential to spell this out in the agreement. Granting this authority also requires the artist to execute a power of attorney for the manager. The power of attorney should be drafted with care, to clearly delineate the scope of the manager's authority to bind the artist. The agreement should also permit the artist to audit the manager's records with regard to any financial transactions that affect the artist.

If the manager is employed by a management company, the artist's management contract should include a "key man" clause. This will enable the artist to continue working with the same individual manager, rather than being subject to the company's authority to assign a different manager.

Some managers may play a dominant role in shaping an artist's sound, style, image, and overall career path. A manager may even start with no artist at all, but only a concept, and then select and guide performers into fitting that concept. Most often these are young performers who have not already established a distinct image or fan base. This is how a "concept group" is formed. *See* Bell v. Streetwise Records, Ltd., 640 F.Supp. 575, 581 & n.18 (D. Mass.

1986) (finding that "New Edition" was not a concept group). Concept groups may be formed by a manager, producer, promoter, or record label. The creator of the concept group can remove and replace group members who no longer fit the concept (typically because they "age out" of the group's youthful image). Many well-known "boy bands" were created as concept groups. Examples include Menudo, New Kids on the Block, Backstreet Boys, and *NSYNC.

A personal manager's compensation is normally calculated as a percentage of the musician's gross or net earnings. Compensation that is based on gross earnings should normally be set at a lower percentage than compensation that is based on net earnings. A typical manager's commission is 10–20% of the gross. If the musician incurs large expenses while touring or making a recording, paying a management fee based on gross earnings can leave the artist with little or nothing in the way of take-home pay. *See, e.g.*, Reznor v. J. Artist Management, Inc., 365 F.Supp.2d 565, 571 (S.D.N.Y. 2005) (manager's 20% share of artist's gross revenues amounted to entire profit from concert tour).

If the artist has revenue streams to which the manager's efforts did not contribute (for example, if the manager facilitates only the artist's work as a performer, but the artist also receives songwriting royalties), these should normally be excluded from the manager's compensation base. Also, the manager's percentage may increase or decrease over time, or when the musician's earnings reach certain benchmarks. These details should be spelled out in the agreement.

The management agreement may entitle the manager to continue receiving a percentage of the musician's earnings even after their relationship has terminated. For example, if the manager represented the musician when the latter signed a publishing agreement, recording contract, or endorsement deal, the manager may be entitled to share in the artist's earnings from that transaction even after their management agreement has terminated. For these "post-term commissions," management contracts typically include a "sunset clause," gradually reducing the manager's percentage commission from these transactions over a period of years, until it eventually reaches zero. Before signing a management agreement, therefore, the artist should have a clear understanding of any financial obligations that will continue after the relationship ends.

While managers can play an important role in negotiating and evaluating business opportunities, musicians should, whenever possible, have their contracts reviewed by an attorney before signing. This is especially important with respect to recording contracts, which are complex agreements with potentially long-term effects on a musician's career. (Recording contracts are discussed in Chapter 10.)

Surprisingly, and unfortunately, management contracts are not always in writing. Frequently they are "handshake" deals. One problem with handshake deals is that, in most cases, the parties have not hammered out all of the terms of their agreement. Even to the extent they have done so, without a full written contract there may be insufficient evidence of the terms to which they agreed. This can lead to disputes and litigation in later years. Also, the very act of putting an agreement in writing typically causes the parties to think more carefully about the important details of their arrangement. The best practice is to have an attorney review the written contract before signing.

Note that a musician's *personal manager* is very different from a *business manager*. (For some artists, especially those just starting out, it is possible that the same person will fill both roles.) The business manager keeps track of the musician's earnings, expenditures, and tax obligations, and may play a significant role in investing the musician's funds. A dishonest or incompetent business manager can decimate the artist's finances; mishandled or stolen funds may be unrecoverable. Therefore, artists should select their business managers carefully, and should remain personally engaged with their finances to the greatest extent possible. Higher-earning musicians should bring in an outside auditor periodically to review the business manager's records.

As an example of what can go wrong if an artist is too disengaged from his or her finances, one songwriter and recording artist ended up having to sue both his personal manager and his business manager for misappropriating his funds. Although the improprieties had gone on for some time, he did not begin to ask questions until his assets had shrunk to almost nothing, and it was another three years before he hired an independent accountant, who uncovered the discrepancies. By the time he filed the lawsuit, the statute of limitations had run on several of his claims, which limited the amount of money he could recover from his former managers. *See,* Malmsteen v. Berdon, 595 F.Supp.2d 299 (S.D.N.Y. 2009), *aff'd,* 369 Fed. Appx. 248 (2d Cir. 2010). If the artist had been more fully engaged with his finances from the start, or had arranged to have his accounts independently audited every year or two, he would have been able to stop the mismanagement sooner, and could potentially have recovered more of the misdirected funds.

Another artist, Ne-Yo, sued his business manager for fraud and financial mismanagement. *See* Shaffer Smith, 2424, LLC v. Foster, 168 F.Supp.3d 654 (S.D.N.Y. 2016). Although the civil suit was dismissed, criminal charges were also brought. The manager was convicted of criminal fraud, received a prison sentence, and was ordered to pay Ne-Yo $6 million in restitution. *See* United States v. Kevin R. Foster, 829 Fed. Appx. 86 (6th Cir. Oct. 2, 2020) (affirming conviction).

§ 2.3 BOOKING AGENTS

Agents generally play a less significant role in the music industry than in other entertainment industries. Typically, musicians use agents to secure bookings for live performances at festivals, at special events, such as weddings and trade shows, and at smaller venues such as clubs and theatres. Agents can also book a series of performances as a tour. However, major tours at arenas and stadiums are usually arranged through concert promoters such as Live Nation or AEG Presents, sometimes with the participation of the artist's record label.

A booking agency will represent multiple artists, but its arrangement with each artist may be exclusive or non-exclusive. If the arrangement is non-exclusive, then the artist is free to use other agents as well, and each agency's commission will be based only on the events that it actually books for the artist. Under an exclusive arrangement, the artist agrees to book only through one agency, and must pay that agency's commission for each live performance, whether booked through that agency or directly. It is also possible for an artist to have several exclusive agents, each operating in a separate geographic territory—e.g., one in the U.S., and another in Canada.

Agents' commissions are typically 10–15% of the gross performance fee, but do not include any portion of the artist's merchandise revenues. Some exclusive agency contracts require artists to continue paying commissions even after the contract expires, if the venues that the agency initially booked for them hire them again for future bookings (either directly or through a new agent).

§ 2.4 PRODUCERS

When making a record, an artist will choose a producer to provide creative direction and supervision. Typically, the producer participates in selecting songs, arrangements, and session musicians, chooses the recording studio, manages the production budget, and helps the artist to cultivate the desired sound.

If the artist has a contract with a record label, the producer may be hired either by the record label or the artist. Like the artist, the producer will be compensated by receiving royalties based on the revenues generated by the recording, but will also receive an advance that is recoupable against those royalties. Typically, the record label makes the actual payments to the producer, but recoups these from the artist's royalties. (When the record label pays the producer's advance, it treats this as an additional advance to the artist.)

An artist that is not signed to a recording contract may enter a contract directly with a record producer or, more often, a production company owned by the producer. Under this agreement, the production company typically pays all of the recording costs; in return, however, it owns the masters, and may also own exclusive rights to the artist's recording services for a period of time (similar to a deal with a record label). The production company can then seek out record labels or distributors interested in buying or licensing the masters. In this situation, the artist must carefully review the production agreement to determine how he or she will be compensated when the masters generate revenue—e.g., how royalties will be split between the artist and the production company, the artist's right to receive an advance either from the production company or from the label or distributor that acquires the masters, and the extent to which the production company will recoup its production costs from the artist. The artist should also assess his or her right to terminate the agreement if the production company fails to deliver the recording or to exploit it successfully within a reasonable time period. As is true of contracts with record labels, artists should have an attorney review a production agreement before they sign.

The producer typically receives an upfront fee in addition to a 3% royalty. If the artist receives an advance from the record label, this may include the producer's upfront fee, but this amount, like the rest of the advance, will be recoupable out of the artist's royalties. The 3% royalty is typically charged against the artist's royalty share, although the artist may negotiate for it to come out of the label's share. (In the case of statutory streaming royalties under § 114, the artist or label, respectively, may send a Letter of Direction directing SoundExchange to make this payment directly to the producer. See Chapter 7.)

Many producers—sometimes called beat makers—actually function as songwriters. Beat makers create instrumental tracks, typically by combining samples licensed from existing recordings under master use licenses. Beat makers then license the resulting "beats" (on an exclusive or non-exclusive basis) to songwriters, publishers, record labels, or other producers, who can then incorporate the beats into new musical works. The license will specify the terms and conditions under which the beat can be used, including the beat maker's compensation. A beat maker may be considered a co-writer of the resulting song, and may negotiate for an ownership share in the song and/or a share of the master recording royalties.

§ 2.5 PUBLISHERS

Songwriters must license their musical works in order to earn royalties. Licensing of musical compositions is referred to in the music industry as "publishing." A music publisher can license a songwriter's work to record labels for use in creating sound recordings, to sheet music companies for producing sheet music and songbooks, and to audiovisual production companies for use in creating films, television programs, karaoke devices, video games, music videos, commercials, and so on.

Songwriters may use the services of a major publisher or an independent publisher, or they may create their own publishing company and use a publishing administrator to track and collect their royalties.

Chapter 4 examines the songwriter's various publishing options, and discusses the most important provisions of a typical publishing contract.

§ 2.6 DISTRIBUTORS

The job of a distributor is to get an artist's sound recordings into the marketplace for retail sale or streaming. If an artist has a recording contract, the record label will handle distribution, either in-house or through outside distributors with which they have an established relationship. However, independent artists will need to engage the services of a distributor.

A reputable distributor will have established relationships with retailers (digital, and in some cases, physical) as well as streaming platforms that will make it easier to get new releases into the marketplace quickly. (Most digital music platforms no longer allow direct uploads from artists.) Distributors send periodic reports to artists, enabling the artists to track their distribution proceeds from each retailer or platform. Some distributors are independent, while others are affiliated with record labels. Some also handle music videos.

Three of the major labels (Sony Music, Universal Music Group, and Warner Music Group) make their distribution services available to independent labels. The major labels distribute in both physical and digital formats. They have expertise in promoting recordings and in developing marketing strategies. The size of their catalogs also gives them significant negotiating power with the interactive streaming services, enabling them to extract higher streaming royalties from those platforms.

There are also a number of top-tier independent distributors that provide a high level of service: They actively promote the artist's recordings, and develop marketing and digital release strategies, much like the major labels. Most provide only digital distribution, while a few offer physical distribution as well. They often pay artist advances, recoupable against future royalties. However, these top-tier services are selective in the artists (and independent labels) they represent, making them less accessible to most new artists. They also take a substantial share of the distribution proceeds—up to 50% in some cases.

The largest number of distributors fall into the "open platform" category, accessible to all recording artists, and offering a more basic level of services at an affordable price. The pricing structure may be a fixed fee per release, a subscription plan, or a commission up to 15%. While the most basic plans offer only digital distribution, some services offer "premium" plans that include physical distribution as well as additional services.

A handful of distributors have emerged under a new hybrid business model. Artists initially sign up for the most basic level of service, which is similar to the basic tier of the "open platform" distributors. The most successful of these artists are invited to upgrade to higher tiers of service (subject to higher fees). At the highest level, the distributor functions as a record label.

To use a distributor's services, the artist enters into a distribution agreement with the company. Distribution contracts are generally more straightforward than recording contracts or production agreements. Unlike record deals, which can last up to seven years, a distribution agreement typically lasts for only one or two years (or even shorter, for the open platform services).

A distributor does not take ownership of the artist's masters. Thus, an artist is free to change distributors after a contract expires. An artist can also use different distributors for different releases.

§ 2.7 CHOICE OF ENTITY

Business involves risks, including the risk of liability arising from debts, mishaps, or legal disputes. While most music professionals begin their careers as individuals ("sole proprietors"), those who begin to achieve some financial success often choose to protect their earnings by forming a limited liability entity through which they will offer their services, borrow funds, and/or manage their copyright interests. These entities are often called "loan-outs."

Typically, the musician will be both the sole owner and the sole employee of the loan-out. Instead of rendering services directly to a third party employer as an employee or independent contractor, the musician will have his or her loan-out enter a contract with the third party, under which the third party will pay the loan-out for lending the services of its sole employee.

Provided that the loan-out is formed as a limited liability entity, any debts or liabilities it incurs can be satisfied only from the assets of the entity, thus insulating the artist's personal assets. When the loan-out receives payments from third parties, the entertainer can withdraw funds from the loan-out as salary, expenses, or a "draw" (depending on the type of entity), thus removing those funds from the reach of the loan-out's creditors. (However, the entertainer should respect the loan-out's status as a separate entity, rather than treat it as a personal pocketbook; failure to respect this separation can lead a court to disregard the loan-out as a sham, leaving the entertainer once again exposed to personal liability.)

A loan-out can be either a corporation or a limited liability company (LLC). Most entertainers use LLCs, largely because fewer formalities are involved. Typically, the entertainer is the sole owner of the loan-out and, if it is a corporation, the sole employee as well. Some entertainers elect to have their LLCs taxed as corporations in order to take advantage of certain federal tax benefits that are available to corporations but not to individuals. Tax rules affecting entertainers change frequently, however, and entertainers should consult with tax advisors to determine whether this option fits their particular circumstances.

For artists who create copyrightable works such as musical works and sound recordings, rendering their creative services through a corporation may not be advisable, for reasons peculiar to copyright law. As discussed in Chapter 3, individual authors who assign or license their copyrights have the legal right to terminate those grants, and get their copyrights back, after a period of time set by statute (for newly created works, typically 35 years from the date of the grant). However, if the work was created as a work made for hire for the artist's loan-out corporation, and the loan-out rather than the individual artist executed the assignment or license to the third party, there is a serious risk that the termination right will not apply. *See, e.g.*, Waite v. UMG Recordings, Inc., 450 F.Supp.3d 430, 441–42 (S.D.N.Y. 2020) (holding that recording artists who granted copyrights to record labels through artists' loan-out companies could not terminate the grants). Therefore, artists who anticipate creating valuable copyrights should seek legal advice before choosing to operate through a corporation, and weigh the tax advantages against the risk of losing their termination rights in later years.

An artist can still achieve a degree of liability protection without using the corporate form, if he or she forms a single-member LLC that operates as a sole proprietorship. In this case, the artist is the owner of the business, not an employee, thus preserving his or her future termination rights. To enjoy limited liability, the artist should keep his or her personal assets separate from those of the LLC. The artist can take earnings out of the business as the owner's "draw."

When a musician, vocalist, or producer offers his or her personal services through a loan-out, the loan-out will be the party that enters contracts with third parties, such as other entertainers or professionals, record labels, concert promoters, publicists, orchestras, or music venues such as clubs. The loan-out then "lends out" the individual's services to these third parties. The individual will still sign the contract with the third party, but will do so in his or her capacity as the chief executive of the loan-out (or the owner, if using an LLC that is a sole proprietorship) rather than as an individual artist.

The party contracting with the loan-out may require the individual artist to sign an "inducement letter" in his or her personal capacity. An inducement letter is the artist's acknowledgment of his or her obligation to perform the services that have been promised by the loan-out. If there is a breach of contract, typically the loan-out, and not the individual artist, will be responsible for any financial consequences. Much depends, however, on the wording of the inducement letter.

For example, in Great Entertainment Merchandise, Inc. v. VN Merchandise, Inc., 1996 WL 355377 (S.D.N.Y. June 27, 1996), a merchandising company (GEM) wanted to license heavy metal artist Vince Neil's trademark rights in order to make and sell T-shirts during his upcoming concert tour. Neil transferred his trademark rights to his loan-out company, which in turn granted the merchandising license to GEM in exchange for a $ 1 million advance. GEM also required Neil to sign an inducement letter.

The contract provided that if Neil's concerts attracted fewer than 800,000 paid attendees, the unrecouped portion of the advance would have to be repaid. When attendance fell short of 800,000, GEM demanded partial repayment. When the loan-out failed to comply, GEM sued both the loan-out and Neil personally. The court looked to the language of the inducement letter to determine whether Neil could be held personally liable for the repayment. However, the letter stated only that Neil approved the terms of the merchandising agreement, including his performance obligations, and guaranteed to perform those obligations "to the best of [his] ability." *Id.* at *2. In the court's view, this fell short of a commitment to personally guarantee the loan-out's financial obligations. (The court's opinion would have allowed further evidence to be presented at trial, but the parties apparently settled.)

Another example is Main Line Pictures, Inc. v. Basinger, 1994 WL 814244 (Cal.App. 2 Dist. Sept. 22, 1994), in which actress Kim Basinger entered a verbal agreement to appear in a film. However, the written contract for her acting services made clear that the agreement was between the production company and Basinger's loan-out. There was also an inducement letter, in which Basinger agreed to be joined as a defendant in any breach of contract action against her loan-out. Before either agreement was actually signed, the production company began pre-production. (Due to the complexity of film contracts and tight filming schedules, it is not unusual for preproduction and even filming to take place without signed contracts.) When Basinger later pulled out of the film, the production company sued both her and her loan-out for breach of contract. Although the jury awarded damages for breach, it failed to specify whether the breach was by Basinger, her loan-out, or both. In addition, the production company did not present any evidence that the inducement letter constituted a personal guarantee. For these reasons, the case was overturned on appeal. As a result, Basinger avoided personal bankruptcy.

As these cases demonstrate, entering contracts through a limited liability entity operating as loan-out can insulate an entertainer from personal liability in the event of a breach. While a letter of inducement can offer third parties a way to hold the entertainer personally liable, they are likely to succeed only if the letter clearly indicates that the entertainer personally guarantees the loan-out's financial obligations.

§ 2.8 SPECIAL CONSIDERATIONS FOR MUSICAL GROUPS

There are added considerations for the artist who is part of a musical group rather than a solo performer. Group members must work together in making important decisions such as selecting a producer, distributor or personal manager, admitting new members, and deciding whether to go on tour or whether to accept a particular recording contract. If they write songs together, they may experience creative differences, and will also have to agree on song splits (that is, their respective copyright ownership shares in each musical work).

The members of musical groups should consider entering an agreement with one another addressing such issues in advance, in order to avoid disputes that could arise at a later date. For example, who will decide on whether to admit a new artist to the group? If the group writes music together, will they agree in advance to the same song split for each of their songs, or will this be decided on a song-by-song basis? (Any delay in agreeing on song splits could delay the songwriters' receipt of publishing royalties.) The agreement can also address ownership of the group's name: If a single member leaves, under the general rule of trademark law the name belongs to the remaining members. (See Chapter 8 on Trademarks.) However, if the group splits up, it is possible that no member would have a superior right under the law. Addressing such issues in the agreement can avoid later disputes that can disrupt the creative enterprise and/or lead to costly litigation. It is best to seek the advice of an attorney in drafting such an agreement.

§ 2.9 LABOR ORGANIZATIONS

Creative workers in the music industry are often entrepreneurs, arranging concert tours through promoters or agents and/or negotiating publishing deals and recording contracts in which they surrender some of their intellectual property rights in exchange for royalties that are contingent on the success of their creative efforts. In these cases, they are acting like business owners, assuming at least some of the risk of success or failure.

Sometimes, however, their work resembles that of a traditional employee, even if they are freelancing, because their compensation is less dependent on the success or failure of the undertaking—for example, when they render their services for pre-negotiated fees in clubs, bars or cabarets, record scores for motion pictures, television shows, video games, and commercials, or perform in an orchestra, as session musicians in a recording studio, or at special events.

When a musician's role resembles that of a traditional employee—even if the performer is technically an independent contractor—under federal law he or she is eligible for union representation. In addition, under the National Labor Relations Board's (NLRB) 2023 decision in Atlanta Opera, Inc., 372 NLRB No. 95 (2023), a worker can still be eligible for union representation even if he or she engages in some amount of entrepreneurial activity. The key inquiry is whether the worker is operating an independent business or is acting as a "common law" employee. The determination of common law employee status involves a fact-specific multi-factor test. In the case of musicians, application of this test can be especially difficult, since many musicians choose when and for whom they want to work at different times, and often for short engagements. *Compare* Lancaster Symphony Orchestra v. NLRB, 822 F.3d 563 (D.C. Cir. 2016) (holding that orchestra members were employees eligible for representation) *with* Lerohl v. Friends of Minnesota Sinfonia, 322 F.3d 486 (8th Cir. 2003) (holding that orchestra members were independent contractors ineligible for representation).

The American Federation of Musicians (AFM) is the labor union that represents musicians (including instrumentalists, vocalists, and arrangers). It operates by entering into collective bargaining agreements with employers to establish minimum standards for pay and working conditions. The agreements may address many other employment details, such as the minimum number of musicians that must be hired for a particular venue, whether the employer can record the musicians' performance, how those recordings can be used, and how the musicians will be compensated for any such uses.

However, the terms established through collective bargaining are binding only on the employers that participate. Unlike most other fields of entertainment, in the music industry many employers do not participate in collective bargaining. This is especially true of smaller businesses, such as clubs and bars, even when they use music on a regular basis. In addition, many musicians perform one-off "gigs" for weddings, birthdays, bar mitzvahs, trade shows, and other special events whose organizers do not engage in collective bargaining.

Under these circumstances, the AFM has been less effective than other entertainment industry unions (or "talent guilds") in improving working conditions for musicians. While symphony orchestras and professional producers of opera, ballet, and musical theatre are likely to be AFM signatories (for example, the producers of shows at Broadway theatres and Lincoln Center), most professional musicians find that they must work for non-signatory employers in order to make a living in their chosen profession.

Joining the AFM gives a musician access to jobs with employers who are AFM signatories. If there are few such employers in the region where the musician works, AFM membership may not be beneficial. However, while technically an AFM member is not allowed to work for non-signatory employers, this rule is generally not enforced (unlike comparable rules in other talent guilds). Therefore, some musicians join the AFM in order to access union jobs, but also feel free to work for non-union employers. Working union jobs enables the musician to qualify for health insurance and to earn credits toward the union's pension plan; both plans are funded by mandatory contributions from signatory employers.

Unlike most other talent guilds, which operate on a nationwide basis, the AFM operates through more than 240 geographic locals in the United States and Canada. Each local has its own membership and engages in collective bargaining only with employers within its geographic jurisdiction. For example, Local 47 operates in Los Angeles, Local 369 in Las Vegas, and Local 802 in the greater New York City area.

While both singers and instrumentalists can join the AFM, some singers are eligible for other talent guilds as well. Which talent guild(s) they can join depends on the kind of work they do. Singers who perform in opera and concert choral performances are eligible for membership in the American Guild of Musical Artists (AGMA). Singers who are recording artists or session performers for major labels can join the Screen Actors Guild/American Federation of Television and Radio Artists (SAG-AFTRA), which has collective bargaining agreements pursuant to its Sound Recordings Code with Universal Music Group, Sony Music Entertainment, Warner Music Group, and Disney Music Group. SAG-AFTRA membership also opens the door to acting roles in major film and television productions.

§ 2.10 INSURANCE

Artists should obtain insurance that will safeguard their assets in the event of lawsuits arising from their professional activities. This is true even if the artist operates through a loan-out. There is always the risk that a court will find a reason to disregard the loan-out, or that the artist will be held personally liable according to the terms of his or her letter of inducement.

Errors and omissions ("E&O") insurance covers liability arising from infringement of various intangible rights. These include copyright, trademark, and right of publicity claims, as well as claims of defamation (libel or slander), invasion or privacy, and breach of contract. In each case, liability can arise even if an artist does not intend to infringe someone's intangible rights.

Publishers, record labels, distributors, venue operators, and tour promoters need E&O insurance as well. They might be joined with the artist as defendants in a lawsuit, or sued individually. (For example, an artist might sue a publisher, or an artist and his or her record label might be joined as defendants by a plaintiff alleging copyright infringement.)

In addition to E&O insurance, artists should obtain general liability insurance to cover other types of claims—such as personal injuries or property damage arising from accidents that occur during a live performance. This type of insurance is important for tour promoters and venue operators as well.

Each insurance policy will spell out the types of claims that will be covered, and any exclusions, as well as the policy's geographic scope and monetary limits. Because the policy language may be difficult to understand, artists should review the terms carefully, and seek advice if needed.

CHAPTER 3
COPYRIGHT LAW

§ 3.1 INTRODUCTION

Almost everyone involved in creating and distributing music needs to know some basic copyright law. This includes writers, producers, performers, publishers, publishing administrators, record labels, performing rights organizations (PROs), venue operators, broadcasters, streaming services, and teachers—as well as the lawyers, publicists, and social media managers who assist them. Whenever creative content is created, copied, adapted, performed, displayed, or distributed, some aspect of copyright law may be involved.

Copyright law is almost exclusively federal. The federal copyright statutes are located in Title 17 of the United States Code (except for a few criminal provisions, which are in Title 18). This text will refer to particular copyright statutes by their section number. For example, § 107 (fair use) is located at 17 U.S.C. § 107.

Except where otherwise indicated, all references to copyright law in this book refer to the *current* federal copyright statutes, collectively known as the Copyright Act of 1976 (even though they have been amended many times since 1976). From time to time, the text may refer to the previous copyright statute, the Copyright Act of 1909. Although most of that statute is now obsolete, a few of its provisions still govern the copyright status (including duration) of older works.

This chapter focuses on the basics of copyright law—for example, what kinds of works are protected, who owns the copyright, how long copyright lasts, which rights are protected, and how these rights are enforced. Because this book is about the music industry, it omits certain aspects of copyright law that are not relevant to music (for example, the protection of architectural works). It is worth noting, however, that certain other aspects of copyright law are occasionally relevant to music—such as the protection of photography and artwork (which might be used, for example, in advertising and promotional materials, on a website, in social media, as cover art for a recording, on merchandise, or in a music video).

Also, every country has its own copyright laws. The copyright laws discussed here apply only within the United States. While most countries' copyright laws are similar in their broad strokes, they are not identical. Therefore, when music, sound recordings, and videos are exploited in other countries, the governing laws and procedures will be somewhat different.

§ 3.2 WHAT WORKS ARE PROTECTED?

Copyright law applies broadly to any "original work of authorship" from the moment it is "fixed" in a "tangible medium of expression." Original works of authorship can include literature, artwork (including photographs), audiovisual works, dramatic works, choreography, musical compositions, sound recordings, software, architectural works, and any other form of creative expression that involves at least a modest degree of originality. 17 U.S.C. § 102. While copyright does not protect ideas or facts, it does protect original ways of *expressing* those ideas or facts.

What is meant by originality? According to the Supreme Court, a work is original if it (1) was independently created and (2) possesses at least a minimal amount of creativity. *See* Feist Publications v. Rural Telephone Service, 499 U.S. 340, 345 (1991). For a work to be independently created, the creator must not simply copy from an existing work: The creator must contribute *something* from the creator's own mind.

Copyright does not protect individual words and musical notes, but it does protect the specific way that a songwriter chooses to combine them. Likewise, copyright does not protect the raw sound of a musical instrument or a person's voice, but it does protect a specific recorded performance by a singer and/or instrumentalist. The relatively low standard of creativity that applies to copyrights means that almost any musical work, musical sound recording, or music video will easily meet the standard.

Originality does not mean novelty. In other words, a work can be original without being completely different from everything that has gone before. It is enough that *something* in the work came from the creator's own mind.

For example, if a composer adds original music to one of Shakespeare's sonnets, the resulting song, considered as a whole, is an original and copyrightable work. The lyrics have been copied, but the new music provides sufficient originality to make the song copyrightable. (Since Shakespeare's sonnets are in the public domain, the composer did not need permission to copy them.) While there is no clear standard for "how much" originality is required for a work to be copyrightable, there is broad consensus that it must be more than trivial.

There is also a broad consensus that at least some of the creativity in a copyrightable work must come from the mind of a *human* creator. Therefore, while a person is free to use computerized tools to assist in creating a musical work, at least some of the creative choices must be made by a human being; this position is reflected in § 802.5(C) of the Copyright Office Compendium. In the context of artificial intelligence (AI), this principle is currently being challenged in court, although the challenge is unlikely to succeed. *See* Thaler v. Perlmutter, 687 F.Supp.3d 140 (D.D.C. 2023), *appeal pending*, Case No. 23–5233 (D.C. Cir. filed Oct. 18, 2023). For works that combine creative choices by humans with creative choices by AI, the courts and the Copyright Office will have to decide whether the human's creative contribution was sufficient to satisfy the legal standard for originality.

Copyright also does not protect any portion of a work that infringes someone else's copyright. In contrast to the composer who sets Shakespeare's public domain sonnets to music, one who adds original music to someone else's copyrighted poetry or lyrics without that person's consent will have no copyright protection in the resulting song, because the music is completely intertwined with infringing lyrics. However, copyright will still protect the instrumental music by itself, since that is original.

In addition to possessing at least minimal originality, to be copyrightable a work must be "fixed" in some tangible form. In the case of a musical composition, it can be written down as sheet music, or it can be recorded in analog or digital formats. Therefore, a songwriter does not have to be able to read or write sheet music in order to make a sufficient fixation of a new composition. Similarly, in the case of a sound recording, fixation occurs as the sounds are being recorded. As the recorded track is mixed and edited, copyright attaches to each new variation that is produced.

§ 3.3 COPYRIGHTS IN MUSIC AND SOUND RECORDINGS

To fully understand how copyrights work in the music industry, it is crucial to distinguish between the copyright in a musical composition (called a "musical work" in the copyright statutes) and the copyright in a sound recording. A sound recording is an audio recording of a specific performance of a musical composition. In the music industry, copyrights in sound recordings are referred to as "masters." (However, this term does not appear in the copyright statutes.) The musical composition and the sound recording are two separate works, with two separate copyrights, frequently owned by two different parties.

For example, Dolly Parton wrote the song "I Will Always Love You." That is a copyrighted musical composition, which can be expressed either in sheet music or in a recorded performance. Dolly Parton herself performed on at least two different audio recordings of "I Will Always Love You." Each of these recorded performances is a separately copyrighted sound recording. Keeping count, so far we have one copyrighted musical composition and two copyrighted sound recordings, for a total of three copyrights. Later, Whitney Houston performed on yet another sound recording of "I Will Always Love You." That sound recording has its own copyright as well. So now we have one copyrighted musical work and three copyrighted sound recordings. In fact, the song has been recorded by many other artists, resulting in quite a few copyrighted sound recordings of the same underlying song. Whenever *any* of these recordings is sold or streamed, regardless of who recorded it, a portion of the revenues goes to the songwriter, Dolly Parton.

Another example is "Nothing Compares 2 U," with music and lyrics written by Prince. This musical composition has been recorded several times, by different artists, including the most well-known version recorded by Sinéad O'Connor. There is one copyright in Prince's underlying musical work, but each of the recorded performances is a separately copyrighted sound recording.

As you can see, every audio recording of a copyrighted musical work involves at least two copyrights—the copyright in the musical work (that is, the music and lyrics—elements which can also be expressed in written form, although they don't have to be) and the copyright in the sound recording (which cannot be expressed in written form). In addition, the musical work and the sound recording typically have *different copyright owners*. The musical work is typically owned by the songwriters and/or their publishers, while the sound recording is typically owned by a record label (unless the recording artist owns his or her own masters). Because almost any exploitation of a sound recording is also an exploitation of the underlying musical work, a party that wants to commercially exploit a sound recording—e.g., through streaming, record sales, or incorporation into a motion picture—typically needs a license from *both* copyright owners.

The term "sound recording" applies only to purely *audio* recordings of a musical work, not audiovisual recordings. Audiovisual recordings include motion pictures, music videos, television programs, karaoke devices, video games, TikTok or YouTube videos, concert videos, and any other recorded works that combine audio and visual elements.

The audio component of an audiovisual work is considered a part of the audiovisual work, even if it contains music; it is *not* a sound recording. Thus, when a song is recorded specifically for a film score, the recording becomes part of an audiovisual work, and does not have its own separate copyright. In contrast, if a film producer licenses a *pre-existing* sound recording for inclusion in a film (under what is termed a "master recording" or "master use" license), that recording continues to have its own separate existence as a sound recording. Sometimes a song that was initially recorded for a film score will later be recorded separately for commercial release as a sound recording (for example, in a "soundtrack album"); that subsequent audio recording stands on its own as a copyrighted sound recording, separate from the copyright in the motion picture.

In one of the more bizarre wrinkles of copyright law, the federal protection of sound recordings differs in several respects from the protection provided for other works of authorship, such as musical works. These differences are noted, where relevant, throughout this chapter. But why are sound recordings treated differently? The reason is historical rather than logical.

Before the 1970s, sound recordings were simply not recognized as works of authorship worthy of federal copyright protection. A sound recording was viewed as a mechanical device that was merely a component of the machine that played the recorded music (initially these were player pianos, later record players). Despite the artistry of the musicians and vocalists who performed on them, records were not recognized as creative works that were separate from the underlying musical compositions. As a result, federal copyright law did not protect them. Finally, in 1971, after extensive lobbying from the recording industry, amid rising concerns over record piracy,

Congress amended federal copyright law to include sound recordings.

Even under the new law, however, federal copyright applied only to sound recordings that were created on or after February 15, 1972. Older sound recordings were still ineligible for federal protection. They were protected, if at all, only by state law (which, in most states, was underdeveloped in this regard).

However, the law changed again in 2018, when Congress enacted a new statute, 17 U.S.C. § 1401, that applies specifically to these previously-excluded sound recordings. While, technically, they are still not protected by "copyright," § 1401 provides them with protection that is nearly identical to copyright. (One significant difference is that copyright termination rights do not apply to these recordings, as discussed in § 3.10[A] below.)

The result of this history is that sound recordings created on or after February 15, 1972, are protected by federal copyright law, and those created before that date receive near-equivalent protection. As discussed in § 3.12 below, however, federal protection for sound recordings is still a "second class citizen" compared to copyright in musical works.

§ 3.4 SECURING COPYRIGHT PROTECTION: WHEN DOES COPYRIGHT BEGIN?

People often ask: "How do I copyright my work?" Unless you created your work before 1989, the answer is: You don't. The law does it for you. However, there are some steps you can take to maximize your protection. The discussion below explains the rules for newly created works.

The rule for newly created works is this: Copyright attaches automatically as the creative work is fixed in tangible form. For example, if a songwriter composes a few bars of music and writes them down or records them, that music is immediately protected by copyright, even if the composition is not yet finished. If a lyricist comes up with a few lines, and writes them down or records them, those lines are copyrighted even if the rest of the lyrics are not finished (and even if there is no melody yet to accompany them). Thus, as the creative process moves forward, copyright attaches to all of the new content as soon as it is fixed. This rule was introduced in the 1976 Act, and applies to all works created in 1978 or later. [1]

As the above paragraph reveals, the current rule is that it is only necessary to *create* the work and *fix* it in some tangible form. At the moment of fixation, the work is automatically protected by copyright *to the extent that the work is original.* 17 U.S.C. § 102.

---

[1] For a brief period, between 1978 and 1989, copyright notice was still required in order to avoid losing copyright protection in a newly created work. Publishing without notice was not fatal, however. If the copyright owner registered the work within 5 years, and placed a copyright notice on all copies publicly distributed in the U.S. in the future, the copyright could be salvaged. 17 U.S.C. § 405(a).

In the contemporary music industry, a musical work and its first sound recording are often created at the same time. While a songwriter might create sheet music first, he or she may instead create an audio recording of the song while creating it. In that case, the act of recording the song is the initial fixation that secures copyright protection for the music and lyrics. At the same time, the initial fixation also creates a copyrighted sound recording. Alternatively, the songwriter might write the lyrics on paper or a laptop, and use an audio recording to fix the actual music during the creative process. In this situation, the lyrics have been fixed on paper, and the music has been fixed through an audio recording. To ensure that the entire song meets the fixation requirement for copyright protection, the songwriter should then make a new recording that includes both the music and the lyrics.

If the songwriter instead makes an audiovisual recording of the creative process, then for copyright purposes the resulting recording is an audiovisual work and not a sound recording. Nonetheless, it meets the fixation requirement for copyright in the musical work as well as the audiovisual work.

As should be clear from this discussion, for newly created works copyright notice and registration are not *required* in order for copyright to attach to a creative work. Copyright attaches automatically as the work is fixed in a tangible medium of expression. As discussed in the next section, however, copyright notice can be helpful as a practical matter, and registration conveys important legal benefits.

§ 3.5 COPYRIGHT NOTICE AND REGISTRATION

But what about copyright notice and registration? Although at one time copyright notice and/or registration were essential to securing or preserving copyright protection (see § 3.9[B] below), today they are optional. Under § 102, a newly created work, once fixed in tangible form, is automatically protected by copyright regardless of whether it displays a copyright notice or has been registered.

Even though notice is no longer required, it is still a good idea to place a copyright notice on a work before making copies (or "phonorecords," the term used for sound recordings) available to others, because it reminds people that the work is legally protected. (Many people erroneously believe that the absence of a copyright notice means that a work is unprotected.) For most works, the standard format for a copyright notice is the copyright symbol © followed by the year of the work's first publication and the name of the copyright owner at the time of publication. For example: © 2025 Joan Smith. For historical reasons, in the copyright notice for a sound recording, the © symbol is replaced with ℗, which stands for phonogram (a synonym for sound recordings, commonly used in international law).

As for copyright *registration*, while it is not essential to copyright protection, it does offer significant benefits, as discussed below.

In most cases, registration is a prerequisite to suing infringers. If someone infringes an unregistered copyright, the copyright owner will have to register the work before he or she can file an infringement claim. 17 U.S.C. § 411. Therefore, while a delay in registration will not cause a loss of copyright protection, it can cause a delay in pursuing an infringer.

There are other advantages to registering a work before infringement occurs: It enables the prevailing copyright owner to recover substantial damages (called "statutory" damages) without having to prove any actual damages such as lost profits. It also makes it possible to recover attorney's fees related to the infringement suit (although these are not guaranteed). See § 3.17 below.

If a work is registered no later than five years after its initial publication, then the certificate of registration is prima facie evidence of the copyright's validity and the facts stated on the certificate (such as authorship). This can be useful in infringement litigation, if the accused infringer challenges the validity or ownership of the copyright.

Registration is also important to monetizing the copyright. Registering a copyright creates a searchable public record that identifies the work's authorship and initial ownership. Potential licensees or purchasers will look to the Copyright Office records to identify the copyright owner(s) of a work, to secure a license, to send legal notices, and/or to pay royalties to the correct parties.

If a copyright is assigned, exclusively licensed, or used as collateral for a loan, the party acquiring the copyright interest will want to record the transaction in the Copyright Office promptly in order to protect against false ownership claims by others, and to enable potential buyers or licensees to identify the current owner. For the acquiring party to get this protection, however, the work must be registered before it can be recorded. Therefore, any third party that wants to acquire an interest in a copyrighted work should insist that the copyright be registered before the transaction takes place.

Copyright registration is a simple process that can be completed online at the website of the U.S. Copyright Office, www.copyright.gov. In registering a work, it is necessary to identify the type of work being registered. Thus, for example, the musical composition "I Will Always Love You" would be registered as a musical work, while Whitney Houston's recording of that song would be registered as a sound recording, and the film "The Bodyguard" would be registered as an audiovisual work.

One complete copy or phonorecord of the work (two, in the case of published works) must be submitted as part of the registration; in the event of an infringement suit, the deposit copy defines the scope of the copyright. In the case of musical works, under current law the deposit copy can be either sheet music or a phonorecord. The copyright owner should choose whichever format reflects the most complete version of the work. If the music was released only in a motion picture, the deposit can be either a copy of the motion picture or a copy or phonorecord of the musical work along with the title of the motion picture and any credits or copyright notice that appeared in the film credits to identify the musical work. In the case of sound recording copyrights, the deposit must include not only the phonorecord but any accompanying visual material, such as album covers, record sleeves, leaflets, and booklets, if any.

There are different copyright registration forms for different categories of copyrightable works: Use Form PA for musical works and audiovisual works, and use Form SR for sound recordings.

The copyright registration identifies the person who owns the copyright *at the time of registration*. Once a copyright has been registered, any change of ownership should be recorded with the Copyright Office. The responsibility for this falls on the new owner(s). (The same rule applies to exclusive licensees and persons who acquire security interests in the copyright.) Having an up-to-date record of ownership interests is essential for future licensees who will need to identify the *current* copyright owner for purposes of obtaining a license, paying royalties, and sending various legal notices.

Preregistration can be a useful option for musical works, sound recordings, and audiovisual works (such as music videos or karaoke recordings) that are being prepared for commercial release. Copyright in these works can be preregistered online (by providing a detailed description of the work using Form PRE) even before the works have been completed. The preregistration option is a valuable tool for copyright owners whose work might be infringed soon after, or even before, its commercial release. (This happens more often with motion pictures and computer software, but the Copyright Office offers the option for music and sound recordings as well.) Preregistration allows the copyright owner to sue an infringer before the work has been commercially released or fully registered. Full registration must be completed in a timely manner after infringement occurs or the work is completed and released. 17 U.S.C. §§ 408(f), 411(a); 37 C.F.R. § 202.16.

§ 3.6 WHO OWNS THE COPYRIGHT?

A. GENERAL RULE

The initial copyright owner of a work is always the author. The author is the actual human being who created the work, except in the case of works made for hire (as explained in § 3.6[B] below). If there are several authors, as in the case of musical works with multiple songwriters, then the initial copyright ownership is shared among them, except in the case of works made for hire.

When a musical work is co-written, the work is considered a "joint work" under copyright law, and each of the co-writers is considered a joint author. This is true regardless of whether one writer creates only the lyrics and another creates only the music, or whether several writers contribute to the lyric-writing and/or the composing.

Generally speaking, for a work to be joint, the amount and nature of each writer's contribution to a song does not matter; as long as each contributes more than a trivial amount of copyrightable expression and they create their contributions with the intention of combining them into a single unitary work. Unfortunately, some courts have refused to recognize creative contributors as joint authors where their contributions are relatively small, absent proof that the "dominant" author intended to share authorship. The Second Circuit first developed this approach in Childress v. Taylor, 945 F.2d 500, 509 (2d Cir. 1991). The Ninth Circuit adopted a variation of this test in Aalhmuhammed v. Lee, 202 F.3d 1227 (9th Cir. 2000) (looking at the extent of each collaborator's control over the creative process, the existence of objective manifestations of intent to share authorship, and whether the audience appeal of the work turns on both parties' contributions and "the share of each in its success cannot be appraised").

For an example of how the *Childress* standard affects songwriters, in Ulloa v. Universal Music and Video Distribution Group, 303 F.Supp.2d 409 (S.D.N.Y. 2004), the plaintiff spontaneously created a countermelody while listening to Jay-Z record a song in the studio. When Jay-Z incorporated this vocal phrase into his song without crediting or compensating the plaintiff, she sued. However, the court rejected her joint authorship claim because she could not prove that Jay-Z intended to share authorship.

Co-writers should reach an agreement on how copyright ownership in the song will be split among them. Music publishers and collecting societies (such as performing rights organizations or the Mechanical Licensing Collective) will need to know this allocation in order to ensure that each writer receives the correct share of any royalties generated by the musical work. Any delay in determining and communicating song splits will delay the writers' receipt of these royalties.

B. WORKS MADE FOR HIRE

The only situation in which the individual who actually creates a work is not considered its author for purposes of copyright law is where the work is created as a "work made for hire." In this situation, the party that hired or commissioned the creator is considered to be its author.

There are two types of works made for hire: those created by employees within the scope of their employment, and certain types of works commissioned from independent contractors under specific circumstances. (The modern statutory definition of a work made for hire is in § 101 of the 1976 Act, but its details have been fleshed out by the Supreme Court.)

Entertainers can be independent contractors for copyright purposes even if they are employees for purposes of union representation. *See* Horror, Inc. v. Miller, 15 F.4th 232 (2d Cir. 2021). Nonetheless, the question whether a particular individual is an employee or an independent contractor for copyright purposes is a fact-intensive analysis. *See* Community for Creative Non-Violence v. Reid, 490 U.S. 730

(1989) (applying a multi-factor analysis derived from the common law of agency).

For an independent contractor's work to qualify as a work made for hire under the current statutory definition, the parties must enter a signed, written contract expressly stating that the commissioned work is a work made for hire, and the work in question must fit certain statutory categories. Contributions to motion pictures, for example, are one such category, and indeed these are typically commissioned as works made for hire, with all creative contributors to the film (actors, writers, directors, designers, editors, etc.) required to sign written work-made-for-hire contracts. Another important category of works made for hire consists of contributions to collective works; these are individual separately copyrightable works (such as newspaper or magazine articles) that are published together in a collection (the newspaper or magazine, respectively).

Therefore, if the creator of a commissioned work is an independent contractor, then even if the contract includes work-made-for-hire language, this clause will not be enforceable unless the work fits one of the eligible categories listed in the work-made-for-hire definition. In the case of musical works, the only relevant categories are contributions to collective works, contributions to motion pictures and other audiovisual works, and translations.

While most musical works are not created as works made for hire, some of them are. For example, if a motion picture production company commissions a composer to create a film score under a properly executed work-made-for-hire contract, then the production company, and not the composer, is the author for copyright purposes. The same is true of music created for other audiovisual works such as televisions shows and video games. If an advertising agency keeps a jingle writer on its staff as a regular employee, then the agency, not the employee, is the author of the resulting jingles.

Some songwriters create music for production libraries. Some of these are owned by the major music publishers, while other are independent libraries. The production library owns the copyright in the musical work, and issues synchronization licenses to producers of audiovisual works such as films, television shows, commercials, sports broadcasts, and video games. The production library also collects public performance royalties when those audiovisual works are streamed or broadcast. (The writer's contract typically allows the writer to retain the standard writer's share (50%) of the nondramatic public performance rights.).

Even if the writer's contract with the production library states that the musical work is a work made for hire, this may not be enforceable because, as noted above, musical works created by independent contractors are not works made for hire unless they fit one of the statutory categories. Although the music created for a production library may eventually be licensed for use in an audiovisual work, it is arguable whether, at the time of its creation, it is specifically intended to be a part of such a work.

For the same reason, if the writer also creates a sound recording of the work for the production library, there are serious questions as to whether the sound recording can qualify as a work made for hire. Typically, however, the writer's contract with the production library will also include language assigning the copyrights in both the musical work and the sound recording to the library. This ensures that production libraries can own and license their masters.

Because the employer or commissioning party is considered the author of a work made for hire, ordinarily that party owns the entire copyright as well. 17 U.S.C. § 201(b). However, the parties to the agreement can override this default rule by contract, dividing the copyright ownership between them. *Id.* For example, if a television production company hires a composer to create music for a television show under a work-made-for-hire agreement, the agreement typically assigns the songwriter's traditional 50% share of nondramatic public performance rights back to the composer so that he or she can collect these royalties through a PRO.

One big problem with the work-made-for-hire doctrine is that, at this time, its application to sound recordings is uncertain. Recording contracts typically state that the sound recordings an artist creates for the record label are works made for hire authored by the record label, not the artist. However, it is not clear that these clauses are enforceable. Artists and record labels generally disagree on whether the recording artists were employees or independent contractors at the time they made their recordings. While the record labels may argue that the artists were employees, this argument might not succeed in court. If the artists were independent contractors, then their recordings can be works made for hire only if they fit within one of the statutory categories of commissioned works can be works made for hire under § 101. These include any work specially commissioned as part of an audiovisual work (such as a motion picture or video game) or as a contribution to a collective work (such as a magazine or newspaper). However, the statute does not list sound recordings among the eligible categories. Therefore, even if an artist's recording contract contains a "work made for hire" clause, it is not clear whether the record label can enforce it. This problem has persisted for a long time. To ensure that the record label owns the masters, recording contracts include a copyright assignment clause as a back-up, in case the work-made-for-hire clause is ineffective.

For works created prior to 1978, the definition of a work-made-for-hire was even less clear than it is today. There was no statutory definition at that time, and many courts interpreted the term quite broadly, compared to the more stringent definition found in the 1976 Act. *See, e.g.,* Martha Graham School & Dance Foundation v. Martha Graham Center of Contemporary Dance, Inc., 224 F.Supp.2d 567 (S.D.N.Y. 2002). Therefore, a work that might not be considered a work made for hire under current law might have qualified as such if it was created before 1978. As a result, during those years it was easier for a record label to establish that it, and not the recording artist, was the "author" of a master recording. *See, e.g.*, Fifty-Six hope Road Music Ltd. v. UMG Recordings, Inc., 2010 WL 3564258 (S.D.N.Y. 2010).

If the artist's recording contract assigns the record label full ownership of the sound recording copyright (the "master"), does it really matter whether a sound recording is a work made for hire? In fact, it does. As discussed in greater detail in § 3.10 below, an author can terminate a copyright assignment after a period of time specified by law (35 years, generally speaking), unless the work was created as a work made for hire. Today, quite a few valuable sound recordings are old enough for their authors to exercise their termination rights, and regain ownership of their masters, and a number of recording artists have sent termination notices to their record labels. Some of these may have resulted in negotiated settlements. However, in many cases it appears that the labels are simply ignoring the notices. In 2020, a group of recording artists filed a class action lawsuit to enforce their rights, but in 2023 the court ruled that they must sue individually. Waite v. UMG Recordings, Inc., 2023 WL 1069690 (S.D.N.Y. Jan. 27, 2023). Due to the high cost of litigation, many of these artists may be unable to proceed with their claims.

If a sound recording is eligible for termination, this raises another thorny authorship problem: Who are the "authors" that are eligible to terminate the grant, and who will own the rights post-termination? Because a sound recording is a highly collaborative work, if it is not a work made for hire then it is probably a work of joint authorship. While the authorship group will certainly include the performing artists featured on the recording, other creative contributors may have authorship claims as well – including the producer, mixer, sound engineer, session musicians, and potentially others. If some of these are employees of the record label, the record label itself may be a joint author.

§ 3.7 ASSIGNMENTS

As noted earlier, the author of a work is its *initial* copyright owner. But authors are free to assign their copyrights to others. An author can assign the entire copyright, or any portion of it. Under current copyright law, an assignment is valid only if it is in writing and signed by the transferor.

In the case of jointly authored works, an assignment of the entire copyright requires the written consent of all of the authors. However, if the joint authors enter a written agreement to divide ownership of the copyright, then each can individually assign his or her share. Therefore, once the co-writers of a song have agreed on their song splits, each is free to assign his or her share of the song to a different publisher, which is a fairly common scenario.

Payment for an assignment may involve a lump sum, fixed installment payments, or periodic payments that are contingent on the revenues that the copyright generates for the grantee. Payments of the latter sort are called "royalties."

Assignments should always be recorded in the Copyright Office. This creates a searchable public record of who owns or controls each part of the copyright in any given work. Maintaining an up-to-date public record of ownership is important for the successful exploitation of the work, as it enables potential purchasers or licensees to identify and contact the current copyright owner(s). For certain licenses imposed by law ("statutory" or "compulsory" licenses), the copyright owner's identity and contact information must be a matter of public record in order for the royalties to reach the party entitled to them.

If authors are free to transfer their copyright ownership to others, then why are work-made-for-hire agreements so popular? Couldn't the party that commissions an artist or writer to create a work simply require that person to assign the copyright? After all, commissioned works have to fit certain specific categories (e.g., contribution to an audiovisual work or a collective work) in order to qualify as works made for hire, whereas copyrights of *all* kinds can be assigned.

Work-made-for-hire contracts remain important because there are a handful of significant differences between authorship and "mere" copyright ownership. In the context of music and sound recordings, the most important difference is that human authors who transfer their copyrights have the option to terminate those transfers and reclaim their rights after several decades have passed. Because this option is inalienable, artists cannot be compelled to surrender it in their recording contracts. In contrast, human authors who create works made for hire do not possess this termination right. Therefore, commissioning parties generally prefer work-made-for-hire arrangements (if the work qualifies) over mere assignments. Individual authors, however, are usually better off assigning their copyrights in order to preserve their termination rights. After all, when creating a musical work or sound recording, it is difficult to predict whether it will enjoy long-term success. Authors who exercise their termination rights can get a "second bite at the apple" if they believe that they sold their rights too cheaply at the time of creation. Upon reclaiming their copyrights, they may be able to resell or re-license their rights at a better price. Termination is so important, and the rules so complex, that this subject is addressed as a separate topic in § 3.10 below.

As noted in § 3.6[B] above, the law is unclear whether, and under what circumstances, a sound recording can be created as a work made for hire. Although record labels are aware of this problem, they still include work-made-for-hire language in their recording contracts in hope that the legal issue will eventually be resolved in their favor. As a backup, however, recording contracts also contain a clause stating that the recording artist assigns the copyright in the master recording to the record label. That way, even if the recording fails to qualify as a work made for hire, the record label will still own the copyright unless and until the recording artist decides to terminate the assignment.

In a valid work-made-for-hire arrangement, although the employer or commissioning party will be recognized as the author for copyright purposes, the parties to the agreement might not intend for the commissioning party to own 100 percent of the copyright. If they want to share ownership of the copyright, § 201(b) of the copyright statutes allows them to make this allocation in their work-made-for-hire contract. In effect, the legal "author" of the work made for hire is assigning part of the copyright back to the work's actual creator. This technique is often used in commissioning film scores to enable the composer to retain certain valuable economic rights, such as the "writer's share" (50%) of nondramatic public performance royalties.

§ 3.8 LICENSES

Several types of copyright licenses are fundamental to the music industry. For musical works, these include mechanical licenses (see Chapter 5), public performance licenses (see Chapter 6), and synchronization licenses (see Chapter 4).

For sound recordings, important licenses include digital audio transmission licenses (see Chapter 7) and master recording (or "master use") licenses. The latter can authorize the licensee to copy and use the copyrighted sound recording in any of a wide variety of ways, such as incorporating it into a motion picture, video game, or commercial, or allowing a portion of the recording to be "sampled" in another sound recording.

A licensed use of a sound recording, however, typically also involves use of the underlying musical work. Therefore, the holder of a master use license or a digital audio transmission license typically will also need a license from the copyright owner of the musical work. There are exceptions, however. For example, as discussed in § 3.13[D] below, a digital sample of a sound recording might incorporate so little of the underlying musical work that a license for the latter is not required.

Before exploring the details of these licenses, it is important to understand the basic rules that govern copyright licenses.

A copyright owner can license any of his or her exclusive rights under § 106. Unlike an assignment, which confers unfettered ownership of the copyright (or a specified portion of it), a license conveys specific rights, subject to specific limits, that are delineated in the license. For example, the license may be limited as to time, may be valid only within particular countries, may apply only to certain types of media or uses, and may be revocable under certain circumstances (such as nonpayment). Payment for a license can be a lump sum, fixed installment payments, or periodic royalties that are contingent on the revenues generated by the licensed work.

Licenses may be exclusive or non-exclusive. An *exclusive* license gives the grantee rights that are exclusive within the time, territory, media, and uses specified in the license. The licensor, therefore, is making a commitment not to grant anyone else an interest in the copyright that overlaps or interferes with the rights of the exclusive licensee. A *non-exclusive* license is merely permission to use the copyrighted work in the manner specified in the license. (They are sometimes referred to as permissions, waivers, or clearances). The copyright owner is therefore free to give overlapping non-exclusive licenses to multiple parties. For example, when PROs give blanket public performance licenses to radio stations, these licenses are non-exclusive. The PRO will license the exact same rights to other radio stations, even within the same geographic territory. That is why multiple radio stations can play the same music, even within the same city.

Like an assignment, an exclusive license requires a writing signed by the licensor, and should be recorded in the Copyright Office in order to create a public record showing who controls the particular rights in question. In contrast, non-exclusive licenses need not be in writing, and frequently go unrecorded. Non-exclusive licenses can even be *implied* licenses, arising from the conduct of the parties. *See* Effects, Inc. v. Cohen, 908 F.2d 555 (9th Cir. 1990); Oddo v. Ries, 743 F.2d 630 (9th Cir. 1984). Nonetheless, if either the non-exclusive license or the copyright itself is valuable, it is in the licensee's best interest to have it reduced to writing and signed by the copyright owner, in order to have proof in the event of a subsequent dispute.

Where a work is jointly authored, as is the case with many musical works, an exclusive license requires the consent of all of the authors. In contrast, each individual joint author is free to grant *non-*

exclusive licenses, subject to a duty to share the profits with the other joint authors. The authors can depart from these rules by entering a written agreement with one another. In another departure from the rules, when the co-writers of a song belong to different PROs, blanket licensees must obtain licenses from each PRO, even though the licenses are non-exclusive. (See § 6.2[A] below.)

§ 3.9 HOW LONG DOES COPYRIGHT LAST?

The general answer is: a long, long time.

More specifically, the answer to this question depends on the time period when the work was created or first published. We will start with the copyright term for newly created works (anything created in 1978 through the present). Then, we will look at the rules for determining the copyright term for works that were copyrighted *before* 1978. The latter rules are important for anyone who owns an interest in one of these older works, as well as anyone who wishes to exploit one of them—for example, by creating a new version, or by sampling.

A. WORKS CREATED IN 1978 OR LATER

As you know, under the 1976 Act copyright attaches to a new work at the moment it is fixed in a tangible medium of expression.[2] That marks the

---

[2] Between 1978 and 1989, even though copyright attached at the moment of fixation, it was possible for the copyright to be forfeited. During this period, publishing a work without a copyright notice could cause the work to enter the public domain.

beginning of the copyright term of protection. But when does that term *end*?

Under the 1976 Act, the answer depends on the authorship of the work. In the case of *works made for hire*, the term is a fixed, predictable number of years: The copyright expires 95 years from the date of first publication (that is, the first public distribution of copies or phonorecords), or 120 years from the date of creation, whichever expires first.

The rules are different for works that are *not* created as works made for hire—in other words, works by individual or joint authors. For these works, the copyright term ends 70 years after the author's death. In the case of joint works, such as co-written songs, copyright ends 70 years after the death of the last surviving author. As you can see, the exact date on which these copyrights will expire cannot be determined until the last joint author has died. Also, it does not matter whether the copyright has been sold. Even if the author no longer owns the copyright, protection will still expire 70 years after the author's date of death.

This is another reason why copyright registration is valuable: It creates a record of the work's creation date and its authorship (individual, joint, or work

---

There were a number of exceptions to this rule, however. Under one exception, the copyright owner could rescue the copyright by registering it within 5 years, and adding a copyright notice to all copies distributed in the U.S. in the future. 17 U.S.C. § 405(a). Fortunately, newly created works today are not subject to the notice requirement.

made for hire). This will enable interested parties to determine when the copyright will expire.

Under these rules, which apply to all works *created in 1978 or later*, writers and performers who create new copyrightable works today will be outlived by their copyrights. Since copyrights can be inherited, just like other property, copyright owners should give serious thought to estate planning.

B. WORKS COPYRIGHTED BEFORE 1978

If a work was copyrighted before 1978 (through publication with a copyright notice or, for some works, through registration), a completely different—and more complicated—set of rules determines its term of protection. And the nature of the authorship (sole, joint, or work made for hire) is not relevant.

Even though these rules do not apply to newly created works, it is necessary to understand them in order to determine the current copyright status of older works. After all, a vast number of musical works published before 1978 are still commercially valuable today.

Because so much great music and literature was created before 1978, a modern creator inspired by one of these older works may want to incorporate it into a new work. Before exploiting one of these older works, it is important to figure out whether that work was ever copyrighted, and, if so, whether it has since lost its copyright protection. The relevant rules are summarized briefly here.

Before 1978, federal copyright did *not* attach automatically at the time a work was first fixed in tangible form. (The rules under the 1976 Act did not take effect until 1978.) Instead, the work began its life with perpetual "common law" copyright rather than limited-term copyright under the federal statutes. The work lost its common law copyright as soon as it was distributed to the public. However, it could still receive federal copyright protection if each of the publicly distributed copies or phonorecords bore a copyright notice in the proper form. If the copies or phonorecords were distributed without copyright notice, then the work lost its copyright completely. In other words, it entered the "public domain." This old rule is the reason why many people today still believe (mistakenly) that copyright notice is essential to copyright protection.

A slightly different rule applied to pre-1978 works that were not intended for public distribution—unpublished screenplays and musical works that were not published as sheet music, for example. Such works still enjoyed perpetual common law copyright protection from the moment of creation (and could lose that protection if publicly distributed without a copyright notice). However, if the copyright owner wanted to trade common law protection for federal protection without publicly distributing copies with notice, the owner could accomplish this by registering the copyright.

Now that you know when copyright attached to pre-1978 works (upon publication with notice, or upon registration), here is some good news: Except for certain sound recordings, if a work was copyrighted in *1929 or earlier*, then it entered the public domain (meaning its copyright term ended) no later than the beginning of 2025 (and in some cases much earlier). And you can roll those numbers forward: A work copyrighted in 1930 will be in the public domain by the start of 2026, and so forth. Essentially, to find the latest possible year in which one of these works becomes part of the public domain, just add 96 years to the year that the work's federal copyright protection began. (This rule is not reliable for pre-1972 sound recordings, however, for reasons explained later.)

This rule of thumb works because, for a work other than a pre-1972 sound recording, the longest possible copyright term it could have enjoyed under pre-1978 law is 95 years. Therefore, if the work was copyrighted more than 95 years ago, whatever copyright it once possessed has expired by now. If it is less than 95 years old, however, it might still be protected by copyright.

For pre-1978 copyrights that have *not* yet expired, there are several variables that affect the copyright term. (The life of the author is *not* one of them.) As described above, the term of protection for these works is measured not from their creation date, but from the date they were first published with copyright notice (or registered, for unpublished works such as screenplays or musical works that were not released as sheet music). This was the moment when federal copyright first attached to the work. To determine the date on which the copyright term *expires*, however, requires some knowledge of the work's history, as discussed below.

In general, copyright for these works lasted for 28 years, 75 years, or 95 years, depending on certain events. Obviously, that's a huge difference. Someone who is interested in using one of these works will therefore want to investigate further.

Originally, all of these pre-1978 copyrights had only 28 years of protection, but the owner had the option to renew the copyright before the end of the 28th year. Some copyright owners failed to renew (sometimes by mistake or because they were unaware of the requirement), which caused their copyrights to enter the public domain after only 28 years. (This happened to the films *Pygmalion* and *It's a Wonderful Life*.) If they renewed by the deadline, however, then they received an additional 28 years of protection, to which Congress eventually added another 19 years, for a total term of 75 years. (In 1992, renewals became automatic, making life easier for copyright owners.) Then, in a 1998 amendment, Congress added yet another 20 years of protection to all existing copyrights. So, if a work's copyright was still in force in 1998, then its copyright lasted for a total term of 95 years. In contrast, if a work had already exhausted its 28 or 75 years of protection before that date, it did not get the 20-year extension.

There are, however, three additional wrinkles affecting the copyright term for pre-1978 works. These special rules apply to sound recordings, certain foreign works, and works that had been created but not federally copyrighted as of January 1, 1978. These special situations are addressed next.

C. SOUND RECORDINGS

Sound recordings created in 1978 or later have the same copyright term as other categories of copyrightable works—the life of the author plus 70 years, or, for works made for hire, the shorter of 95 years from publication or 120 years from creation. In contrast, sound recordings created *before* 1978 have several different terms of protection, depending on when the master recording was created.

The reason for this complexity is that sound recordings created on or after February 15, 1972, are treated as copyrighted works, subject to the same copyright terms as other works, while those created *before* that date are protected by a separate statute—§ 1401, as discussed in § 3.3 earlier—which has a slightly different term of protection. Here are the terms of protection for each group of sound recordings:

If a sound recording was publicly distributed with notice between February 15, 1972, and January 1, 1978, it received 95 years of copyright protection. (This figure takes full account of automatic renewal and the 20-year extension that took effect in 1998). Note that, during this period, a copyright notice was required in order to keep the work out of the public domain.

However, if a sound recording was created *before* February 15, 1972, then, under § 1401, its term of protection expires *at least* 95 years from its first public distribution, but in many cases it lasts longer. How much longer depends on the year in which the recording was first published; § 1401 spells this out in detail. There is, however, an outer limit to this protection: § 1401 does not protect any sound recordings beyond 2067. (Because these works were distributed at a time when no federal protection was available, it does not matter whether they bore a copyright notice.)

Since § 1401 does not affect the copyright term of newly created recordings, its details generally need not concern artists and record labels with respect to their new works. However, if a new recording were to contain a "sample" from one of these older recordings, then § 1401 would be highly relevant to determining whether a sampling license is required.

D. FOREIGN WORKS

Normally, once a work has lost its copyright, it remains in the public domain forever. However, there is one big exception to this rule: In the case of certain *foreign* works that were at one time in the public domain in the U.S., their copyrights have been restored. This unusual scenario came began in 1994, when Congress changed the law to comply with a series of international treaties in which the U.S. participates.

It will require some research to determine whether a particular foreign work was affected by this change in the law. The rules are fairly complex. (They are found in § 104A.) Generally speaking, however, if a work of foreign origin entered the U.S. public domain because the U.S. had no copyright treaty with that country, or because the foreign copyright owner failed to comply with various formalities (notice, registration, and/or renewal) that were once required by U.S. copyright law, there is a good chance that the foreign work's copyright was restored in 1996 or later. The same is true of foreign sound recordings that did not receive federal copyright protection because they were created before the critical date (February 15, 1972).

The lesson here is to proceed with caution in utilizing a work of foreign origin that appears to be in the public domain (or a derivative work that incorporates it); even if the foreign work was in the public domain at one time, this might no longer be the case, in which case a license may be required. This precaution, however, does not apply to *domestic* works that entered the public domain due to noncompliance with formalities; those works remain forever in the public domain.

E. WORKS CREATED BUT NOT FEDERALLY COPYRIGHTED AS OF JANUARY 1, 1978

So far, we have talked about the copyright term for works *created* in 1978 or later, and the copyright term for works *published or registered* before 1978. But there is one group of works that falls between the cracks: Copyrightable works created before 1978 but neither copyrighted nor in the public domain as of January 1, 1978. Mostly, these are works that were created but still unpublished as of that date. You can think of these as works that were sitting in a desk drawer, gathering dust, as of the critical date. What is the term of protection for those works?

In general, these works are subject to the copyright term created by the 1976 Act: the life of the author plus 70 years, or else the fixed term of years (95 or 120) for works made for hire. For long-deceased authors, this general rule meant that their works would have entered the public domain immediately on, or shortly after, January 1, 1978. Thus, they would have gone very quickly from having perpetual common law copyright to having no copyright at all, dealing a harsh blow to the heirs of these authors. To help heirs avoid this abrupt loss of protection, Congress created a special rule: If such a work was published by the end of 2002, its copyright would last until at least 2047. (Note that sound recordings created before February 15, 1972, are not covered by this rule, since they are protected by § 1401 rather than by copyright, as discussed in § 3.9[C] above.)

§ 3.10 TERMINATION RIGHTS

A. IN GENERAL

Subject to only a few exceptions, federal law gives the author the right to terminate any copyright assignment, exclusive license, or non-exclusive license, and to reclaim his or her copyright interest, after a period of time established by law. The author does not have to compensate the grantee for exercising the termination right. In addition, the right is unwaivable. Therefore, the author cannot surrender it by contract, even if the grantee offers additional consideration to include such a waiver in the grant. As a result, even if the written instrument for the copyright assignment or license states that the rights received by the grantee are "perpetual," or endure for the entire remaining term of copyright, free of any termination right, as a matter of federal law this language is not enforceable.

Songwriters routinely exercise their termination rights with respect to their publishing agreements. Historically, most songwriters have assigned the copyrights in their musical compositions to publishers, in exchange for royalties. (See Chapter 4.) As each such grant becomes eligible for termination, songwriters send termination notices to their publishers. Sometimes the parties successfully renegotiate their publishing agreement, and continue their relationship. In other cases, the songwriters reclaim their copyrights and either self-publish or find a new publishing partner.

There are actually three different termination rights in the copyright statutes, each created for a different time period and a different purpose. These provisions are found in §§ 203, 304(c), and 304(d). Contemporary authors are most likely to utilize § 203, while earlier generations of authors (and their heirs) will find their rights addressed in §§ 304(c) and (d).

All of the termination provisions have several things in common. First, they do not apply to works made for hire. Congress's purpose in allowing terminations was to benefit individual creators and their families, especially when the value of the copyright has increased since the time of the grant. Because individual creators are not considered "authors" of their works made for hire, they do not receive this benefit. Therefore, songwriters who create music for films, television shows, video games, or other audiovisual works under valid work-made-for-hire contracts (see § 3.6[B] above) typically have no termination right with respect to those works. In the case of sound recordings, although a number of recording artists are attempting to use the termination right to regain ownership of their masters, record labels are resisting these attempts by arguing that the masters were created as works made for hire. If the record labels succeed, then the artists and their heirs will have no termination rights. (This issue does not arise with respect to pre-1972 recordings that are protected by § 1401 rather than by copyright; termination is not available at all for those works, because, by their own terms, the termination provisions apply only to "copyright" grants.)

Second, all terminations are subject to a "derivative works" exception, which permits the grantee to continue exploiting a derivative work that was lawfully created under the terms of the grant, provided that the derivative work was created before the effective date of termination. Thus, for example, if a songwriter assigns his or her copyright to a publisher, who then grants a mechanical license to a record label and a synchronization license to a motion picture producer, the resulting sound recording and motion picture are derivative works. If the songwriter later terminates the publisher's assignment, the record label and the owner of the motion picture's copyright can continue to exploit the derivative works. The termination of the publisher's rights in the underlying work simply means that the publisher cannot create or authorize any further derivative works based on the underlying work.

When a songwriter terminates the publisher's grant, but the record label or film company lawfully continues to exploit the derivative work, who is entitled to the publisher's share of the post-termination royalties generated by the derivative work? Generally speaking, the original publisher can continue to receive those royalties. The Supreme Court held in Mills Music, Inc. v. Snyder, 469 U.S. 153 (1985), that the derivative works exception preserves all of the contractual rights arising from the original license to create the derivative work.

In Woods v. Bourne Co., 60 F.3d 978 (2d Cir. 1995), the Second Circuit applied this rule to public performance royalties generated by television performances of a film that incorporated a musical work pursuant to a pre-termination synchronization license. Because the film was a licensed derivative work created prior to termination, the public performance royalties that ASCAP collected under its blanket license to the television broadcaster were payable to the original publisher, even for post-termination broadcasts. However, the court reached the opposition conclusion with respect to the performance royalties that ASCAP collected for radio performances of sound recordings created before termination. (See § 7.1 below.) Even though sound recordings are derivative works, the court reasoned, they do not enjoy a public performance right in the context of radio broadcasts. Therefore, the court treated the sound recording's derivative work status as irrelevant, and treated the radio performance of the recording the same as a live performance of the music, generating royalties only for the post-termination owner of the musical work.

In 2024 the Copyright Office determined that the *Mills Music* analysis does not apply to royalties generated by the blanket compulsory mechanical license for streaming recordings of musical works. (This blanket license is discussed in Chapter 5). Therefore, any post-termination streaming royalties generated by the blanket compulsory mechanical license belong to the party that owns the copyright in the musical work *after* the effective date of termination. This will be the songwriter(s), their statutory heirs, or any publisher to which they assign the post-termination copyright.

In the case of a deceased author, the surviving family members or the author's estate can exercise the termination right and reclaim the remainder of the copyright. However, the termination statutes are quite particular about *which* family members have this right, and in what proportions, and at what point the right belongs to the author's estate. Therefore, the question of who owns the author's postmortem termination right is not necessarily governed by the author's will or by state inheritance laws.

Under each of the termination provisions, the party seeking to terminate the grant must serve the grantee with a signed, written termination notice 2–10 years before the effective date of termination. The notice's content and manner of service must comply with Copyright Office regulations, and a copy must be recorded with the Copyright Office.

Regardless of which termination provision applies, termination affects only the grantee's interest in domestic copyright. If the original grant covered foreign copyrights as well (and many copyright assignments are "worldwide" in scope), the grantee's interest in those foreign copyrights will be unaffected.

B. WHICH GRANTS CAN BE TERMINATED, AND WHEN

1. Post-1977 Grants

The termination right under § 203 is the one most relevant to contemporary artists, because it applies to grants made by authors on or after January 1, 1978.

If the grant covers the right to publicly distribute copies or phonorecords of the work ("publication," within the meaning of copyright law), then it can be terminated 35–40 years after the work's publication date, or 40–45 years after the execution of the grant, whichever term ends first.

If the grant was made by a single author, that author can terminate. If the grant was made by two or more authors of a joint work (such as a co-written song), then the grant can be terminated only by a majority of the authors who executed it. If any author is deceased, his or her termination right can be exercised by surviving family members, or the estate, in a specific order of priority spelled out in the statute.

Congress created the § 203 termination right to give authors (or their surviving family members) a "second chance" to capture the full value of their copyrighted works. Because it can be difficult to assess the full economic value of a copyrighted work when it is first created, and new authors often have little bargaining power relative to publishers or other grantees, many authors find, in retrospect, that they extracted too low a price when they initially assigned or licensed their copyrights. § 203 gives them the opportunity to reclaim their copyrights and issue new grants at prices that are more commensurate with the value of the works.

2. Pre-1978 Grants

Under § 304(c), grants that were executed before 1978 can be terminated after the work in question has ended its 56th year of copyright protection. There is a good reason for this timing: As discussed in § 3.9[B] above, works copyrighted before 1978 had an initial copyright term of 28 years, followed by a 28-year renewal term, but that renewal term was eventually extended to 47 years in the 1976 Act, thus creating a "windfall" of 19 additional years of copyright protection (the "extended renewal term").

Because many authors had already conveyed their entire renewal term before the 19-year extension took effect, Congress had to choose who would get the economic benefit of the additional 19 years. Congress decided that the benefit should go to the authors (and their families) rather than to the grantees. Therefore, it gave the authors and their families the right to terminate these grants *before* the copyright in the work entered its 19-year extended renewal term.

Because Congress later extended the renewal term once again, adding another 20 years in 1998, for many of these older works a termination under § 304(c) actually reclaims 39 years of copyright protection rather than only 19. That makes it extremely valuable for many works.

The termination right under § 304(c) is not limited to grants that were executed by authors; it also applies to grants that were executed by a deceased author's family or estate. (The statute specifies the order of priority among the eligible heirs.)

If the grant was executed by one or more of the work's authors, each author that executed it can terminate it to the extent of that author's ownership share of the renewal copyright. If an author is dead, the surviving family members or the estate can terminate that author's share, according to the order of priority specified in the statute. If the grant was executed by a deceased author's family or estate, the surviving person(s) who executed it can terminate it.

Termination can be effective at any time during a 5-year period beginning at the end of the 56th year of copyright protection.

The most recently enacted termination provision applies to pre-1978 grants that were eligible for termination under § 304(c) but were not terminated, but only if the termination deadline was before 1998. The copyright must also have been in its 47-year renewal term as of 1998, the year that Congress added another 20 years to all subsisting copyrights, bringing the renewal term to a total of 67 years.

Why did Congress decide to give these authors, and their families, a second chance to terminate? If they had exercised their rights under § 304(c) before those rights expired, they would have received the 19-year extended renewal term. Having passed up that opportunity, they would also have missed out on the additional 20 years that Congress added to all subsisting renewal terms in 1998. Congress decided that the authors and their heirs should have the opportunity to capture this 20-year windfall rather than have it go automatically to the grantee. Therefore, beginning in 1998, authors and their families can reclaim the remaining 20 years of copyright by terminating under § 304(d).

Termination under this new rule may be effective during a 5-year window beginning in the 75th year of copyright protection. In other respects, terminations under § 304(d) are subject to the same rules as § 304(c) terminations.

3. "Gap" Grants

Some grants of musical works and sound recordings will fall into the problematic category of "gap" grants. A gap grant is an assignment or license that was executed before 1978 with respect to a work that was not actually created until 1978 or later.

For example, if a songwriter signed a publishing contract before 1978 that assigned the copyrights in his or her future works to the publisher, some of those works might not have been created until 1978 or later. Similarly, an artist that signed a recording contract before 1978 may have delivered one or more albums in 1978 or later. (This is an especially interesting situation because, as discussed in § 3.6[B] above, post-1977 sound recordings are less likely to qualify as works made for hire than recordings made earlier.)

These arrangements present a problem, because §§ 304(c) and (d) govern pre-1978 grants, but termination under §§ 304(c) or (d) is not possible for a work created in 1978 or later (since those works do not have renewal terms).

The Copyright Office has decided that gap grants can be terminated under § 203. Even though § 203 applies only to post-1977 grants, the Copyright Office has reasoned that a copyright grant cannot be effective until the work of authorship has come into existence. Therefore, for termination purposes, the "execution" date of a gap grant is the date on which the work was created (and fixed in a tangible medium of expression). 37 C.F.R. § 201.10(f)(1)(ii)(C).

§ 3.11 OWNERSHIP UNDER FOREIGN LAW

Note, however, that the federal copyright rules pertaining to authorship, ownership, assignments, licenses, and terminations reflect only domestic copyright law. Since most copyrighted works in the music industry are intended for international exploitation, it is important to recognize that the authorship, ownership, assignment, and licensing laws of other countries may be different, and that terminations under federal copyright law are unlikely to affect grants of rights in foreign countries.

Even if a work was created in the U.S., it is possible that another country might analyze the work's authorship and/or ownership differently. For example, many countries do not recognize the concept of a work made for hire, or may define or apply the concept differently. (This is another reason why a work-made-for-hire contract should also include a copyright assignment as a back-up.) Also, a foreign country may approach joint authorship differently, applying different rules to determine who qualifies as a joint author and what rights each joint author can exercise.

Therefore, before exploiting a copyrighted work in a foreign country, it may be necessary to do some research to determine who controls the relevant portion of the copyright in that country. If the work incorporates an underlying work under a derivative work license (such as a sampling license), it is also important to determine whether that license conveys the necessary rights in the other countries where the derivative work will be exploited.

§ 3.12 EXCLUSIVE RIGHTS OF COPYRIGHT OWNERS

The copyright owner of a work has several exclusive rights with respect to that work. These are found in § 106.

This part of the chapter presents a general overview of these rights, with a focus on their application to musical works and sound recordings. Several of the rights receive additional attention in subsequent chapters devoted to publishing rights, public performance licenses, and mechanical licenses.

Although the exclusive rights recognized in § 106 are subject to a long list of exceptions and limitations, we will begin by simply listing the rights. They are:

(1) The right to reproduce the work in copies or phonorecords;

(2) The right to create adaptations (or "derivative works");

(3) The right to distribute copies or phonorecords to the public;

(4) The right to publicly perform certain types of works;

(5) The right to publicly display certain types of works; and

(6) The right to publicly perform sound recordings by digital audio transmission.

Right away, you may notice an apparent redundancy: There seem to be two public performance rights. Indeed, there are. The general public performance right (§ 106(4)) applies to musical works (and several other types of works), but it does *not* apply to sound recordings. Instead, the public performance right for sound recordings is much narrower: It is limited to public performance by way of digital audio transmissions (§ 106(6)).

Under § 106(4), the public performance right for musical works applies to performances that occur in places that are open to the public, or where members of the public are actually gathered (even if they are gathered in a private space like someone's home, unless they are just a normal circle of family and friends). It also applies to *transmissions*, such as radio and television broadcasts, streaming, and webcasting, even if members of the public receive the transmission in different places or at different times (for example, through on-demand streaming services).

Under § 106(6), however, the public performance right for sound recordings is much narrower. It applies only to satellite radio (SiriusXM), music streaming services, and webcasting (FCC-licensed radio broadcasts that are simultaneously streamed).

Why are sound recordings treated differently? Recall that they had no copyright protection at all until 1972. When Congress finally agreed that sound recordings needed protection, its only concern (and that of the recording industry) was record piracy—that is, the unauthorized copying and distribution of copyrighted sound recordings. So, when Congress amended the copyright law in 1971 to extend copyright protection to sound recordings for the first time, it granted them protection against unauthorized *copying and distribution,* but not against unauthorized public performances. In contrast, musical works (meaning the music and lyrics, if any, that are performed on a sound recording) already enjoyed a full public performance right, and continue to do so today.

In later years, the recording industry lobbied heavily to extend the public performance right to sound recordings, but its efforts were stymied by opposition from the broadcasting and music publishing industries, both of which were concerned that they would suffer economic harm if broadcasters were required to pay royalties not only for musical works but also for sound recordings. (Also, the broadcasting industry argued that radio play actually stimulated record sales, and for many years this was probably true.) With the advent of music streaming services and satellite radio, however, these services began to pose a serious threat to record sales. In 1995, the recording industry finally persuaded Congress to create a *digital* public performance right for sound recordings (§ 106(6)), applicable only to streaming services and satellite radio (today encompassing webcasting as well). Given the explosive growth of these music services since that time, digital performance royalties now represent a substantial income stream for the U.S. recording industry. The digital public performance right, however, is surprisingly complex; the details are addressed in Chapter 7.

Since 1995, the domestic recording industry has continued its efforts to broaden the public performance right for sound recordings to include traditional radio and television broadcasts, and it may one day succeed. For now, however, the U.S. remains one of the only countries in the world that fails to recognize a full public performance right in sound recordings. As a result of foreign reciprocity requirements, the U.S. recording industry has lost out not only on domestic performance royalties, but on foreign performance royalties as well. Considering the worldwide popularity of U.S. sound recordings, this is a significant revenue loss.

You may have noticed one other oddity in the list of exclusive rights under § 106: the phrase "copies or phonorecords." For arcane historical reasons, Congress uses the term "phonorecords" to refer to copies of sound recordings. Copies of other kinds of works are simply called "copies." As a result, you will find the cumbersome phrase "copies or phonorecords" throughout the copyright statutes.

All of these exclusive rights are subject to limitations and exceptions. (These are found in §§ 107–122.) The most important exceptions for the music industry are addressed in detail later in this chapter.

For now, one fairly straightforward limitation is worth mentioning. It involves the right to reproduce a work in copies or phonorecords, as well as the right to create derivative works. And it is another example of how sound recordings do not receive the same level of copyright protection that is afforded to other works (including musical works).

For all works *other than* sound recordings, the right to reproduce a work, or to incorporate it into a derivative work, includes both verbatim (exact) copying *and* close imitations. (The test is whether the imitation is "substantially similar" to the copyrighted work.) In the case of sound recordings, however, mere imitation—no matter how close—does not infringe the reproduction right or the right to create derivative works. Instead, the exclusive reproduction and adaptation rights for sound recordings are limited to the right to duplicate the existing recording (or portions thereof) by capturing the actual sounds fixed in that recording—for example, by using analog or digital copying technology.

Thus, from a copyright perspective, it is perfectly okay for an artist to make a "soundalike" recording of an existing recording by independently creating sounds that are similar or identical to those in the recording—provided, of course, that the artist has a mechanical license for the underlying musical work (which is not usually a problem, under the § 115 compulsory mechanical license). The copyright statute, § 114(b), refers to a soundalike recording as an "independent fixation" of sounds that "imitate or simulate" the sounds in the earlier recording. You can think of it as "re-creating" the sounds. This is why Taylor Swift was within her legal rights to re-record the same songs ("Taylor's Version") that she had already released on earlier masters that she created while under contract to her former record label. She delivered a new live performance of each song, and recorded that new performance. Under copyright law, she was free to imitate her previous masters as closely as she wished. (If an artist makes a soundalike recording that imitates *another artist's* voice without permission, however, this could run afoul of the other artist's right of publicity under state law. See Chapter 9.)

The same rule applies to derivative works that incorporate portions of pre-existing sound recordings. If the derivative work actually "samples" the previous recording, this implicates the reproduction right as well as the right to create derivative works. Therefore, the party wishing to sample an existing recording must obtain a master use license from the copyright owner of that recording (typically a record label). The master use license authorizes the licensee to duplicate the actual sounds fixed in the earlier recording, and to include them in a derivative work. However, no master use license is required in order to merely imitate the sounds from the previous recording by independently re-creating them, because this does not infringe the copyright in that recording, no matter how perfect the imitation. (But note that the imitation might still infringe the copyright in the musical work itself, unless a mechanical license—negotiated or compulsory—was obtained.)

§ 3.13 INFRINGEMENT

A. IN GENERAL

To infringe a copyright is to exercise one or more of the copyright owner's exclusive rights without legal authorization. That authorization can take either of two forms: (1) the copyright owner's consent (in other words, a license), or (2) one of the exceptions or limitations found in §§ 107–22 of the copyright statutes (the most pertinent of which are discussed in § 3.15 below).

Infringement may be direct or indirect. A direct infringer is the person who actually engages in the infringing conduct (e.g., reproducing or publicly performing the work). Direct infringement is based on strict liability: The person that carries out the infringing activity will be liable regardless of whether he or she realizes that the work is copyrighted and the activity is infringing. Indirect infringement, or "secondary liability," holds a defendant responsible for direct infringement by another party, based on either (1) the defendant's conduct and state of mind, or (2) the defendant's relationship to the direct infringer.

B. ELEMENTS OF INFRINGEMENT LIABILITY

As noted above, direct infringement is the unauthorized exercise of one or more of the exclusive rights of the copyright owner, and is based on principles of strict liability. Thus, a defendant may be liable for direct infringement without ever realizing that the work was copyrighted or the activity was infringing.

The copyist's work need not be identical in order to infringe. The legal standard is "substantial similarity," not verbatim copying. Two works are substantially similar if "an average lay observer would recognize the alleged copy as having been appropriated from the copyrighted work." Ideal Toy Corp. v. Fab-Lu Ltd., 360 F.2d 1021 (2d Cir. 1966). Thus, a defendant that copies only *portions* of someone else's words or melody may still be liable for infringement if the average lay observer would recognize those elements as coming from the other person's work. This is how an unauthorized adaptation ("derivative work") can infringe: Even if though the adaptation as a whole is different from the underlying copyrighted work, it will still infringe if portions of it are substantially similar to copyrighted portions of the other work.

For infringement to occur, there must be substantial similarity of *copyrightable expression*. Because copyright does not extend to facts or ideas, a songwriter may borrow ideas or information from any source without fear of infringing. However, copying another's lyrics or melody may constitute infringement.

Some courts permit the copying of a "de minimis" amount of expression. Although it can be hard to predict what a particular court will consider to be de minimis, generally the amount should be small enough that the audience would not recognize its source. *See* VMG Salsoul, LLC v. Ciccone, 824 F.3d

871, 878 (9th Cir. 2016) (holding that Madonna's *Vogue* copied a single horn hit from the *Love Break* musical composition and recording, but that the copying was de minimis). De minimis copying is discussed in § 3.13[D] below.

The essence of infringement is *copying*. Direct infringement occurs only if the defendant actually copied someone else's copyrighted expression without authorization. (In the infringement context, courts use the term "copying" as a shorthand for any activity that implicates one of the copyright owner's exclusive rights, such as the public performance right.) There is no infringement if the defendant created something that is substantially similar or even identical to the copyrighted work, if the defendant did so completely independently, that is, without ever having had access to the other work. This is because, without access to the other work, copying is impossible. Thus, if two writers, working completely independently, write similar or identical lyrics, neither has infringed the other's copyright. (And, indeed, each one owns a copyright in his or her set of lyrics.) This type of parallel independent creation can occur by coincidence, or where real-life events or developments in popular culture inspire two creators to develop similar works, without either having copied from the other.

Because direct infringement is based on strict liability, a person who distributes or performs an infringing work may be held liable even if he or she was not aware that the work contained infringing content. For example, if a songwriter infringes the work of another songwriter, a record label may be held liable for distributing a recording of the infringing song even if it knew nothing of the infringement. For this reason, most copyright licenses and assignments, as well as recording contracts, include representations, warranties, and indemnification provisions that make the creator or copyright owner financially responsible for any infringements that are later discovered.

Proving that copying occurred is relatively easy in cases where the defendant admits to copying or where there is other direct evidence that the defendant actually used the plaintiff's copyrighted work rather than creating something independently. Absent such direct evidence, however, courts require (1) evidence that the defendant had some degree of *access* to the plaintiff's copyrighted work, plus (2) sufficient similarity to suggest copying rather than independent creation. Some courts take the position that "striking similarity" is sufficient to prove copying even if there is no evidence of access.

In the case of musical works or sound recordings, access is easy to prove if the plaintiff's work has been published or publicly performed, especially on radio, television, or a streaming service, since these performances are widely available to the public. However, it is also possible to show that a defendant had access if the work was circulated to publishers, record labels, producers, artists, music supervisors, or other parties that might have shared it with the defendant.

Even if the evidence shows access plus sufficient similarity to suggest that the defendant copied from the plaintiff's work, there is no infringement without substantial similarity of *copyrightable expression*. Therefore, the similarities that are sufficient to raise an inference that *copying* took place may not always be sufficient to establish copyright *infringement*. For example, if the copied elements were not original enough to be copyrightable, they may support an inference of copying, but there will be no infringement, because infringement requires copying of *copyrightable expression*.

Substantial similarity of copyrighted expression can be especially difficult to assess in the context of music. Songs within the same genre will often have common characteristics, but style and genre are not copyrightable elements. On the other hand, songs that sound quite different overall may have particular passages (of music or lyrics) that sound similar.

To show substantial similarity, it is not necessary that the songs be similar in their entirety; one song may infringe another even if only a small portion was copied. But the portion copied must itself be copyrightable expression. For example, individual words, notes and chords are not copyrightable; they are simply the public domain "building blocks" which a songwriter can assemble and arrange to create a copyrightable song.

Musical elements that courts have held to be unoriginal, and therefore unprotectable, include key, meter, tempo, common song structures, common chord progressions, harmonic progressions, common melodies, and common percussive rhythms. *See* Skidmore v. Led Zeppelin, 952 F.3d 1051, 1070–71 (9th Cir. 2020); Swirsky v. Carey, 376 F.3d 841, 845 (9th Cir. 2004); Griffin v. Sheeran, 351 F.Supp.3d 492, 497 (S.D.N.Y. 2019); McDonald v. West, 138 F.Supp.3d 448, 454 (S.D.N.Y. 2015), *aff'd*, 669 Fed. Appx. 59 (2d Cir. 2016); Jean v. Bug Music, Inc., 2002 WL 287786, at *6 (S.D.N.Y. Feb. 27, 2002); Tisi v. Patrick, 97 F.Supp.2d 539, 543–44 (S.D.N.Y. 2000).

The Copyright Office Compendium (an internal manual that does not have the force of law) lists several examples of "common property musical material" that, in its view, do not constitute original authorship. The examples include diatonic or chromatic scales, arpeggios, and "chord symbols based on standard chord progressions." Compendium of U.S. Copyright Office Practices, § 802.5(A) (3d ed. 2021). While "there is no predetermined number of notes, measures, or words that automatically . . . qualifies for copyright registration," the Compendium states that "short musical phrases are not copyrightable . . . just as words and short textual phrases are not copyrightable. . . ." *Id.* § 802.5(B); *see also id.* § 313.4(B)–(C) (three-note musical phrase is not copyrightable).

Note, however, that even if individual elements of a song are not original, the specific manner in which a songwriter *combines* those elements (the "selection and arrangement" of uncopyrightable components) may be original enough to be copyrightable. *See* Three Boys Music Corp. v. Bolton, 212 F.3d 477, 484

(9th Cir. 2000) (upholding jury's finding that defendant's song infringed plaintiff's original combination of 5 unprotectible elements).

In many cases, the parties will retain expert musicologists to analyze the works and testify as to whether their similarities pertain to copyrightable expression or unoriginal components. In recent years, a number of music infringement cases have featured a "battle of the experts" in which musicologists for each side offer disparate opinions on whether particular elements of a song are copyrightable, and whether the works at issue are substantially similar.

In Gray v. Hudson, 28 F.4th 87 (9th Cir. 2022), the plaintiffs alleged that Katy Perry's song *Dark Horse* infringed the copyright in their song *Joyful Noise* by copying an ostinato. After a jury awarded the plaintiffs $2.8 million in damages, the district court vacated the award on the ground that, based on the evidence presented by the parties' musicologist experts, there was insufficient evidence the ostinato was original expression. The Ninth Circuit affirmed, holding that the two songs' similarities arose from unoriginal combinations of ostinatos that were "commonplace musical elements." *Id.* at 101–02.

In two cases, Marvin Gaye's estate alleged that Ed Sheeran's *Thinking Out Loud* infringed Gaye's *Let's Get It On* by copying the combination of a specific harmonic rhythm with a specific chord progression that allegedly was widely used even before Gaye's song was released. In each case, the parties' musicologist experts reached opposite conclusions with respect to both originality and substantial similarity. As a result, both courts held that these questions could not be answered on a motion for summary judgment, and would have to be resolved at trial. *See* Structured Asset Sales, LLC v. Sheeran, 632 F.Supp.3d 192 (S.D.N.Y. 2022); Griffin v. Sheeran, 351 F.Supp.3d 492 (S.D.N.Y. 2019).

In Williams v. Gaye, 895 F.3d 1106 (9th Cir. 2018), the Ninth Circuit upheld a jury's verdict that the song *Blurred Lines* by Pharrell Williams, Robin Thicke, and Clifford Harris, Jr. infringed Marvin Gaye's *Got To Give It Up*. The Gaye family's musicologist expert identified multiple similarities, including signature phrases, hooks, bass melodies, word painting, placement of rap and "parlando" sections, and structural similarities on a sectional and phrasing level.

The jury in *Skidmore v. Led Zeppelin* rejected the claim that Led Zeppelin's *Stairway to Heaven* infringed the opening notes of the song *Taurus*, written by Spirit band member Randy Wolfe and recorded by Spirit. The plaintiff's infringement claim was based on five elements: "minor chromatic line and associated chords; duration of pitches of minor chromatic line; melody placed over the descending chromatic line consisting of combination of arpeggios and two-note sequences; rhythm of steady eighth note beats; and pitch collection." Skidmore v. Led Zeppelin, 952 F.3d 1051, 1074 (9th Cir. 2020). However, some of these elements were unprotectible. Skidmore v. Led Zeppelin, 905 F.3d 1116, 1126 (9th Cir. 2018). Because the plaintiff alleged only that these five elements were *present* in both works, the "death knell" for the substantial similarity claim was the plaintiff's failure to argue that Wolfe's *selection and arrangement* of these elements was original and therefore copyrightable. *Skidmore*, 952 F.3d at 1074–75.

Skidmore also highlighted a problem that has arisen in a number of infringement cases involving musical works created under the Copyright Act of 1909 (which was in force until December 31, 1977). Under the 1909 Act, phonorecords did not satisfy the deposit requirement for musical works; instead, the copyright owner was required to deposit sheet music. *Skidmore,* 905 F.3d at 1132. According to the Ninth Circuit, this means that the scope of copyright protection for pre-1978 musical works that were released in recordings but not in sheet music form (and were therefore considered "unpublished" at the time) is determined by the deposited sheet music rather than by the original sound recording. *Id.* at 1134. Unfortunately, the sheet music submitted as the deposit copy was often skeletal, failing to reflect the full composition that was recorded. Many songwriters did not read or write sheet music (as is still true today), and therefore had to have their recordings transcribed after-the-fact into sheet music in order to register their copyrights. In some cases, the transcriptions captured only the vocal melody and chords, omitting elements such as piano, drums, guitar, and bass line. If the music is infringed, these omissions from the deposit copy can impede the copyright owner's ability to establish the protectible elements of the work and prove substantial similarity.

Because sound recordings and musical works are separate copyrightable works, and the sound recording of a musical work may contain performance elements (contributed by vocalists, musicians, engineers, and mixers) that were not present in the underlying musical work, this can present a problem when an infringement question goes to a jury. Since juries typically do not read sheet music, in order to assess whether two musical works are substantially similar the jury will need to hear recordings—or, alternatively, live performances—of both works. However, in some cases a court may decide not to allow the jury to hear a commercial recording of a plaintiff's song, because the jury would have difficulty separating the song's creative expression from the creative expression added by the creators of the recording. This has been especially problematic in the case of musical works copyrighted before 1978 because, as noted earlier, under the Copyright Act of 1909 phonorecords could not be used to satisfy the deposit requirement for registering a musical work, and the sheet music that was deposited did not always reflect the fully developed musical composition. If the court does not allow the jury to hear the original recording of the music, this can make it difficult for copyright owners of music from that era to prove infringement.

Most music infringement suits are litigated in the Ninth and Second Circuits. These jurisdictions have different approaches to determining whether two works are substantially similar.

In the Ninth Circuit, the assessment of substantial similarity occurs in two stages, using two distinct test. At the first stage (the "extrinsic" test), the court compares the objective similarities of the two works. The court may consider expert testimony (for example, from musicologists) and analytical dissection of the music into its technical elements. If the court finds no substantial similarity of the objective elements, then a summary judgment of non-infringement is appropriate. If there is substantial similarity of objective elements, or if the question is especially close, then the case must go to the factfinder—usually a jury. At this stage (the "intrinsic" test) the factfinder considers whether, from the perspective of an ordinary reasonable observer, the two works are substantially similar in "total concept and feel." Substantial similarity must be found under both tests in order for there to be a finding of infringement. *See* Skidmore v. Led Zeppelin, 952 F.3d 1051, 1064 (9th Cir. 2020).

In contrast, the Second Circuit uses only a single test—the "ordinary observer" test. Expert testimony is relevant only to establish that copying occurred. Then, after separating out the unprotectable elements of the plaintiff's work, the court asks whether an "ordinary lay observer" would recognize that the defendant's work was copied from the plaintiff's. The court generally does not allow expert testimony in making this determination. Arnstein v. Porter, 154 F.2d 464, 473 (2d Cir. 1946).

C. SUBCONSCIOUS COPYING

Because direct infringement is based on strict liability, and can be proven based on access plus substantial similarity, songwriters can be—and indeed have been—held liable for infringement based on *subconscious copying* (also called "unconscious" copying). A songwriter that has been exposed to a particular musical work in the past—sometimes the distant past—may unconsciously reproduce a portion of it when endeavoring to write something completely new. When confronted with the similarities, the songwriter may not even remember having encountered the earlier work. This scenario has led to judgments of infringement against a number of high-profile songwriters. *See, e.g.,* Williams v. Gaye, 885 F.3d 1150 (9th Cir. 2015) (Pharrell Williams, Robin Thicke, and Clifford Harris's *Blurred Lines*); Three Boys Music Corp. v. Bolton, 212 F.3d 477 (9th Cir. 2000) (Michael Bolton and Andrew Goldmark's *Love is a Wonderful Thing*); ABKCO Music, Inc. v. Harrisongs Music, Ltd., 722 F.2d 988 (2d Cir. 1983) (George Harrison's *My Sweet Lord*).

D. DE MINIMIS COPYING

Although the concept of de minimis copying is not found in the copyright statutes, it can be understood as a corollary of the "substantial similarity" test for infringement. If the portion copied is so small that an ordinary person would not recognize the work from which it was copied, then it is probably de minimis. Fisher v. Dees, 794 F.2d 432, 434 n.2 (9th Cir. 1986).

In music and other contexts, courts have rejected de minimis arguments where the portion copied was substantial enough that it would be recognized by those familiar with the sampled work. *See, e.g.,* Ringgold v. Black Entertainment Television, Inc., 126 F.3d 70, 77 (2d Cir. 1997); *Fisher,* 794 F.2d at 434 n.2; Elsmere Music, Inc. v. National Broadcasting Co., 482 F.Supp. 741, 744 (S.D.N.Y.), *aff'd per curiam*, 623 F.2d 252 (2d Cir. 1980).

The de minimis concept plays an important role in infringement claims based on unauthorized sampling. The term "sampling" refers to using a short excerpt from a copyrighted sound recording and/or musical work by incorporating it into a new sound recording, thereby creating a derivative work. If the use of the sample is authorized by its copyright owner or qualifies under the fair use exception (discussed in § 3.15[B] below), then the new derivative work does not infringe. However, if the sample is unauthorized and not a fair use, then incorporating it into the new work may give rise to infringement liability. Indeed, it is possible that the person doing the sampling has infringed two works: (1) the underlying sound recording from which the sample was duplicated, and (2) the musical work embodied in the underlying sound recording.

With respect to the underlying sound recording, recall that copyright law defines the exclusive reproduction right more narrowly for sound recordings than for other copyrighted works (see § 3.12 above). Merely *imitating* a sound recording (or portion thereof) by making an independent fixation of sounds (a "soundalike" recording) does not "reproduce" that sound recording, even if the new recording sounds exactly like the original. (Remember Taylor Swift's lawful re-creation of her previously released masters.) To *reproduce* a sound recording (or portion thereof) means to mechanically or electronically duplicate the actual sounds fixed on that recording. 17 U.S.C. § 114(b). Therefore, if someone samples a portion of an existing sound recording merely by *imitating* it through a new fixation of similar sounds, this does not infringe the sound recording. (However, if the imitation of the sound recording also replicates the underlying musical work without a license to do so, this may infringe the musical work by creating an unauthorized derivative work.) Therefore, the "sampling" that potentially gives rise to liability for infringing a sound recording is a mechanical or electronic duplication of the sounds actually fixed in a copyrighted sound recording. Typically, this involves digital copying.

As discussed in § 2.4 earlier, beat makers typically sample existing recordings in order to create their beats; this constitutes sampling, and the resulting beats are derivative works. When songwriters and recording artists use these beats to create new musical works and sound recordings, these new works are derivative works as well. Beat makers typically obtain master use licenses for their samples. When they do not, however, they face potential infringement liability.

When a recording artist or beat maker samples the sounds of an existing recording without a license, this is an unauthorized reproduction and adaptation of the existing recording as well as any elements of the musical work that are discernable from the sampled sounds. This can lead to infringement liability (for the beat maker, the songwriter, and the publisher, as well as the recording artists and their record label), unless a court determines that either (1) the amount sampled is de minimis, or (2) the sampling qualifies as fair use. These possibilities apply to both the sampled portion of the copyrighted sound recording and any portion of the underlying musical work that is incorporated in that sample.

A number of courts have used the de minimis concept to reject infringement claims based on sampling of sound recordings and/or musical works. *See* VMG Salsoul, LLC v. Ciccone, 824 F.3d 871 (9th Cir. 2016) (horn segment sampled in Madonna's *Vogue* recording was de minimis portion of plaintiff's sound recording and underlying musical work); Saregama India Ltd. v. Mosley, 687 F.Supp.2d 1325 (S.D. Fla. 2009), *aff'd on other grounds*, 635 F.3d 1284 (11th Cir. 2011) (finding no substantial similarity where defendant sampled two seconds of sound recording); Lil' Joe Wein Music, Inc. v. Jackson, 245 Fed.Appx. 873, 875 (11th Cir. 2007) (short phrase sampled from lyrics was de minimis); Jean v. Bug Music, Inc., 2002 U.S. Dist. LEXIS 3176 (S.D.N.Y. Feb. 25, 2002) (sample of three-word phrase and three accompanying notes from musical work was de minimis).

A particular sound recording sample could be a significant part of the sound recording but only a de minimis part of the underlying musical work. This was the case in the Beastie Boys' recording of *Pass the Mic,* which sampled James Newton's recording of his own song *Choir.* Although the Beastie Boys obtained a sampling license from ECM Records, that license covered only the recording; they neglected to obtain a license for the song itself, which was still owned by Newton. The sample lasted six seconds, and was repeated 40 times in the Beastie Boys' recording. (It is easy to see why they felt that a license for the sound recording was necessary.) When Newton sued for infringement, expert testimony was needed to identify which elements of ECM's sound recording were components of Newton's musical work and which elements were created by Newton's performance. Based on this testimony, the court found that the sample incorporated a three-note sequence that was not a qualitatively significant part of Newton's musical work. Finding this sequence to be de minimis, the court ruled that the Beastie Boys did not infringe the musical work. *See* Newton v. Diamond, 388 F.3d 1189 (9th Cir. 2004).

One court has held that the de minimis concept does not, as a matter of law, apply to sampling a sound recording (as distinguished from a musical work). Bridgeport Music, Inc. v. Dimension Films, 410 F.3d 792 (6th Cir. 2005). Although that opinion was poorly reasoned and has been widely criticized (and expressly rejected in the *VMG Salsoul* and *Saregama* cases), it still precedential in the Sixth

Circuit, which includes Nashville, an important judicial venue for the music industry.

When the amount copied does not qualify as de minimis, it may still qualify as fair use. *Bridgeport Music*, 410 F.3d at 805; *Ringgold,* 126 F.3d at 77; *Fisher*, 794 F.2d at 434 n.2. This topic is discussed in § 3.15[B] below.

E. GENERATIVE ARTIFICIAL INTELLIGENCE

Many copyrighted works are used in "training" generative artificial intelligence (AI) systems. Infringement questions have arisen with respect to both the training phase and the outputs generated by these systems. At the training phase, the question is whether the copyrighted inputs are being copied and stored, and whether these activities constitute fair use. (Fair use is discussed in § 3.15[B] below.) In some cases, the operators of AI systems may also have removed copyright management information (CMI) from the works, in violation of 17 U.S.C. § 1202. At the output phase, the question is whether any of the content *generated* by the AI system is substantially similar to any of the copyrighted inputs, in which case there could be liability for unauthorized copying and/or creation of derivative works.

A large number of lawsuits have already been filed by copyright owners, including music publishers and record labels, and these suits are still pending. *See, e.g.,* Concord Music Group, Inc. v. Anthropic PBC, No. 5:24–cv–03811 (filed N.D. Cal. June 26, 2024); UMG Recordings, Inc. v. Suno, No. 1:24–cv–11611 (filed D. Mass. June 24, 2024); UMG Recordings, Inc. v. Uncharted Labs, Inc., No. 1:24–cv–04777 (S.D.N.Y. filed June 24, 2024). Although there have been no decisions on the merits as yet, a similar suit brought by visual artists recently survived a motion to dismiss. *See* Andersen v. Stability AI Ltd, 2024 WL 3823234 (N.D. Cal. Aug. 12, 2024).

In the meantime, several of the companies operating AI platforms have begun to negotiate licenses with the owners of large copyright catalogs. As the availability of licenses increases, courts may become increasingly skeptical of the defendants' fair use arguments. In all likelihood, operators of AI systems will eventually have licensing agreements with the largest copyright owners (e.g., major publishers and record labels). However, copyright owners with less bargaining power are likely to be left out of these arrangements. Their rights will have to be addressed by Congress and the courts.

In an egregious illustration of how generative AI can be abused, in 2024 a federal indictment was issued against an individual who allegedly used AI to generate hundreds of thousands of songs, then used automated "bots" and fake subscriber accounts to continuously stream these recordings on various streaming platforms, collecting $10 million in streaming royalties. If the allegations are true, these royalties depleted the pool of streaming royalties available to legitimate songwriters, publishers, recording artists, and record labels.

F. SECONDARY LIABILITY

A defendant who did not *directly* exercise one of the exclusive rights without authorization may still face contributory or vicarious liability for infringement. A *contributory* infringer is one who induces or knowingly assists in the infringing activity. A *vicarious* infringer is someone who has the right and ability to supervise or control the infringing activity, and derives a direct financial benefit from it. These doctrines cannot be found in the copyright statutes; they arise from common law. Copyright owners often bring contributory or vicarious infringement claims rather than direct infringement claims where the direct infringers have no money, are difficult to identify or locate, and/or are too numerous to sue individually, or where suing direct infringers would generate negative publicity (for example, where the direct infringers are fans or potential customers).

1. Contributory Liability

The Second Circuit established the standard for contributory liability in Gershwin Publishing Corp. v. Columbia Artists Mgt., Inc., 443 F.2d 1159, 1162 (2d Cir. 1971):

> One who, with knowledge of the infringing activity, induces, causes or materially contributes to the infringing conduct of another, may be held liable as a "contributory" infringer.

Thus, whereas direct infringement is based on strict liability, contributory liability arises only where the defendant *knowingly* facilitates or induces direct infringement.

However, merely providing an ordinary device (either a physical device or software) or a service that can facilitate infringement does not necessarily give rise to contributory liability, even if the company providing the device or service knows that some of its customers are likely to use it for infringing activities. The Supreme Court first articulated this exception in a case involving the sale of home recording devices used by consumers to copy television shows (in other words, the predecessors of modern DVRs):

> [T]he sale of copying equipment, like the sale of other articles of commerce, does not constitute contributory infringement if the product is widely used for legitimate, unobjectionable purposes. Indeed, it need merely be capable of substantial noninfringing uses.

Sony Corp. v. Universal City Studios, Inc., 464 U.S. 417, 442 (1984). This rule, commonly known as the "staple article of commerce" doctrine, was later expanded to services and software.

However, in 2005 the Supreme Court clarified that the staple article of commerce doctrine does not immunize a defendant that provides products or services with the intent to *induce* infringement:

> *Sony*'s rule limits imputing culpable intent as a matter of law from the characteristics or uses of a distributed product. But nothing in *Sony* requires courts to ignore evidence of intent if there is such evidence, and the case was never

meant to foreclose rules of fault-based liability derived from the common law.

Thus, where evidence goes beyond a product's characteristics or the knowledge that it may be put to infringing uses, and shows statements or actions directed to promoting infringement, *Sony*'s staple-article rule will not preclude liability.

. . .

[O]ne who distributes a device with the object of promoting its use to infringe copyright, as shown by clear expression or other affirmative steps taken to foster infringement, is liable for the resulting acts of infringement by third parties. We are, of course, mindful of the need to keep from trenching on regular commerce or discouraging the development of technologies with lawful and unlawful potential. Accordingly, just as *Sony* did not find intentional inducement despite the knowledge of the VCR manufacturer that its device could be used to infringe, mere knowledge of infringing potential or of actual infringing uses would not be enough here to subject a distributor to liability. Nor would ordinary acts incident to product distribution, such as offering customers technical support or product updates, support liability in themselves. The inducement rule, instead, premises liability on purposeful, culpable expression and conduct, and thus does nothing to compromise legitimate commerce or discourage innovation having a lawful promise.

Metro-Goldwyn-Mayer Studios, Inc. v. Grokster, Ltd., 545 U.S. 913, 934–37 (2005).

2. Vicarious Liability

An employer can be vicariously liable for infringement by its employees. In addition, vicarious liability is a significant concern for venues where live or recorded music is performed—for example, the operator of a club where a band or DJ publicly performs music, a bar that hosts karaoke nights, a coffee shop where local musicians perform, or a hotel, retail store, trade show operator, sports venue, or athletic club that plays background music.

The Second Circuit established the rule governing vicarious liability:

> [E]ven in the absence of an employer-employee relationship one may be vicariously liable if he has the right and ability to supervise the infringing activity and also has a direct financial interest in such activities.

Gershwin Publishing Corp. v. Columbia Artists Mgt., Inc., 443 F.2d 1159, 1162 (2d Cir. 1971); *see also* Polygram Int'l Pub., Inc. v. Nevada/TIG, Inc. 855 F.Supp. 1314, 1332 (D.Mass. 1994) (trade show); Famous Music Corp. v. Bay State Harness Racing and Breeding Ass'n, 554 F.2d 1213, 1214 (1st Cir. 1977) (race track).

The vicarious liability rule explains why clubs, bars, restaurants, stores, hotels, athletic clubs, and other venues where live or recorded music is performed (either onsite or through a streaming service) need to obtain public performance licenses. Even when a live band performs, it is the venue, and not the band, that must obtain the public performance license, because copyright owners find it more practical to enforce their rights against the venue rather than the itinerant (and probably less-than-wealthy) performers.

As discussed in Chapter 6, venue operators typically obtain blanket public performance licenses from performing rights organizations (PROs). However, if a business subscribes to certain commercial music services (as opposed to *personal* streaming services), the service itself will have obtained a commercial public performance license that extends to its customers. The major streaming services, as well as SiriusXM, offer both personal and commercial options.

In addition to public performances, many vicarious liability cases have involved "flea markets" or similar venues where infringing copies of CDs have been sold. *See, e.g.,* Fonovisa, Inc. v. Cherry Auction, Inc., 76 F.3d 259 (9th Cir. 1996); Shapiro Bernstein and Co. v. H.L. Green Co., 316 F.2d 304 (2d Cir. 1963). This application of the rule has become less significant since the music industry and consumers have transitioned away from physical media.

Online services can also be vicariously liable for making unauthorized copies of sound recordings available for download or streaming, even if the infringing materials are provided by individuals who are not employed by the service. *See* A&M Records, Inc. v. Napster, Inc., 239 F.3d 1004 (9th Cir. 2001).

As discussed in § 3.16 below, however, the safe harbor provisions of § 512 offer significant protections for online platforms that host user-provided content.

§ 3.14 NO EXTRATERRITORIAL REACH

Federal copyright law applies only within the U.S. (including its territories). Therefore, copyright owners who object to the unauthorized use of their works outside the U.S. will need to consult the copyright laws of the countries where the unauthorized activities are taking place in order to determine whether their works have been infringed. If so, they may be able to bring copyright claims under the laws of those countries. In most cases, they will have to bring those suits in the courts of the relevant country rather than in U.S. courts. Under limited circumstances, however, U.S. courts will agree to hear cases in which U.S. defendants are accused of violating foreign copyright laws. *See, e.g.*, Boosey & Hawkes Music Publishers, Ltd. v. Walt Disney Co., 145 F.3d 481 (2d Cir. 1998) (considering claims that Disney's foreign distribution of musical film *Fantasia* infringed copyright in music that was still copyrighted outside the U.S.).

§ 3.15 EXCEPTIONS AND LIMITATIONS

There are many exceptions and limitations to the exclusive rights of copyright owners. These are found in 17 U.S.C. §§ 107–122. Two of the most important ones—the first sale rule and fair use—apply to all categories of copyrightable works. Several others have particular relevance to musical works and/or sound recordings.

A. FIRST SALE

Subject to a notable exception of special relevance to the music industry, the first sale rule allows the owner of a lawfully made copy or phonorecord of a work to sell, lend, or otherwise dispose of that copy without the consent of the copyright owner(s). 17 U.S.C. § 109(a). Thus, for example, the owner of a music CD (assuming it was lawfully made) can sell or lend that CD to someone else without the consent of the record label or the copyright owners of the songs included on the CD.

The first sale rule is narrower, however, for sound recordings and software than for other copyrighted works, such as book and motion pictures. While copies of books and motion pictures can be offered for commercial rental, this is not the case for sound recordings or software. Because, at one time, the main reason why people rented sound recordings or software was to make unauthorized copies, Congress amended the first sale rule to exclude commercial rentals of these works. *Id.* § 109(b)(1)(A). The copyright owners still have the option to authorize such rentals, but in most cases they do not.

The importance of the first sale rule for music consumers has greatly diminished, however, with the transition from physical phonorecords to digital downloads and music streaming. With streaming, the consumer never obtains a lawfully made copy of the work. Even with digital downloads, the terms of sale (which consumers never bother to read) specify that the consumer is not the owner of the download, but a mere licensee. The terms of the license typically prohibit copying or selling the download.

Even if the consumer is the owner of the downloaded music file, courts have held that the first sale rule does not apply to digital resales, at least those accomplished through currently available technology. In Capitol Records, LLC v. ReDigi, Inc., 910 F.3d 649 (2d Cir. 2018), the Second Circuit considered whether the first sale rule permitted the sale of digital music files by uploading them to the defendant's server, from which the buyer could download or stream them. The court found that the upload process created a new copy (technically, a "phonorecord") of the work. Even if the seller promptly deleted his or her copy (which was difficult to verify), the creation of the new copy was an unauthorized reproduction. Under this analysis, the only lawful way to sell a digital music file without a license is to sell the device in which it is stored (such as a CD, iPod, smartphone or flash drive). Otherwise, the sale of a digital music file would require a license from the copyright owners of both the musical work and the sound recording.

B. FAIR USE

Among the many exceptions and limitations in §§ 107–122 of the copyright statutes, fair use is one of the best known. It applies to all categories of copyrightable works, including musical works, sound recordings, and audiovisual works such as music videos, videogames, motion pictures and television shows.

Fair use is an affirmative defense that was originally developed by courts but was later codified at § 107 of the 1976 Act. Even after codification, its scope remains flexible (some would say vague), and its interpretation evolves constantly with each new court decision, including multiple decisions from the Supreme Court.

Because of the fluid and indeterminate nature of fair use, it is difficult to predict with certainty whether any particular activity will qualify. As a result, fair use questions are frequently litigated. If an artist wishes to use another's work in a manner that could infringe the other's copyright, the only way to be certain that the use is non-infringing is to obtain a license. If a license is not available or its not affordable, then an artist that still wishes to use the work should seek advice from legal counsel in order to assess the likelihood that the use will be considered fair, and determine whether the use of the work is worth the risk of costly infringement litigation and potential liability.

While the outcomes in fair use cases are hard to predict, and the decisions do not always seem consistent, a recurring theme in court opinions ruling in favor of fair use is that the public benefits of a particular unauthorized use outweigh the copyright owner's property rights. While there are no hard-and-fast rules, the statute itself lists certain general categories of use that are deemed to serve the public interest. These include criticism, comment, news reporting, teaching, scholarship and research. Even a use that falls within these categories, however, must be scrutinized under the statutory criteria to determine whether it is fair.

Section 107 lists four factors that must be considered in every fair use analysis:

(1) The purpose and character of the use, including whether such use is of a commercial nature or is for nonprofit educational purposes;

(2) The nature of the copyrighted work;

(3) The amount and substantiality of the portion used in relation to the copyrighted work as a whole; and

(4) The effect of the use upon the potential market for or value of the copyrighted work.

In any given case, after deciding the extent to which each factor favors or disfavors fair use, a court must weigh them against one another to conclude whether the use is fair. No single factor is dispositive. Because this list is non-exhaustive, courts may consider other relevant factors as well. However, most decisions focus predominantly or exclusively on these four factors. Over time, the case law has added an interpretive gloss to each of these factors.

1. Purpose and Character of the Use

One element of the first factor is the extent to which the challenged use is commercial. In the context of music and entertainment, of course, most works are commercial in the sense that their makers hope to be commercially rewarded for their efforts. However, for fair use purposes these works are considered less commercial than works created purely for advertising purposes—e.g., commercial jingles. Campbell v. Acuff-Rose Music, Inc., 510 U.S. 569, 585 (1994). Not surprisingly, when a well-known song is adapted to promote goods or services on a television commercial, a license is required. (These licenses are discussed in Chapter 4.)

Although the fair use analysis generally looks more favorably on noncommercial uses, commerciality (or lack thereof) is not dispositive. Courts also consider the extent to which a use is "transformative." Unfortunately, this term has no precise definition.

In 1994, the Supreme Court concluded that 2 Live Crew's commercially-released rap parody of the country pop song *Oh, Pretty Woman* was transformative, explaining that the transformativeness inquiry asks "whether the new work merely supersede[s] the objects of the original creation, or instead adds something new, with a further purpose or different character, altering the first with new expression, meaning, or message." *Campbell,* 510 U.S. at 579 (internal quotes and citations omitted). In 2023, however, the Court cautioned against reading this definition too broadly, because it threatened to turn every derivative work into a fair use, which would squarely conflict with the copyright owner's exclusive right to create derivative works: "[T]he degree of transformation required to make 'transformative' use of an original must go beyond that required to qualify as a derivative." Andy Warhol Foundation for the Visual Arts, Inc. v. Goldsmith, 598 U.S. 508, 529 (2023) (holding that, where a magazine licensed a Warhol silkscreen of Prince, without also licensing the photograph on which it was based, use of the image to illustrate an article about Prince was not transformative, because in this context it served the same purpose as a photograph). Even under this heightened standard, the musical parody in *Campbell* would still be transformative, because a parody serves the purpose of criticizing or commenting on the underlying work—a completely different purpose from that of the underlying work (and a purpose which the copyright owner is not allowed to monopolize).

2. Nature of the Copyrighted Work

The second fair use factor considers the nature of the plaintiff's copyrighted work. If the work is highly creative—such as music, sound recordings, motion pictures, and works of fiction—this factor is more likely to weigh in favor of the copyright owner. When the work is less creative—such as fact-based works and computer software, this factor is more likely to weigh in favor of fair use. Thus, for example, in *Campbell v. Acuff-Rose*, this factor favored the copyright owner, because the song *Oh, Pretty Woman*—like most music—is very creative. *Campbell*, 510 U.S. at 586. In contrast, in a case where the plaintiff's work consisted of a particular piece of software that the Supreme Court considered barely worthy of copyright protection, this factor favored fair use. *See* Google, LLC v. Oracle America, Inc., 593 U.S. 1, 29 (2021).

3. Amount and Substantiality of the Portion Used

This factor considers the portion of the copyrighted work that the defendant used, relative to the plaintiff's entire work. This is both a quantitative and qualitative assessment. The amount taken may be quantitatively small—a few words, a few notes, a single guitar riff—but may still be a qualitatively significant component of the plaintiff's work—for example, if it is especially memorable, valuable, or distinctive. In *Campbell v. Acuff-Rose*, the Supreme Court found this factor especially challenging. Because the defendant's work was a parody, and a parody must copy enough of the original to enable the audience to identify the work it is targeting, the Court recognized that 2 Live Crew must be allowed to copy some of the most distinctive and memorable elements of *Oh, Pretty Woman*. However, even a parody must not copy more than is reasonably necessary to "conjure up" the original; if the copying is excessive, this factor can weigh against fair use. Walt Disney Productions v. Air Pirates, 581 F.2d 751, 758 (9th Cir. 1978). In *Campbell*, the Court concluded that the copying of the lyrics (the opening line, and the repetition of the phrase "pretty woman") was not excessive. *Campbell*, 510 U.S. at 589. With respect to the amount of *music* that was copied, however, the Court did not reach a conclusion, and remanded to the lower court for a determination "whether repetition of the bass riff is excessive copying" in light of the other fair use factors. *Id.*

Although, generally speaking, copying large portions of a work weighs against a fair use finding, the amount copied must always be considered in light of the other fair use factors. Even when a work is copied in its entirety, courts have occasionally ruled in favor of fair use. *See, e.g.,* Sony Corp. v. Universal City Studios, 464 U.S. 417 (1984) (finding fair use where consumers, for their own noncommercial personal use, recorded television programs for viewing at later times).

4. Effect on the Market for the Copyrighted Work

The fourth factor considers the extent to which the defendant's activity provides a market substitute for the copyrighted work or for licensed derivatives of that work. This inquiry does not consider the defendant's activity in isolation; instead, it considers the impact of the defendant's activity if it were to become widespread. For example, even if distributing a single unauthorized copy of a work would have little or no impact on the plaintiff's market, the fair use analysis considers the impact of distributing thousands or millions of copies.

As noted above, the "effect on the market" refers to the market substitution effect. A scathing parody could reduce the public demand for the parodied work, but this type of market effect is not relevant to the fourth factor, because the copyright owner has no right to control the public's opinion of the work.

Indeed, as a form of criticism, parody advances First Amendment values.

Following this principle, the Supreme Court in *Campbell v. Acuff-Rose* recognized that the copyright owner of *Oh, Pretty Woman* had no exclusive right to produce parodies of the work. *Campbell,* 510 U.S. at 591–92. However, the Court recognized that 2 Live Crew's adaptation of the song was not only a parody but also a rap song, and that the market for rap versions of *Oh, Pretty Woman* should be considered separately from the market for parodies. The right to adapt a song for different styles and genres of music falls squarely within the scope of the copyright owner's exclusive rights. Accordingly, the Court remanded the case for a determination whether and to what extent 2 Live Crew's song served as a market substitute for a licensed rap version of the plaintiff's song. *Id.* at 592–94.

C. OTHER EXCEPTIONS AND LIMITATIONS OF SPECIAL RELEVANCE TO MUSIC

The copyright statutes contain many exceptions and limitations in addition to fair use. Unlike fair use, these are narrowly circumscribed. While a complete survey of these exceptions is beyond the scope of this book, exceptions that are particularly relevant to musical works are discussed below. Where noted, several of these exceptions are the subject of separate chapters.

1. Limitations Specific to Sound Recordings

Several limitations that are specific to sound recordings have already been mentioned: The exclusive rights to reproduce and create derivative works (17 U.S.C. § 114(b)) and to publicly perform the recording (*id.* §§ 106(6), 114(a)) are defined more narrowly than for other works. The public performance right in sound recordings is explored more fully in Chapter 7.

As noted earlier, sound recordings fixed prior to February 15, 1972, are not protected by federal copyright law; instead, they receive similar but not identical protection under § 1401. Generally speaking, *noncommercial* uses of such recordings are permitted if the rights owner is not exploiting them and has not filed an ownership record with the Copyright Office, the recordings are not commercially available for purchase or streaming, and the user notifies the Copyright Office of the intended use. (The details of these rules are in § 1401(c).) This exception is a type of "orphan works" provision, designed to ensure that these older works can still be preserved and made available to the public even if it is not possible to contact their owners for consent. (Note, however, that this limitation applies only to the sound recordings; the musical works embodied in these older recordings are still subject to the normal rules of copyright law.)

2. Limitations Specific to Musical Works

Several limitations are specific to musical works. As noted below, the more significant or complex limitations are the subject of separate chapters.

One of these is the compulsory mechanical license to make and distribute sound recordings (through record sales, downloads, or on-demand streaming) of copyrighted musical works. 17 U.S.C. § 115. A compulsory license is available to users as a matter of law; while the copyright owner cannot veto the license, he or she is entitled to royalty payments established by law. For a detailed discussion of this license, see Chapter 5.

Another is the licensing provision in § 116, which applies to "coin operated phonorecord players" in business establishments that allow customers to select and play recorded music from a list of available titles—in other words, "jukeboxes." Since these are public performances, the jukebox company must have a license from the copyright owner of each musical work on offer. These licenses can be negotiated. If the parties do not reach agreement, however, a compulsory license will apply, under rates and terms established by the Copyright Royalty Judges.

Section 110 of the copyright statutes imposes a number of different limits on public performance rights in musical works, each tied to very specific circumstances, and each applicable to public performances of live as well as recorded music. The most complex of the limitations—§ 110(5)—will be addressed last.

As noted where relevant below, several of the § 110 limitations apply only to *nondramatic* musical works. A *dramatic* musical work is one that was created as an integral part of a dramatico-musical work, meaning a work that tells a story and is intended to be performed, such as a musical comedy, opera, or operetta. All other musical works are considered *nondramatic*; therefore, this category encompasses most classical music as well as most popular music such as jazz, rock, country, rap, hip-hop, and blues. (There are exceptions, of course; the scores of some contemporary stage musicals such as *Hamilton* correspond to a variety of these modern genres rather than more traditional "show tunes," but they are still dramatic musical works.) Music that begins as a nondramatic musical work may later be incorporated into a dramatico-musical work (such as *MJ: The Musical,* featuring Michael Jackson's songs); however, this does not alter the music's character as a nondramatic work.

Teaching activities: Music can be performed during classroom instruction (and, in the case of nondramatic musical works or limited portions of other musical works, during online instruction, provided that certain technological controls are in place) at a nonprofit educational institution. *Id.* §§ 110(1)–(2).

Religious services: Nondramatic musical works, and dramatico-musical works of a religious nature, may be performed during services at a place of worship or other religious assembly. *Id.* § 110(3).

Certain nonprofit performances: Nonprofit public performances must meet certain requirements in order to qualify for this exception, which applies only to nondramatic musical works. The performance must not be transmitted to the public, there must be no admission charge and no purpose of direct or indirect commercial advantage, and no compensation can be paid to anyone involved. Any proceeds must be used exclusively for educational, religious, or charitable purposes. *Id.* § 110(4).

Nonprofit veterans' and fraternal organizations: This exception applies to performances of nondramatic musical (or literary) works at social functions organized and promoted by these organizations, even if admission is charged, if the event is limited to invitees rather than open to the public, and only if the proceeds (after reasonable costs) are used for charitable purposes. (If the organization is a collegiate fraternity or sorority, the purpose of the social function must be solely to raise funds for a specific charitable purpose.) *Id.* § 110(10).

Agricultural fairs: A government body or a nonprofit organization is not liable if an infringing performance of a nondramatic musical work takes place at its annual agricultural or horticultural exhibition. (Essentially, this exception insulates the organization from contributory or vicarious liability.) However, the individual person or business that performed the work may be liable. *Id.* § 110(6).

Vending establishments: A store that sells records or record-playing equipment may play music for the sole purpose of promoting such sales, provided that no admission is charged and the performance is not transmitted beyond the store. *Id.* § 110(7). This provision was more important in the days before streaming supplanted physical records.

Transmissions received in a public place: This exception, § 110(5), is one of the most complex. As originally enacted in 1976, it permitted the performance of a copyrighted work in a place open to the public (typically, a store or restaurant) if the performance took the form of a transmission (which, at that time, would have been a radio or television broadcast) that was received on a "single receiving apparatus of a kind commonly used in private homes," as long as there was no direct charge for hearing the transmission and no further public transmission of the performance. (The general idea was that a small business could turn on a radio or television for the enjoyment of its customers and/or staff without having to pay for a public performance license.) Today, of course, an establishment can also receive a "transmission" via cable, satellite, webcasting, or streaming. Although no court has ruled on whether the original exception applies to these later-developed technologies, the subscriber agreements offered by these services typically prohibit commercial use.

In 1998, § 110(5) was broadened. The original exception was preserved as § 110(5)(A), but a new exception was added as § 110(5)(B). The new exception applies only to transmissions of nondramatic musical works. Unlike the original exception, it is not limited to a "single receiving apparatus of a kind commonly used in private homes." Instead, it allows a business establishment to use multiple loudspeakers and audiovisual devices. (The maximum number depends on several factors.) However, eligible transmissions are limited to radio and television broadcasts by FCC-licensed stations (in other words, traditional terrestrial broadcasts), except that if the music is incorporated in an audiovisual work, eligible transmissions can include cable systems and satellite carriers. In either case, a transmission is eligible only if it was licensed by the copyright owner of the musical work. As in the original exception, there must be no direct charge to hear the transmission, and the transmission must not be further transmitted beyond the establishment.

The broadened scope of § 110(5)(B) provoked a group of Irish songwriters and publishers to complain that the U.S. was violating its copyright protection obligations under international law—specifically, the intellectual property provisions of the World Trade Organization (WTO) Agreement. A dispute panel of the WTO agreed, but the U.S. paid only a modest amount of reparations, and § 110(5)(B) continues in force.

Despite the breadth of the § 110(5) exceptions, many businesses do not want to rely on radio or television transmissions for their ambient music. They are willing to pay commercial music services to provide a more predictable and uninterrupted stream of music that is specially tailored to their needs.

D. AUDIO HOME RECORDING ACT

The Audio Home Recording Act (AHRA), a copyright limitation applicable to both musical works and sound recordings, was enacted in 1992 but quickly became obsolete due to changes in technology. Although it still remains in the copyright statutes (§§ 1001–10), it warrants only limited discussion.

When the technology first became widely available for making high quality digital copies of commercially released sound recordings, Congress attempted to strike a compromise between the rights of copyright owners and consumers' interest in the convenience of making copies of their purchased recordings in different formats—e.g., copying a vinyl record or DVD onto a digital audio tape. Under this compromise, consumers were allowed to make copies for personal use, but importers and manufacturers of digital recording devices and blank media had to comply with certain conditions. Each digital recording device had to include copy control technology that prevented making second-generation copies, and the importer or manufacturer of each digital recording device or medium was required to pay a royalty that was split among the copyright owners of musical works and sound recordings.

Not long after the AHRA's enactment, however, it became possible for consumers to use computer technology rather than specialized digital recording devices to make copies of sound recordings. In 1999, a ruling by the Ninth Circuit made the AHRA inapplicable to the use of computers to copy sound recordings. Recording Industry Ass'n of America v. Diamond Multimedia Systems, 180 F.3d 1072 (9th Cir. 1999). Manufacturers and importers of computers and computer storage media therefore do not have to incorporate copy controls or pay royalties to the Copyright Office. Also, the AHRA does not exempt consumers from infringement liability when they use computers to copy sound recordings, even for personal use. As a result, the AHRA today has little impact on the rights of copyright owners or music consumers.

§ 3.16 WEBSITES HOSTING USER-PROVIDED CONTENT

Musical recordings and audiovisual works such as music videos are available on a wide variety of digital platforms that host user-provided content, including YouTube, TikTok, Instagram, Facebook, and many others. Some of this content is licensed, while some is infringing.

Several of the major platforms, such as YouTube (through its Content ID system) and TikTok (through its Music Library and Commercial Music Library), have established licensing arrangements with major labels and publishers. They are not comprehensive, however, and many independent artists have found themselves excluded. Some copyright owners also authorize free-standing licensing services (such as Lickd) to issue licenses to users that want to incorporate music in videos they post on digital platforms. However, these arrangements do not cover all of the copyrighted musical works, sound recordings, and audiovisual works that are posted by users. As a result, there is a high incidence of copyright infringement in user-posted content.

Digital platforms may be liable for copyright infringement even if they are not *directly* responsible for making the infringing content available. They can be liable under theories of contributory liability if they knowingly induce or facilitate the infringement (as in *Grokster*, discussed in § 3.13[F][1] above) or vicarious liability if they financially benefit from the infringement and have the ability to curtail it (as in *Napster*, discussed in § 3.13[F][2] above).

In 1998, when platforms hosting user-provided content were in their infancy, Congress addressed concerns that, even when these platforms played a purely passive role, and did nothing to induce infringement, they still faced significant threats of secondary liability because they lacked the practical ability to pre-screen the large volumes of content that users were constantly posting. In an effort to protect copyright owners without forcing these platforms to shut down, Congress in the Digital Millenium Copyright Act (DMCA) enacted a series of safe harbors that protect eligible platforms from infringement liability for passively hosting infringing content, provided that the platforms comply with certain requirements that are designed to reduce the incidence of infringement by their users. The safe harbors, found in 17 U.S.C. § 512, are quite complex.

Therefore, only the most relevant provisions are discussed here.

When a digital service provider (DSP) satisfies the requirements for the safe harbor, it is immune from claims for damages, as well as most forms of injunctive relief, arising from infringement suits. However, a court can still order it to block access to infringing content residing at a particular location on its network, and to terminate the account of a specific identified user. The court can also order the "least burdensome" injunctive relief necessary to prevent infringement of specific copyrighted content at particular online location. *Id.* § 512(j)(1)(A).

The safe harbor most relevant to DSPs that store user-provided content, such as YouTube, TikTok, or Instagram, is 17 U.S.C. § 512(c). To be eligible, a DSP must have a policy of terminating "repeat infringers" and must accommodate "standard technical measures" that copyright owners use to protect their digital content. Its website must also display contact information identifying the agent it has designated to receive "takedown" notices from copyright owners. *Id.* § 512(c)(2).

The concepts underlying this safe harbor resemble the concepts underlying contributory and vicarious liability, with some modifications. If users post infringing content, the safe harbor protects the DSP only if it does not have "actual knowledge" of the infringing activity and "is not aware of facts of circumstances from which infringing activity is apparent," or if, upon obtaining such knowledge or awareness, it "acts expeditiously" to remove or disable access to the infringing material. In addition, if the DSP has the "right and ability to control" the infringing activity, it must not receive a financial benefit "directly attributable to" the infringement. And, under what has become known as the "notice and takedown" regime, if a copyright owner sends the DSP a legally sufficient notice of infringement, the DSP must act "expeditiously" to remove or disable access to the material claimed to infringe. To satisfy the statute, the takedown notice must, among other requirements, identify both the copyrighted work and the infringing material, and provide information "reasonably sufficient" to enable the DSP to locate the infringing content. *Id.* § 512(c)(3). The person who posted the content can send a counter-notification, in which case the DSP must make the content available again unless the copyright owner files an infringement suit in federal court. *Id.* § 512(g)(2).

The most litigated aspect of this safe harbor is what kind of "knowledge" the DSP must have in order to be held liable for failing to remove or disable content. A DSP's general awareness that its platform hosts infringing content is not sufficient. Instead, courts have held that the knowledge must pertain to "specific and identifiable incidents of infringement." *See* Viacom Int'l, Inc. v. YouTube, Inc., 676 F.3d 19, 31 (2d Cir. 2012). This requirement applies both to "actual knowledge" and awareness of "facts and circumstances from which infringing activity is apparent" (also known as "red flag" knowledge). *Id.*

Courts have also considered what it means for a DSP to have the "right and ability to control" its users' infringing activity. It is not sufficient that the DSP has the ability to locate and remove infringing material, or to terminate users' access, because the DSP must possess this ability in order to carry out its obligations under the safe harbor. Instead, courts require proof of "something more," such as the exercise of substantial influence over user activities or purposeful conduct such as inducing the infringements. *See id.* at 38; UMG Recordings, Inc. v. Shelter Capital Partners LLC, 718 F.3d 1006, 1030 (9th Cir. 2013).

Neither copyright owners nor DSP users are particularly happy with the current functioning of the notice-and-takedown regime. Copyright owners complain of a "whack-a-mole" problem, where infringing content is repeatedly re-posted by users after being taken down. DSP users complain that the automated systems used by the entertainment industry to detect suspected infringements and generate takedown notices are overzealous, prompting takedowns of non-infringing materials, including content that qualifies as fair use. The European Union has adopted a more stringent regime, placing an affirmative burden on major DSPs to pre-screen user-provided content. Congress is likely to consider a shift in this direction as well.

§ 3.17 INFRINGEMENT PROCEEDINGS AND REMEDIES

The federal courts have exclusive jurisdiction over copyright infringement claims. Civil suits must be filed within three years after the claim accrues. 17 U.S.C. § 507. However, the circuits are currently divided on whether the claim accrues (1) as soon as the infringement occurs or (2) when the copyright owner discovered or reasonably should have discovered it. Because there is no laches defense in copyright law, mere delay in bringing suit will not bar the plaintiff's claim, provided it is brought before the statute of limitations expires. Petrella v. Metro-Goldwyn-Mayer, Inc., 572 U.S. 663 (2014).

Once the suit is filed, a court may grant a request for a preliminary injunction even before the full trial, if it believes that the copyright owner is likely to win the case and that preliminary relief is necessary to prevent irreparable harm. If the copyright owner prevails at trial, the court will typically issue a permanent injunction. Injunctions have nationwide effect. 17 U.S.C. § 502. A court may also order seizure or destruction of infringing articles. *Id.* § 503.

A court may award either actual or statutory damages. Actual damages are measured by the economic harm suffered by the copyright owner and the defendant's profits arising from the infringement. If, before the infringement occurred, the copyright was registered or preregistered, or if the copyright owner otherwise satisfied the registration requirements of § 412, then the copyright owner can avoid having to prove the amount of actual damages or profits by electing statutory damages instead. Statutory damages are measured per work infringed. They generally range from $750 to $30,000, but can be as low as $200 for innocent infringements, or as high as $150,000 for willful infringements. *Id.* § 504.

A court, at its discretion, can award attorney's fees to the prevailing party (plaintiff or defendant). However, attorney's fees can be awarded to copyright owners only if they satisfied the same § 412 registration or preregistration requirements that apply to statutory damages. *Id.* § 505.

In certain cases involving willful infringements, the federal government can pursue criminal charges. *Id.* § 506. A person found guilty of criminal copyright infringement may be fined or even imprisoned, depending on the circumstances. Criminal prosecutions, however, are normally reserved for large-scale commercial infringements.

As an alternative to litigation in federal court, the Copyright Office operates a small claims court, called the Copyright Claims Board (CCB), which offers a low-cost streamlined proceeding to resolve infringement claims involving up to $30,000 in damages. Participation is voluntary for both plaintiff and defendant. The CCB can also hear claims of misrepresentation involving the DMCA notice-and-takedown process.

§ 3.18 USE OF MUSIC AND SOUND RECORDINGS IN POLITICAL CAMPAIGNS

Politicians often wish to use copyrighted music in their live campaign events as well as in political ads airing on radio, television, or social media. Questions can arise as to whether these uses are permissible. In most cases, they require a license.

The use of copyrighted music or sound recordings in a political campaign, when unauthorized, will rarely qualify as fair use. Due to their high degree of creativity, music and sound recordings receive strong copyright protection, and the uncontrolled use of such works by politicians for their own political advantage would undermine the copyright owners' ability to capture the economic value of these works in the marketplace. *See* Grant v. Trump, 2024 WL 4179057 (S.D.N.Y. Sept. 13, 2024) (use of Eddy Grant's *Electric Avenue* by 2020 Trump campaign was not fair use). Therefore, the crucial question in these cases will be whether the political use was covered by a license.

The type of license needed will depend on the nature of the use. In most cases, the use involves recorded music, meaning that copyrights in both the musical work and the sound recording may be involved. Performance of music at a live political event involves the public performance right in the musical work, while the use of music in political advertising involves the right to create derivative works as well the public performance right. Each of these uses will be considered in turn.

Generally speaking, an unauthorized performance of music in the kind of public spaces where political rallies take place will infringe the exclusive public performance right in the *musical work*. However, even if recorded music is used at the event, this does not infringe the copyright in the *sound recording*, because the exclusive public performance right for sound recordings applies only to digital audio transmissions, not performances in public venues.

With respect to the musical work, it is possible that the performance of the work at the political event has been authorized by a blanket license that the songwriter's performing rights organization (PRO) has issued to the venue or the event organizer. (PROs are discussed in Chapter 6.) If so, then the public performance does not infringe. In many cases, however, the blanket licenses issued to venue operators exclude events organized by third parties, such as political campaigns. The campaign itself may obtain a blanket license from the PRO—e.g., the ASCAP Political Campaign License and the BMI Music License for Political Entities or Organizations. However, individual songwriters may ask their PRO to exclude their music from this particular license, and the PRO will then notify the licensee of this exclusion. If a campaign intends to use only a small number of musical works, it may simply request an individual license for each work from the music's publisher (although there is no guarantee that the request will be granted).

In addition to performing a musical work at live events, political campaigns may wish to record those events and post them on the Internet or use them in campaign ads. Also, the campaign may wish to include the musical work in specially-created campaign ads. However, both of these uses go beyond the scope of a public performance license, because they incorporate the music into an audiovisual work (which requires a "synchronization license" for the musical work), and the audiovisual work is then publicly performed whenever the campaign ad is broadcast or made available on the Internet, which requires a public performance license. Therefore, the campaign will need to obtain licenses specifically authorizing these activities.

If the campaign wishes to play a specific *sound recording* at a live event, it will not need a copyright license to perform the recording itself, because there is no general public performance right in sound recordings. However, in order to record the events for broadcast or streaming, or to use the sound recording in campaign ads, the campaign will need to obtain a license from the owner of the rights in the sound recording, which is typically a record label (but could be a recording artist who owns his or her own masters).

If a campaign uses a musical work or sound recording without obtaining the necessary licenses, it can be held liable for copyright infringement. A court will enjoin the campaign from any further use of the copyrighted work, and it is also likely to award damages to the copyright owner(s).

For example, in Isaac Hayes Enterprises, LLC v. Trump, 2024 WL 4148758 (N.D. Ga. Sept. 11, 2024), the co-owners of the copyright in Isaac Hayes' song *Hold On, I'm Coming* obtained a preliminary injunction to prevent the Trump campaign from continuing to perform Hayes' song at campaign events. BMI, which was Hayes' PRO, had issued the campaign a Music License for Political Entities or Organizations, but Hayes' song was excluded from that license. Even after being notified of the exclusion, the campaign continued using the song. Finding a likelihood of infringement and irreparable harm to the copyright owners, the court enjoined the campaign from any further use of the song at public events.

In another recent case, Grant v. Trump, 2024 WL 4179057 (S.D.N.Y. Sept. 13, 2024), songwriter and recording artist Eddy Grant sued former President Trump and his campaign organization for tweeting a campaign-related video that incorporated Grant's recording of the song *Electric Avenue*. Grant, through his wholly owned company Greenheart Antigua, owned the copyright in both the song and the sound recording. When the campaign failed to take down the video even after receiving a cease-and-desist letter, Grant and his company sued for copyright infringement. After rejecting the defendants' fair use arguments, the court held them liable for infringement. The amount of damages has yet to be determined.

If a campaign has obtained the necessary licenses to use a musical work and/or sound recording, but the songwriter or recording artist still objects to the use, he or she may still be able to persuade the campaign organizers to stop using the music. Many politicians will wish to avoid the bad publicity that will be generated if the aggrieved party goes public. If the campaign is still uncooperative, the songwriter or artist should consult an attorney to determine whether the music is being used in a way that violates his or her right of publicity and/or infringes his or her trademark rights by falsely suggesting endorsement or affiliation. (See Chapter 8.)

CHAPTER 4
PUBLISHING

§ 4.1 PUBLISHING BASICS

As commonly used in the music industry, the term "publishing" has a broader meaning than it does in federal copyright law. In copyright law, to "publish" a musical work is to distribute copies (or "phonorecords") of the work to the public; the term does not include public performances or the creation of derivative works. 17 U.S.C. § 101. In the music industry, however, publishing refers to all of the ways in which a musical composition can be exploited, including not only copying and distribution, but also public performances and the creation of derivative works such as sound recordings and audiovisual works. That is how the term is used throughout this chapter.

Once a songwriter (or group of songwriters) has created a musical work (that is, the music along with any lyrics), ordinarily the next step is to find ways to generate income from that song through licensing. Pursuing these licensing opportunities is what publishing is all about. Due to the complexity of the task, most songwriters use publishers or publishing administrators to handle their licensing.

§ 4.2 MAJOR SOURCES OF LICENSING REVENUE

The major income streams that a musical work might generate come from several types of licenses. The major categories are:

(1) Public performance licenses

(2) Mechanical licenses

(3) Synchronization licenses

(4) Electrical transcription licenses

Here is a brief explanation of each:

A. PUBLIC PERFORMANCE LICENSES

A musical performance requires a license only if it is *public*. Copyright owners do not have the right to prevent *private* performances of music. According to copyright law, a performances is public if it occurs (a) at a place open to the public (e.g., concert halls, arenas, shopping malls, skating rinks, airports, bars, and restaurants) or where members of the public (outside of a normal social circle) are actually gathered (e.g., schools or prisons) or (b) in a transmission to members of the public (e.g., radio, television, cable, satellite, webcasting, or streaming). 17 U.S.C. § 101.

The most common type of public performance license for music permits only *nondramatic* performances—that is, the performance of music other than in a context where the music advances the storyline of a dramatic work. Nondramatic public performances include live musical performances as well as performances of sound recordings. Examples of nondramatic public performances include radio play, streaming, background music services, and concerts, as well as musical performances at clubs, restaurants, bars, ballrooms, sporting events, political rallies, and trade conventions.

Typically, nondramatic public performances are the subject of blanket licenses issued by performing rights organizations (PROs). In contrast, a dramatic performance license allows music to be incorporated into a dramatic context—which means a context in which the music advances the public performance of a story (either live or recorded).

Public performance licenses are the subject of Chapter 6.

B. MECHANICAL LICENSES

A mechanical license authorizes (1) the creation of a sound recording that embodies a performance of the licensed musical work and (2) the public distribution of phonorecords (e.g., vinyl records, tapes, CDs, and digital music files) of that sound recording. Thus, in order for a record label to make and distribute a recording of a particular song, the record label must obtain a mechanical license from the copyright owner of the musical work, or the owner's publishing representative. Mechanical licenses are also required for certain types of music streaming. Mechanical licenses are addressed in Chapter 5.

C. SYNCHRONIZATION LICENSES

Synchronization (or "sync") licenses permit the creation of audiovisual works that incorporate the licensed musical work. The audiovisual works could be motion pictures, television shows, music videos, karaoke devices, video games, television commercials, YouTube or TikTok videos, or any other work that synchronizes the music with a series of visual images (and, in many cases, other sounds, such as dialog or sound effects).

Because music is used in such a wide variety of audiovisual works, and in such a wide variety of ways, sync licenses are always individually negotiated. For example, the music may be audible for just a few seconds in the background of a scene, it may play in the background throughout a longer scene, or a band performing the music may be the focus of the scene. The music may play during opening or closing titles of a film, or it may become the theme song for a television series. The music may be used in a trailer promoting an upcoming film, regardless of whether it is used in the film itself. It may be used in a television commercial as background music, or it may be featured as an advertising jingle in a series of commercials (perhaps with altered lyrics referencing the product or service being advertised). The song may be relatively unknown, or the licensee may want a song that it is already popular and/or nostalgic for the targeted audience.

A full-service music publisher will actively pursue synchronization opportunities for its songwriters' music. An audiovisual production company, in turn, will typically employ a music supervisor, whose job it is to select the music that will be licensed for particular productions.

When music is licensed for use in a film, television show, or other audiovisual work, the production company is required to prepare a "cue sheet" for the finished work. The cue sheet identifies the title of each musical work used, its songwriters and publishers together with their PRO affiliations, the duration of the musical sequence, and the way in which the music is used (e.g., during the title sequence, or as background music during a scene). The production must submit the cue sheet to the PROs representing the songwriters and publishers. Because PROs issue blanket public performance licenses to television and cable broadcasters, as well as audiovisual streaming services (see Chapter 6), when the audiovisual work is broadcast or streamed the cue sheet enables the PRO to allocate the proper share of royalties to each composer and publisher whose work was used.

D. ELECTRICAL TRANSCRIPTION LICENSES

An electrical transcription license is similar to a mechanical license, but applies only to sound recordings that are intended for radio broadcast, such as radio advertising or theme music, rather than for public distribution or streaming. Because these licenses are not standardized, their terms will vary depending on the use. Some songwriters choose not to authorize the use of their works in commercial advertising.

E. OTHER SOURCES OF LICENSING REVENUE

A musical work may generate income through other types of licensing as well. Income streams may come from licensing the work for sheet music (for distribution as an individual song or as part of a collection), lyric reprints, digital samples, the creation of new arrangements (e.g., for different instruments or for larger or smaller orchestras) or other derivative works, and music box rights (the right to produce a product like a music box or toy that plays a recording of the music). Additional royalties may be generated by subpublishing, which refers to authorizing publishers to license the work in specific foreign territories. (See § 4.5 below.)

§ 4.3 THE SONGWRITER'S PUBLISHING OPTIONS

In order to pursue the licensing opportunities described above, a songwriter must determine who will take on the role of publisher. A songwriter may either (1) enter an agreement with a full-service music publisher or (2) self-publish and use the services of a publishing administrator. Each of these options is explored below.

A. TRADITIONAL PUBLISHERS

Many songwriters—including both established writers and those new to the profession—will prefer to work with a full-service publisher that has the relevant experience and knowledge, as well as sufficient personnel, to maximize the revenue potential of their musical works. Full-service publishers will actively "pitch" the songwriter's music to recording artists, record labels, film studios, television production companies, and advertising agencies, in an effort to secure mechanical, synchronization, and other licenses. A publisher may also pursue co-writing opportunities for its songwriters.

The three "major" music publishers are especially large organizations that are associated with (but still separate from) the three major record labels. The major publishers are Universal Music Publishing Group (UMPG), Sony Music Publishing (formerly Sony/ATV Music Publishing), and Warner Chappell Music. In general, these publishers represent only well-established songwriters.

Publishers that are not affiliated with the three major record labels are referred to as "independent" publishers. An independent publisher may or may not be affiliated with one or more record labels. Newer songwriters will typically work with independent publishers. While there are hundreds to choose from, some of the largest and best-known independents are BMG Music (which also owns a large number of record labels), Kobalt Music Publishing, Concord, RoundHill, and Peermusic.

A songwriter that works with a full-service publisher will enter into a songwriter agreement that establishes the respective rights and obligations of the writer and the publisher. Under the traditional arrangement, the songwriter assigns the copyright in his or her work to the publisher in exchange for a specified share (the "writer's share") of royalties from each stream of income that the work generates. The publisher keeps the remaining portion of the royalties (the "publisher's share"). Publishers will promote the music to potential licensees, negotiate and execute the licensing agreements, collect the resulting royalties, distribute the writer's portion of those royalties (along with a report showing the sources of the various royalty streams), and enforce the copyright through litigation where necessary.

Because the publisher owns the copyright, a publishing deal is a long-term commitment for the songwriter. Unless the contract includes a termination or reversion option, the songwriter cannot get his or her copyrights back until the grant is eligible for termination under 17 U.S.C. § 203, or §§ 304(c) or (d) for pre-1978 contracts. (Termination is discussed in § 3.10 above.)

In a standard publishing deal, the royalties generated by the work (except for print royalties) are split equally between the writer's share and the publisher's share. However, a songwriter with bargaining power can often negotiate for more than half of the total royalties. This is referred to as a "co-publishing" deal. In a co-publishing arrangement, the songwriter is entitled to receive not only the writer's share (50% of the royalties) but also a portion of the publisher's share (the other 50%). The most typical of these arrangements is the "50/50" co-publishing deal, in which the songwriter receives the writer's 50% share plus half of the publisher's 50% share, for a total of 75% of the royalty stream, leaving the publisher with only 25%.

Most publishers will pay the songwriter an advance that is recoupable against future royalties. The advance is therefore analogous to a loan. For example, if a publisher pays the songwriter a $10,000 advance, the publisher will retain the first $10,000 of royalties that it would otherwise have disbursed to the songwriter.

B. SELF-PUBLISHING

Some songwriters will choose to forego a traditional publishing arrangement, and self-publish instead, typically using the services of a publishing administer to track and collect their royalties. The advantage of self-publishing is that the songwriter retains ownership of his or her copyrights and does not have to split the royalties with a publisher. Also, most publishing administration agreements terminate after 1–5 years, enabling the songwriter to end the relationship if he or she finds a better option. The disadvantage, however, is that the songwriter does not get the benefits of a full-services publisher's marketing services and industry connections (such as relationships with music supervisors) that can open up opportunities such as synchronization licensing and attract the attention of recording labels and recording artists.

Many self-publishing songwriters will engage the services of a publishing administrator in order to facilitate royalty collection. A publishing administrator is a company that administers publishing rights for many different songwriters as well as for some of the independent publishers. In most cases, publishing administrators do not actively market music for purposes such as synchronization licensing. Instead, the administrator will ensure that the work is properly registered with the Copyright Office (and any foreign copyright offices within the administrator's territory), the relevant collecting societies, and any foreign sub-publishers, and will track and collect the royalties due from these sources as well as from direct licensees, then disburse these royalties to the songwriter along with periodic reports that identify and quantify each royalty stream. Some administrators also offer synchronization licensing as an additional option.

As compensation for the administrator's services, the songwriter will pay an administration fee, typically calculated as a percentage (usually 10–20%) of the gross publishing income collected by the administrator. The percentage will be higher for additional services such as synchronization licensing. The administration agreement typically allows the administrator to deduct its costs.

Well-known publishing administrators include Songtrust, TuneCore, Sentric, and CDBaby Pro. Some full-service publishers also offer the option of an administration agreement in place of a publishing agreement.

A self-publishing songwriter should form a separate publishing entity in order to license his or her music and/or enter into agreements with administrators or subpublishers. The separate entity should be a corporation or limited liability company (LLC), in order to shield the songwriter's personal assets from any liabilities that might arise from publishing activities (for example, damages liability or other expenses arising from legal disputes).

In the case of licenses that separately pay out a "writer's share" and a "publisher's share" of royalties, such as the blanket public performance licenses granted by PROs, the self-publishing songwriter is entitled to receive both shares. However, to collect both shares, the songwriter must register his or her publishing entity with the PRO, unless the songwriter has hired a publishing administrator for this function.

Forming a separate publishing entity is also important for songwriters who enter co-publishing deals with full-service publishers. As noted earlier, in a 50/50 co-publishing deal the songwriter receives not only the writer's standard 50% royalty share, but also half of the publisher's 50% share. To collect this part of the publisher's share, the songwriter's publishing entity should register as a publisher with his or her PRO, unless the songwriter engages a publishing administrator.

Songwriters who self-publish or enter co-publishing deals are also entitled to receive some or all of the publisher's share of mechanical royalties. To collect the publisher's share of compulsory mechanical royalties (see § 5.2 below), the songwriter's publishing entity should register its ownership rights with the Copyright Office as well as the Mechanical Licensing Collective (MLC).

§ 4.4 PUBLISHING AGREEMENTS

If a songwriter chooses to work with a full-service publisher, the parties must sign a publishing agreement (also called a "songwriter agreement"). The agreement may cover one or more musical works. It may convey rights in compositions that have already been written, and, in a situation where the writer is likely to continue producing new compositions, it may cover all songs that the writer will create during a specified term of years.

Every songwriter should have the publishing agreement reviewed by his or her attorney before signing. The information provided in this chapter is offered merely as a general guide to the most typical provisions of the agreement.

The key provisions of a standard publishing agreement are (1) the copyright grant to the publisher, (2) the publisher's right to make certain changes to the work, (3) the writer's right to restrict the publisher's exploitation of the work, and (4) the writer's compensation (the advance and the royalty share).

A. COPYRIGHT GRANT

Traditionally, the songwriter's grant to the publisher includes the entire copyright in the musical work (as well as all rights in its title), subject only to the nonexclusive public performance rights that the writer grants to his or her PRO. (PROs are discussed in Chapter 6.) The agreement may convey only the work's U.S. copyright, or the copyright in several countries, or even worldwide copyright. Although copyright is protected by each individual country according to (and to the extent of) its own laws, it is possible for the songwriter to convey all of the song's copyrights throughout the world in a single conveyance. Rather than granting each national copyright individually, such an agreement simply states that it conveys worldwide copyright. If the publishing agreement conveys only the U.S. copyright, then the writer will need to enter agreements with other publishers for exploiting the work outside the U.S.

The agreement may specify which party has the obligation to register the copyright in any country where registration is desired. While registration may be unimportant (or non-existent) in many countries, it is still very important in the U.S., where it is essential to filing infringement claims and maximizing remedies.

Ordinarily, the publishing agreement assigns the copyright for its entire term of copyright protection. In some cases, however, the grant may be for a limited term, at the end of which the copyright automatically reverts to the writer. (Technically, this transfer is a license rather than an assignment.) Alternatively, the writer may retain a *reversion* right, which gives the writer the option to reclaim the copyright under specific circumstances, such as a publisher's failure to achieve certain benchmarks in licensing the work within a specified time period.

Because the publisher receives the entire copyright (domestic or worldwide), the publisher is empowered to grant a wide variety of licenses to third parties in exchange for royalties. The next question is: What does the writer receive in return?

B. WRITER'S COMPENSATION

The publishing agreement spells out the writer's entitlement to share in the proceeds generated by the exploitation of the copyright. In addition to an advance, the writer will receive a percentage of the royalties that the publisher receives from commercializing the work through various licenses. The writer and publisher split these royalties equally unless they have agreed to a co-publishing deal (as described above.)

The agreement should also address advances that the publisher *receives* from licensees. (These advances are usually recoupable against royalties that the licensee is obligated to pay the publisher.) Typically, the agreement will state that the publisher is not obligated to share the advance with the writer; rather, the publisher will pay the writer's share of the royalties as the publisher earns its advance. However, depending on the circumstances, the writer may negotiate to receive 50% of the publisher's advances.

The agreement should specify how often the publisher will remit the writer's royalty payments, and should also require the publisher to provide the writer with periodic accounting statements that show how these payments were calculated. In addition, the writer should be entitled to audit the publisher's records (using a certified public accountant) at specified intervals (typically no more than once a year) to determine whether any underpayments have occurred.

1. Writer's Advance

The writer should negotiate for an advance, payable upon executing the agreement and/or at agreed-upon future dates (in which case it may be termed a "draw" rather than an advance). The advance should be nonrefundable, but recoupable against future royalties payable *by the publisher* (and thus not recoupable against the writer's share of nondramatic public performance royalties payable by the writer's PRO, as discussed below). By requiring the publisher to pay a nonrefundable advance against royalties, the writer incentivizes the publisher to begin promoting the musical work assiduously to potential licensees in order to begin earning royalties. The amount of the advance is negotiable, and depends in large part on the writer's bargaining position. If the agreement covers multiple songs, the total amount of the advance should be allocated on a per-song basis.

The agreement should specify which royalty streams can be tapped for recoupment of the advance. For example, an advance for one song might be recoupable only against publishing royalties generated by that song. Alternatively, if the agreement covers multiple songs, the advance for one song might be recoupable against royalties generated by the other songs. If the parties have entered multiple publishing agreements covering different songs, the advance under one contract might be recoupable against royalties owed to the writer under a different contract. Finally, in the case of major publishers affiliated with record labels, a publishing advance might be recoupable against recording royalties, or a recording advance might be recoupable against publishing royalties.

This practice of recouping an advance from royalty streams generated by different songs or different contracts is called *cross-collateralization*. It enables the publisher (or record label, where applicable) to recoup an advance paid for a less successful song by tapping royalty streams generated by a more successful song. Thus, even though an advance may be nonrefundable, if it is cross-collateralized the publisher can save money by withholding the appropriate amount of royalties from a variety of songs. Writers should seek the advice of an attorney to ensure that they understand the scope of any cross-collateralization provisions in their publishing agreements and, depending on their bargaining power, they may be able to negotiate more favorable terms.

2. Nondramatic Public Performance Royalties

Royalties from nondramatic public performances are paid out differently from other royalties generated by musical works, in that each writer receives 50% (the "writer's share") of these royalties directly from the writer's performing rights organization (PRO), whereas other types of royalties are paid in full to the publisher, which then pays out the writer's share according to the publishing agreement. The reason for this difference is that each writer can (and should) join a PRO that issues blanket licenses to the venue operators, broadcasters, and streaming services that perform the music. Each blanket license permits the licensee to engage in nondramatic public performances of all of the musical works in that PRO's catalog. The PRO collects the blanket license fees, allocates them among the various musical works in its catalog, and then pay the writer(s) and publisher(s) of each song directly. In most cases, the PRO splits the payout equally between the writer and the publisher. Therefore, the writer's share never passes through the publisher's hands. As a result, any advance that the publisher has paid to the writer should not be recoupable against the writer's share of the nondramatic public performance royalties. (For more on PROs, see Chapter 6.)

3. Print Publication Royalties

Unlike other music royalties, print royalties traditionally are not split equally between the writer's share and the publisher's share. In the case of sheet music, it is customary for the publisher to pay the writer 7 cents for each copy sold. If the music is included in a print collection, such as a songbook, typically the publisher pays the writers 12-1/2% of the wholesale price, split equally among all of the songs in the collection.

4. Other Royalties

With the exception of print publication royalties, the writer's and publisher's shares of mechanical, synchronization, dramatic public performance, electrical transcription, and other royalties are split 50/50. Because the technologies and business models for exploiting music change constantly, the agreement should not be silent with respect to royalties that fall outside of any of the categories specifically listed in the agreement. There should be a provision addressing the split for any such royalties, whether it is the conventional 50/50 or something else.

C. PUBLISHER'S RIGHT TO REVISE THE WORK

Typically, the agreement gives the publisher the right to make changes to the work and/or its title. Some potential licensees, for example, may want new musical arrangements or lyric changes, may wish to translate the lyrics, or may want to adapt the work in other ways to suit a particular recording artist or to incorporate the composition into a derivative work such as a motion picture, dramatic work (such as a musical play), or video game. Publishers generally prefer to be in a position to approve such changes without the delay that might occur if the writer's consent was required. The writer, however, may negotiate to retain some degree of creative control.

D. RESTRICTIONS ON PUBLISHER'S EXPLOITATION RIGHTS

The agreement may impose certain restrictions on the publisher's authority to license the work. For example, some writers may specify that their music cannot be licensed for use in pornographic films, political advertising, or commercial advertising (of any kind, or only for certain goods or services), without their written consent. Some writers may also want a broader right to approve any use of their music in dramatic or audiovisual works.

§ 4.5 INTERNATIONAL SUBPUBLISHING

Some music publishers may operate only domestically, some may operate worldwide, and others may extend their operations to some foreign territories but not others. Publishers that do not operate worldwide can engage subpublishers to represent them in certain territories. Foreign subpublishers provide publishing services outside the United States, either in individual countries or in multinational territories. In the case of smaller independent publishers as well as self-publishing songwriters, subpublishers are especially valuable because of their knowledge, expertise, and industry connections in foreign markets, and their familiarity with foreign collecting societies and legal systems. (The rules that govern copyright licenses and copyright enforcement can differ from country to country.) In addition, many subpublishers will pay an advance, recoupable against the royalties that will be generated in their territories.

A subpublisher's fee is a percentage (usually 15–25%) of the publishing revenues it generates. The subpublisher's expenses typically come out of this share.

International music publishing has undergone significant changes in recent years. Streaming has largely replaced physical distribution, and domestic publishers are increasingly able to register directly with foreign collecting societies, making subpublishers less crucial than in the past. To ensure flexibility as the industry changes, the duration of a subpublishing agreement should be relatively short. Three to five years is typical, but even shorter terms can be negotiated. For this and other reasons, a subpublishing agreement should not include a copyright assignment.

CHAPTER 5
MECHANICAL LICENSES

§ 5.1 IN GENERAL

One of the most important licenses for a musical work is the mechanical license. This license authorizes the creation and distribution of sound recordings embodying the musical work. Publishing agreements normally split mechanical royalties 50/50 between songwriter and publisher.

There is a reason why the mechanical license has an old-fashioned-sounding name: The first mechanical licenses were for the manufacture and distribution of piano rolls that enabled player pianos to perform copyrighted musical compositions. That technology is, of course, obsolete, and today's mechanical licenses for musical works authorize a different type of copying—specifically, recording a specific performance of the musical work in a sound recording, which is then replicated and streamed and/or distributed to the public in phonorecords (another old-fashioned-sounding term that originated in the piano-roll era but which today includes vinyl records, analog or digital audio tapes, CDs, digital music files, and any other purely audio recording medium which might be invented in the future).

Copyright law defines "sound recordings" as works resulting from the fixation of a series of musical, spoken, or other sounds, other than the sounds incorporated into a motion picture or other audiovisual work. 17 U.S.C. § 101. A mechanical license therefore authorizes the licensee to record a performance of the musical composition in a sound recording (the "master" recording) and to reproduce and distribute that sound recording in phonorecords. However, a mechanical license does not authorize the use of a sound recording in an *audiovisual* work such as a motion picture, music video, or video game. That is the realm of *synchronization* licenses. (These are discussed in Chapter 4.)

In addition to phonorecords that consumers typically purchase or stream, mechanical licenses are required for any other activity that involves creating an audio-only recording of a musical work—ringtones, for example. A karaoke device will require a mechanical license if it uses audio-only recordings of musical works. In contrast, if it synchronizes the audio with visual effects, it will require a synchronization license.

A mechanical license is required not only for physical phonorecords and digital downloads, but also for certain types of music streaming. As discussed in further detail below, a mechanical license is required for interactive streaming—that is, streaming services which allow the user to choose which recording will play at a given time. However, no mechanical license is required for non-interactive (or "radio-style") streaming. Nor is such a license required for SiriusXM satellite radio or for terrestrial broadcasts. (Note, however, that the maker of any sound recording transmitted by one of these services was required to get a mechanical license to create the recording in the first place.)

The copyright owner's consent is always required in order to make the *first* sound recording of a particular musical work. Therefore, this license constitutes a "negotiated" or "voluntary" mechanical license. Whoever controls the publishing rights in the musical work (e.g., the publisher or self-publishing songwriter) is therefore free to accept or reject a mechanical license request from a particular record label or recording artist that wants to make the first sound recording of the work. The owner of the publishing rights can also set conditions on this license (e.g., setting the royalty fee and the time frame for commercial release, and allowing or disallowing any changes in the overall style or lyrics), with the final terms dependent on the parties' respective bargaining power. By exercising this control over the first sound recording of the work, the copyright owner can maximize the chances that the recording will lead to commercial success for the musical work.

When a record label negotiates for a voluntary mechanical license to record a particular musical work, it can request a "pass-through" license. This license passes through to any third party that the record label authorizes to deliver permanent downloads of the recording. Without the pass-through license, the download service would have to obtain a mechanical license of its own (either voluntary or compulsory).

As discussed below, however, for nondramatic musical works the copyright owner's veto power over making and distributing sound recordings embodying the work is typically limited to the *first* authorized distribution. After that, the compulsory license becomes available, provided that the prospective licensee complies with the terms and conditions imposed by law.

§ 5.2 COMPULSORY MECHANICAL LICENSE

Although the copyright owner's consent is required for the *first* sound recording of a musical work, the situation changes once the musical work has been lawfully recorded for the first time. At this point, additional record labels may wish to obtain licenses to make and distribute their own recordings of the work, typically by different artists—so-called "cover" recordings. In addition, digital music services may wish to distribute the original or cover recordings by offering downloads or interactive streaming. For nondramatic musical works, the compulsory mechanical license makes this possible.

In the case of *dramatic* musical works, licenses for cover recordings and digital deliveries are similar to licenses for the initial recording. That is, they must always be negotiated; there is no compulsory license.

However, in the case of *nondramatic* musical works, the rules are different. Individual negotiation is not required. Instead, a party wishing to make a cover recording or to offer digital phonorecord deliveries of the music has two options: (1)

negotiating for a mechanical license, or (2) electing to use the compulsory mechanical license under 17 U.S.C. § 115.

The § 115 license permits the creation and public distribution of a cover recording, or the digital delivery of lawfully made phonorecords embodying the music, without the consent of the copyright owner of the musical work. It also sets the price for the license, provided that certain statutory conditions are satisfied. Finally, it establishes the procedures that must be followed in order to obtain the license.

Under § 115, a musical work is eligible for compulsory licensing in *physical or digital* formats if it has previously been recorded in phonorecords that have been distributed to the public in the United States under the authority of the musical work's copyright owner. In other words, § 115 authorizes the creation of *cover* recordings for either digital or physical distribution.

In contrast, for a compulsory license for *digital distribution* only (including both downloads and interactive streaming), it is enough that the musical work has been fixed in a sound recording with the copyright owner's consent, and the copyright owner has authorized the sound recording copyright owner to make digital phonorecord deliveries of that recording to the public in the United States. *Id.* § 115(a)(1)(A)(i)–(ii). For digital-only distributions, therefore, the compulsory license can permit the public distribution of the first authorized sound recording embodying the musical work; it need not be a cover recording.

The compulsory mechanical license regime grew out of Congress's concerns—again, dating back to the piano roll era—that a single company should not be able to monopolize a popular musical work simply because it was the first to record it. Therefore, Congress wanted to prevent individual companies (today, record labels) from obtaining exclusive rights in one or more musical works.

While most cover recordings today are the result of voluntary rather than compulsory licenses (simply because the voluntary licenses are less cumbersome to obtain), these voluntary licenses typically mirror the exact terms of the compulsory license, and are issued (by publishers or their representatives, such as HFA (formerly the Harry Fox Agency) promptly upon request, with no actual negotiation. The compulsory royalty rate set by § 115 effectively sets a ceiling on the mechanical royalty rate that a publisher can demand from a record label in order to authorize a cover recording.

In contrast, as explained below, most mechanical licenses for interactive streaming and limited downloads today are obtained through the compulsory licensing process. (Limited downloads are digital music files available to the user for a limited period of time, unlike permanent downloads.)

A. SUBSTANTIVE RULES

All compulsory mechanical licenses must meet the following requirements:

(1) The licensee's primary purpose is to make phonorecords of the work and distribute them to the public for private use, including by means of digital phonorecord delivery; and

(2) Although the licensee can arrange the musical work to conform it to the "style or manner of interpretation" of the performance, the arrangement must not change the melody or "fundamental character" of the work, and is not eligible for copyright protection as a derivative work, without the copyright owner's consent.

17 U.S.C. § 115(a)(1)(A).

There are additional conditions as well. However, these differ depending on the type of "phonorecord delivery" the licensee plans to undertake. Until 2018, the same rules governed both physical formats (vinyl records, tapes, and CDs) and "digital phonorecord deliveries" (a term that encompasses both downloads and interactive streaming). Under the Music Modernization Act of 2018 (MMA), however, however, the rules for these two types of phonorecord deliveries have diverged. These changes are both substantive and procedural.

The *substantive* difference lies in the eligibility rules for the compulsory license. To use the compulsory license for distribution of phonorecords in *physical* formats, the pre-MMA eligibility rule still applies: Phonorecords of the musical work must have previously been distributed to the public in the United States, in physical formats and/or by digital delivery, with the consent of the musical work's copyright owner. *Id.* § 115(a)(1)(A)(i). With respect to physical phonorecords, therefore, the compulsory license permits only traditional "cover" recordings.

In contrast, if the potential licensee intends to use the license for *digital phonorecord deliveries* of the musical work, then the compulsory license is not restricted to "cover" recordings. Instead, it can be obtained for digital deliveries of the *original licensed sound recording* that musical work's copyright owner authorized for distribution, provided, of course, that the digital delivery service also obtains the consent of the copyright owner of the sound recording it intends to distribute. *Id.* § 115(a)(1)(A)(ii). Thus, for digital phonorecord deliveries, the compulsory license can authorize the digital distribution of a musical work in phonorecords by downloads or interactive streaming, even if the phonorecord is not a cover recording.

There are also differences in the royalty rates for different types of phonorecord deliveries. The Copyright Royalty Judges establish the rates for compulsory mechanical licenses periodically through administrative proceedings. The rates are different for physical phonorecords and permanent downloads, on the one hand, versus limited downloads and interactive streaming on the other.

As of January 2024, the current rate for physical phonorecords and permanent downloads is 12.4 cents per musical work for recordings of 5 minutes or less, or 2.38 cents per minute of playing time for recordings lasting more than 5 minutes, for each unit sold. For ringtones, the rate is 24 cents per ringtone delivery. These rates are adjusted annually based on increases in the Consumer Price Index. 37 C.F.R. § 385.11.

The rates for limited downloads, interactive streaming, and certain other digital music services are determined by formulas established in 37 C.F.R. § 385.21, and depend on the nature of the service provided. For certain promotional and free trial offerings, the royalty rate is zero. *Id.* § 385.31.

In March of 2024, to the dismay of songwriters and publishers, Spotify announced a strategy that would significantly reduce its mechanical royalty obligations under three of its subscription plans. By bundling audiobooks into the plans, Spotify can make them eligible for a lower payout formula under § 385.21, reducing its U.S. mechanical royalty obligations by $80–150 million in the first year, according to various estimates. This represents a reduction in the royalties that otherwise would flow to music publishers and songwriters. If Spotify's strategy succeeds, other interactive services may follow suit.

B. PROCEDURES

Different procedures are used for obtaining compulsory licenses for physical phonorecords versus digital phonorecord deliveries. The MMA did not change the longstanding procedures for obtaining a compulsory license for vinyl records, tapes, or CDs.

Under these rules, the party seeking the license—typically a record label—must notify the copyright owner of its intent to use the compulsory license. If the records of the Copyright Office do not provide the copyright owner's identity and an address for serving this notice, then the record label can send the notice to the Copyright Office instead. 17 U.S.C. § 115(b)(1). No royalties are owed unless and until the copyright owner is identified in Copyright Office records. *Id.* § 115(c)(1)(A).

In practice, however, most record labels seeking compulsory mechanical licenses for vinyl records, tapes, or CDs have exercised the more efficient option of bypassing the statutory process by obtaining voluntary licenses through HFA (formerly the Harry Fox Agency), which has long acted as a mechanical licensing agent on behalf of the major music publishers. HFA (which is today owned by SESAC) issues the licenses on request, applying the royalty rate and other conditions established by § 115; it also collects the royalties and disburses them to the publishers. This practice continues today.

In contrast, the process for obtaining compulsory mechanical licenses for digital phonorecord deliveries changed dramatically under the MMA. To understand these changes, some background is necessary.

Interactive streaming services initially took the position that they did not need mechanical licenses at all. However, as streaming became increasingly popular, it became apparent that interactive streaming was displacing sales of phonorecords (including not only records, tapes, and CDs, but also permanent downloads). This decrease in phonorecord sales meant that songwriters and music publishers were losing out on the mechanical royalties those sales would have generated. The controversy was resolved in 2008, when the streaming services, music publishers, and record labels reached an industry-wide agreement that interactive streaming and limited downloads should be subject to the compulsory mechanical license. Today, the compulsory mechanical royalties for physical phonorecords and permanent downloads continue to be based on the number of phonorecords distributed (either physically or by download), while the royalties for interactive streaming and limited downloads are based on the revenues that the digital music provider derives from these activities. Noninteractive (that is, radio-style) streaming services continue to be exempt from mechanical licensing requirements.

Although the substantive question was resolved, procedural problems remained. Prior to the MMA, the compulsory licensing process for streaming and digital downloads was the same as the process for vinyl records, tapes, and CDs. With the explosive growth of interactive streaming, however, it became clear that this process did not work well for the new technologies. In their haste to add new recordings to their repertoires, interactive streaming services often failed to send notices to the copyright owners of the musical works, instead sending notices *en masse* to the Copyright Office. The streaming services often failed to follow up by paying the license fees to the copyright owners, due in part to problems in identifying and/or locating the owners. This led to a number of lawsuits that ended in settlements requiring the streaming services to pay substantial amounts of overdue mechanical royalties to songwriters and publishers.

Congress addressed this problem in the MMA. Although it retained the previous rules for record labels making and distributing phonorecords in traditional physical media (vinyl records, tapes, and CDs), it adopted a new approach for services that provide interactive streaming or digital downloads. The new system allows digital music services to obtain the volume of licenses they need without delay, while ensuring that they pay the compulsory license fees promptly.

The new rules apply to services that provide "digital phonorecord deliveries." A digital phonorecord delivery is the "delivery of a phonorecord by digital transmission of a sound recording that results in a specifically identifiable reproduction" by or for the recipient of the transmission. The term includes permanent downloads, limited downloads (where the downloaded file is accessible only for a limited time), and interactive streaming (that is, music on demand). It does not include non-interactive (that is, radio-like) streaming. *Id.* § 115(e)(10). (The distinction between interactive and non-interactive streaming is explored more fully in Chapter 7.)

Under the new rules, providers of digital phonorecord deliveries can no longer obtain a compulsory license by sending a notice of intent to the Copyright Office. Instead, they must follow one of two procedures, depending on the type of license required.

A "record company" (the copyright term for, essentially, a record label) can obtain a compulsory license for *permanent downloads* of a specific *individual* musical work, by following the procedure for an "individual download license." *Id.* § 115(b)(3). To obtain this license, the label must send a notice of intent to the copyright owner (not the Copyright Office) either before or no later than 30 days after the first phonorecord delivery. *Id.* Thereafter, it must send the monthly royalty payments and account statements to the copyright owner. *Id.* § 115(c)(2)(I). This option is available only to record companies. Individual download licenses can also be obtained through HFA.

For *all other digital phonorecord deliveries*, including interactive streaming, limited downloads, and permanent downloads not covered by individual download licenses, the music service must send a "notice of license" to a nonprofit collecting society that was created especially for this purpose by the MMA. This organization, known as the Mechanical Licensing Collective (MLC), began operations on January 1, 2021. The MLC also collects the mechanical royalties and disburses them to the copyright owners.

C. THE MECHANICAL LICENSING COLLECTIVE

Federal copyright law dictates most aspects of the MLC's governance and operations. The MLC administers *blanket* compulsory mechanical licenses covering all musical works in its repertoire, much like the blanket public performance licenses provided by the various PROs. Unlike the PROs, however, the MLC is the *only* organization authorized to administer blanket compulsory mechanical licenses for digital music services. The MLC also differs from the PROs in another respect: it is not a voluntary membership organization. On the contrary, the MLC's "repertoire" includes *all* nondramatic musical works that are eligible for the compulsory license for digital phonorecord deliveries—regardless of who owns the copyright.

In addition to the blanket compulsory license for interactive streaming and limited downloads, the MLC can also administer voluntary licenses and individual download licenses. *Id.* § 115(d)(3)(c)(iii). (As noted above, a record label seeking a compulsory license only for permanent downloads of a specific individual musical work is not required to obtain a blanket license. It may instead opt for an "individual download license" by serving a notice of intention on the copyright owner of that work and complying with the other requirements for an individual compulsory license.)

To obtain a blanket compulsory mechanical license, the digital music provider must send a "notice of license" to the MLC. *Id.* § 115(d)(2)(A).

Unless the MLC rejects the notice within 30 days, the blanket license will take effect automatically, effective as of the date the notice was sent. *Id.* § 115(d)(2)(A)(ii). The MLC can reject a provider's notice of license only if the provider or the notice fails to meet the requirements of § 115 or the applicable regulations, or if the MLC has terminated the provider's blanket license within the preceding three years. *Id.* § 115(d)(2)(A)(iii). A provider whose notice is rejected can seek federal court review. *Id.* § 115(d)(2)(A)(v).

In a further departure from the pre-2018 rules governing the compulsory mechanical license, digital music services may obtain blanket licenses through the MLC for interactive streaming or digital downloads regardless of whether the musical work in question has previously been recorded and distributed on phonorecords. Thus, in contrast to the compulsory licensing rules that continue to apply to traditional physical phonorecords, licenses obtained through the MLC are not limited to "cover" recordings of a musical work, and can therefore be used for streaming or providing downloads of the first lawfully made sound recording of the work. *Id.* § 115(a)(1)(A).

Because the MLC's blanket compulsory license applies only to digital phonorecord deliveries, the MLC is not involved with compulsory licenses for vinyl records, tapes, or CDs. Record labels seeking a compulsory license to record and distribute musical works in these traditional physical media must continue to utilize the pre-2018 process for obtaining such licenses. As noted earlier, this requires sending notice to the copyright owner or, if the Copyright Office does not have the owner's contact information, sending notice to the Copyright Office instead. *Id.* § 115(b)(1). Voluntary licenses, either direct from the publisher or through organizations like HFA, are also an option.

The MLC's blanket license covers only the mechanical rights in nondramatic musical works. It does not grant public performance rights in those works; streaming services must obtain those rights separately, through blanket licenses from the PROs. (See Chapter 6.) Nor does it grant any rights in the sound recordings that incorporate the musical works. The rights to publicly perform a sound recording via streaming, and to reproduce a sound recording as a digital download, are outside the scope of the mechanical compulsory license. Therefore, streaming and download services must acquire the sound recording rights separately.[1]

The MLC does not determine the fees for blanket mechanical licenses. Instead, the royalty rate is set by the Copyright Royalty Judges based on a willing buyer/willing seller standard. *Id.* § 115(c)(1)(F). The

---

[1] The service providing the digital phonorecord deliveries will need the consent of the rights holder of the copyrighted sound recording, since the latter is being publicly performed and/or reproduced in the course of the digital phonorecord delivery. *Id.* §§ 115(a)(1)(A)(ii)(II)–(B), (c)(2)(F). As discussed in Chapter 7, digital public performance rights in sound recordings are addressed in §§ 106(6) and 114. The rights to reproduce a sound recording (or "master") and to distribute it by digital download (or in vinyl records, tapes or CDs) fall under the general rights of reproduction and distribution in §§ 106(1) and 106(3), respectively.

Copyright Royalty Judges periodically conduct rate-setting proceedings at which the copyright owners and digital services present evidence and arguments in support of their requested rates. *Id.* § 115(c)(1)(C). The MLC's role in this process is limited to supplying information. *Id.* § 115(d)(8)(A). It is also prohibited from engaging in any lobbying activities. *Id.* § 115(d)(3)(C)(iv).

In addition to receiving the notices for the blanket compulsory licenses, the MLC also collects the blanket license fees from the digital music providers and distributes them to the copyright owners. *Id.* § 115(d)(3)(C)(i)(II). This involves (1) identifying the copyright owners of the licensed works, and (2) determining how the total blanket license fees should be allocated among them. The methods for accomplishing these tasks are discussed below.

As required by the MMA, the MLC has created—and maintains—the "Musical Works Database," a searchable public database of information about musical compositions, the identity and contact information of their copyright owners (and their respective ownership shares in the case of jointly owned works), and the specific sound recordings that embody those compositions. *Id.* § 115(d)(3)(E)(i). This database is essential to allocating and distributing the blanket license fees among the various copyright owners. HFA shares its own musical works data with the MLC to assist in building the latter's database.

One must register as a member of the MLC in order to be included in the MLC's database and claim a share of the blanket license fees. Fortunately, membership is free. It is open to publishers, publishing administrators, self-publishing songwriters, and foreign collective management organizations (CMOs). As new members register, they are added to the database and matched to the sound recordings that embody their works, thereby becoming eligible to receive their royalty shares.

Where the Musical Works Database has complete information about the copyright ownership of a particular song, the song is considered a "matched work." *Id.* § 115(e)(17). If the ownership information about a particular musical work is missing or incomplete, it is "unmatched" to the extent of the unidentified ownership share. *Id.* § 115(e)(35). The MLC still collects mechanical royalties attributable to unmatched ownership shares, but it retains those royalties until it is able to identify the owners entitled to receive them. *Id.* § 115(d)(3)(H)–(I). The MLC conducts outreach to identify those parties and encourage them to become registered members. *Id.* § 115(d)(3)(E)(i). If successful, it adds them to the database and pays out their respective royalty shares, *id.* § 115(d)(3)(I).

The MLC must hold accrued unmatched royalties for at least three years, during which time the owners may come forward to register and claim their shares, with interest. *Id.* § 115(d)(3)(H). To the extent that any accrued royalties are still unclaimed after the holding period expires, the MLC allocates those royalties, with interest, to the other copyright owners in its database according to their relative market shares for the respective reporting period. *Id.*

§ 115(d)(3)(J). Those copyright owners, in turn, are required to share at least 50 percent of the unclaimed royalties they receive with the songwriters of the works they own, to be allocated according to the reported usage of each work by digital service providers during the reporting period. *Id.* § 115(d)(3)(J)(iv). The songwriters' share may not be waived by contract. *Id.*

In order to allocate the blanket license fees accurately among the many different musical works and their respective copyright owners, the MLC must know how frequently each musical work has been streamed or downloaded. For this, the MLC relies on usage data submitted by its licensees. *Id.* § 115(d)(4)(A).

Each licensee must submit to the MLC a monthly data report that includes: (1) identifying information for the sound recordings it has utilized; (2) to the extent possible, identifying information for the musical works embodied in those recordings as well as their ownership and authorship; and (3) the number of limited downloads and interactive streams it has delivered for each sound recording.[2] *Id.* Licensees are required to make good faith commercially reasonable efforts to obtain from their sound recording licensors the information necessary to match the sound recordings to the songwriters and

---

[2] A 2024 federal indictment describes how one individual allegedly manipulated this data by using automated bots to continuously stream hundreds of thousands of AI-generated songs on several streaming platforms. See § 3.13[E] above. Under the federal regulations governing the MLC, manipulated streams are not eligible for mechanical royalties. 37 C.F.R. §§ 385.2, 385.21.

copyright owners of the underlying musical works. *Id.* § 115(d)(4)(B).

Two sets of unique internationally recognized code numbers are used to identify which musical work corresponds to each recorded track. The International Sound Recording Code (ISRC) identifies the recorded track, and the International Standard Musical Work Code (ISWC) identifies the musical work. When a streaming service reports its usage data, these numbers help the MLC to identify which musical works have been performed.

In determining the blanket license fee payable by each licensee based on its usage report, the MLC must separate out any uses that are covered by voluntary licenses and individual download licenses, because the licensees pay for those licenses separately. *Id.* § 115(d)(3)(G)(i). The licensee reports must therefore separately identify usage data for musical works covered by voluntary licenses and individual download licenses. *Id.* § 115(d)(4)(A)(ii).

Both the MLC and copyright owners have audit rights. To verify the accuracy of royalty payments, the MLC can audit each blanket licensee once every three years. *Id.* § 115(d)(4)(D). Copyright owners, in turn, have the right to audit the MLC, once per year, either individually or collectively, in order to verify that they have received accurate royalty payments. *Id.* § 115(d)(3)(L).

The MLC has a dispute resolution mechanism to address disputes involving copyright ownership interests or the allocation and distribution of royalties. *Id.* § 115(d)(3)(K). Copyright owners and digital music providers may obtain legal remedies against the MLC only for gross negligence. *Id.* § 115(d)(11)(D).

Although *voluntary* mechanical licenses can be negotiated between digital music providers and copyright owners without the involvement of the MLC, the parties to such voluntary licenses may elect (for a fee) to have the MLC administer their licenses by collecting and distributing the royalties; the parties to an individual digital download license have the same option. *Id.* § 115(d)(3)(C)(iii). Some of the digital music providers that operate under voluntary mechanical licenses or individual download licenses are also required to submit usage reports to the MLC. *Id.* § 115(d)(6)A). This requirement applies only to services that provide relatively high volumes of interactive streaming or downloads ("significant nonblanket licensees"). *Id.* § 115(e)(31)(A).

The MLC's Board of Directors, which is dominated by music publishers, consists of fourteen voting and three nonvoting members. All of the voting members represent copyright owners; ten of them represent music publishers, and four are songwriters who have retained ownership of the mechanical rights in their songs. *Id.* § 115(d)(3)(D). The nonvoting members represent (1) a music publishers' nonprofit trade association, (2) a songwriters' nonprofit trade association, and (3) a nonprofit entity (the "digital licensee coordinator") that represents the digital music services holding blanket licenses. *Id.* § 115(d)(3)(D), (d)(5).

Funding for the MLC comes from an administrative assessment imposed on the blanket licensees and significant nonblanket licensees, as well as voluntary contributions determined through private agreements among these parties. *Id.* § 115(d)(7)(A)–(B). The amount of the administrative assessment is determined in a proceeding before the Copyright Royalty Judges. *Id.* § 115(d)(7)(D). If the administrative assessment and voluntary contributions are insufficient to cover its costs, the MLC can use unclaimed royalties to defray expenses as an interim measure, but must reimburse those royalties from future payments of the assessment. *Id.* § 115(d)(7)(C).

If a blanket licensee defaults on its obligations (by failing to submit payments or usage reports, or by failing to comply with other material conditions of its license), the MLC must send a notice of default. If the licensee fails to remedy the default, its license will terminate. Terminated licensees can seek judicial review in a federal district court. *Id.* § 115(d)(4)(E).

The MLC is also authorized to take legal action as necessary in carrying out its statutory functions. *Id.* § 115(d)(3)(C)(i)(VIII). In its first enforcement action, the MLC in 2024 filed suit against streaming provider Pandora, alleging that Pandora had failed to pay the full amount of mechanical royalties it owed. The dispute turns on whether the "Pandora Free" service should be characterized as *interactive* or *noninteractive*. *See* Mechanical Licensing Collective v. Pandora Media LLC, No. 24–168 (M.D. Tenn., filed Feb. 12, 2024). This is the same distinction that affects eligibility for statutory licensing of digital audio transmissions of sound recordings under § 114, as discussed in Chapter 7.

CHAPTER 6

PERFORMANCE RIGHTS IN MUSICAL WORKS

§ 6.1 INTRODUCTION

Perhaps the most valuable right owned by the copyright owner of a musical work is the exclusive right to publicly perform that work, or to authorize public performances. Publicly performed music is ubiquitous—on television and radio, on cable channels, on YouTube and TikTok, on music streaming services, in arenas, theatres, stadiums, clubs, bars, restaurants, offices, elevators, and stores, and even over the telephone while a caller is placed on "hold." The public performance right in a musical work encompasses both live performances and performances of recorded music.

The public performance right addressed in this chapter is the right that attaches to the musical composition itself. The public performance right in *sound recordings* is quite different, and is covered in Chapter 7.

Under copyright law, a performance is public if (1) it takes place at a place open to the public or where members of the public are gathered, or if (2) it is transmitted to the public, by any device or process, regardless of whether the members of the public receive it in different places or at different times. 17 U.S.C. § 101. Under part (2) of the definition, then, a television broadcast received by millions of people in their private homes is a public performance, and so is music that is streamed on demand to individuals at different times and in different places, even if only one person is streaming it at a given moment.

Some public performances of music do not require the consent of the copyright owner, because they fall under specific statutory exemptions. These exemptions are discussed in Chapter 3.

Non-exempt public performance rights generally fall into three categories—dramatic, grand, and nondramatic rights. Nondramatic public performances are generally authorized under blanket licenses issued by performing rights organizations (PROs). (The role of PROs is discussed in § 6.2 below.) However, these licenses do not cover dramatic or grand rights.[1]

Although not defined in copyright law, *dramatic* public performances are generally understood as public performances in which the music is intertwined with a story line and carries the plot forward. It does not matter whether the music itself was created as part of a dramatic work. The category of dramatic performances thus includes performances of a musical composition in a dramatic context such as a film, television show, or live theatrical production, or in a dance performance. These performances occur much less frequently than nondramatic public performances, and are licensed individually. A dramatic public performance license must therefore be negotiated with the copyright

---

[1] In fact, an antitrust consent decree expressly prohibits one PRO, ASCAP, from licensing dramatic or grand rights.

owner of the work or the copyright owner's authorized licensing agent.

For example, the film *The Adventures of Priscilla, Queen of the Desert* involved dramatic public performances of songs written by ABBA. Although they were originally written as nondramatic musical works, in the film they were intertwined with the story; therefore, the film producers needed the dramatic performance rights (as well as synchronization rights). When the film became a Broadway musical, the stage producers were unable to secure the rights to the ABBA songs, and had to obtain dramatic public performance licenses for other period-appropriate pop songs to replace them.

A *grand* performance is a public performance in which a dramatico-musical work (such as an opera or a musical play), or a substantial part of that work, is publicly performed. A good example of grand rights can be found in Frank Music Corp. v. Metro-Goldwyn-Mayer, Inc., 772 F.2d 505 (9th Cir. 1985). In that case, a Las Vegas resort staged a musical revue that included six minutes of songs from the musical play *Kismet,* performed by singers who were identified and costumed as characters from the play. Even if the performance was not dramatic, because it contained no story or dialogue, it still exceeded the scope of the resort's blanket public performance license from ASCAP, because that license expressly excluded the performance of "dramatico-musical works, or songs [accompanied by] visual representation of the work from which the music is taken. . . ." *Id.* at 511.

Thus, licenses for both dramatic and grand rights must always be obtained by negotiating with the copyright owner of the musical work (often through a licensing agent).

In contrast, nondramatic public performances are too numerous, as a practical matter, to be individually licensed. To self-administer nondramatic public performance rights, a copyright owner would have to negotiate licenses, monitor usage, collect royalties, and enforce the copyrights against infringers that publicly perform the works without obtaining a license. These tasks would be overwhelming if the only option were to carry them out individually, song by song, for every venue, radio and television station, cable network, streaming service, and digital platform. For that reason, owners of music copyrights—that is, songwriters and publishers—typically rely on performing rights organizations (PROs), which act on their behalf to negotiate, collect, and distribute royalties arising from nondramatic public performances of their compositions.

§ 6.2 PERFORMING RIGHTS ORGANIZATIONS

Four such organizations are well-established in the United States: the American Society of Composers, Authors, and Publishers (ASCAP), BMI (formerly "Broadcast Music, Inc."), SESAC (formerly "the Society of European Stage Authors and Composers," but now representing United States copyright owners as well), and Global Music Rights.

A fifth PRO, called AllTrack, is still in its early stages; because there is currently very little public information about AllTrack, this discussion focuses on the other four PROs.

Every songwriter whose music is publicly performed should join a PRO, but a songwriter can join only one. In contrast, because music publishers and publishing rights administrators represent large numbers of songwriters who are likely to be members of different PROs, they must join every PRO to which their songwriters belong.

If a song is co-written, the co-writers must notify their respective PROs how they have agreed to split the songwriters' share of the blanket license royalties. (For example, if there are two songwriters, their split might be 50/50, 70/30, or something else.) Each PRO remits the proportionate share(s) to its affiliated writer(s).

Songwriter membership in SESAC and Global Music Rights is by invitation only. In contrast, ASCAP, BMI, and AllTrack maintain open membership policies.

By joining a PRO, the songwriter authorizes it to include that songwriter's music in its catalog. The PRO executes "blanket licenses" permitting each licensee (that is, each of the various broadcasters, streaming services, platforms, and venues described above) to perform the PRO's entire catalog of musical compositions in exchange for a single licensing fee, which is then distributed among the PRO's members.

These blanket licenses apply only to nondramatic public performances ("small" rights).

The two oldest and largest of these collecting societies, ASCAP and BMI, are both subject to antitrust consent decrees dating back to 1941. Under these decrees, ASCAP and BMI are not completely free to negotiate the prices or other terms under which they grant blanket licenses, unlike their newer competitors SESAC, GMR, and AllTrack. Also, the activities of ASCAP and BMI are subject to federal judicial oversight in the Southern District of New York (also known as the "rate court"), which resolves rate-setting disputes as well as other disputes involving their licensing policies.

PROs charge their blanket licensees a fee that is a percentage of the licensee's revenues. Although each PRO has its own approach, the percentage is generally determined by the category of the licensee's business, with more music-intensive businesses (e.g., radio stations and dance halls) paying a higher rate than businesses that do not rely as heavily on music to generate revenues (e.g., retail stores and restaurants). ASCAP, BMI, and SESAC also give licensees the option of a per program license, a type of blanket license where the fee is a percentage of the revenues generated only by the programs in which the PRO's music is used; this can be useful for radio and television broadcasters that need music licenses for some programs but not others. *See* Buffalo Broadcasting Co., Inc. v. ASCAP, 744 F.2d 917, 922 (2d Cir. 1984).

For songwriters, choosing a PRO can be difficult, as the PROs do not disclose the exact methods they use to calculate blanket license fees and to allocate them among their songwriter members. Although a songwriter may change to a different PRO, the window for resigning from the current PRO is a matter of contract. In addition, the process of changing PROs can be labor-intensive, and may involve lengthy delays, because every one of the songwriter's compositions must be deleted from the first PRO's catalog and re-registered with the new PRO. The songwriter could miss out on some royalties during the changeover. Therefore, a songwriter should choose his or her PRO carefully (perhaps after consulting with experienced songwriters in the same music genre), with the expectation of maintaining that affiliation indefinitely, and should change only when presented with a clearly superior opportunity. This appears to have happened with the creation of Global Music Rights, which attracted its high-profile songwriter members away from their previous PROs with promises of better payouts. Only the songwriters know whether those promises have been fulfilled.

ASCAP is the only nonprofit PRO. Although BMI began as a nonprofit, it switched to for-profit status in 2022.

Each of the four major PROs maintains a searchable public database listing all of the song titles in its catalog. This information is valuable to potential licensees, because it enables them to determine which PROs offer the songs they wish to license. It is also helpful to potential songwriter members, who can search the catalogs to assess whether other songwriters in similar genres have chosen one PRO over the others.

Songwriters and publishers normally split a song's nondramatic public performance royalties 50/50 (with the songwriter's 50% shared among all of the song's writers according to their agreed-upon splits). Once a PRO determines the share of its total blanket license fees that it will distribute for a particular song, it remits half to the songwriter(s) and half to the publisher(s), unless the songwriter(s) and publisher(s) notify the PRO that they have agreed to a different arrangement. PROs remit the songwriter's share directly to the songwriter; it does not pass through the publisher.

A songwriter that does not have a publisher (or a publishing rights administrator) will receive only the songwriter's 50%, with the PRO withholding the publisher's share. These songwriters should therefore register twice with their PRO—once as a writer, and once as a publisher—in order to receive their full allocation of the blanket licensing fee. Songwriters who co-publish with their publishers should do the same, in order to ensure that the PRO sends them their portion of the publisher's share.

It is important to remember that ASCAP, BMI, SESAC, Global Music Rights, and AllTrack represent only the owners of copyright in *musical compositions*. They do not represent the owners of copyright in specific *sound recordings* of those compositions—typically, record labels. As discussed in Chapter 7, licensing public performance rights for sound recordings is an entirely different matter.

A. FRACTIONAL LICENSING

If a song is co-written by two or more songwriters that belong to different PROs, then the song will be included in the catalog of each of the PROs. As a result, licensees seeking a blanket license that includes the co-written song must obtain blanket licenses from *each* of those PROs, in a practice known as "fractional licensing."

In 2016, the Department of Justice, in reviewing the ASCAP and BMI consent decrees, proposed a new interpretation of the decrees that would have replaced the practice of fractional licensing with "full work" or "100%" licensing, under which blanket licensees could have obtained full public performance rights in a song from any PRO that had any fraction of the song in its catalog. However, the Second Circuit (which has jurisdiction over both consent decrees) rejected this change. *See* United States v. Broadcast Music, Inc., 720 Fed. Appx. 14 (2d Cir. 2017). Thus, fractional licensing remains in place.

B. ALLOCATING FEES

Each PRO has its own method for determining how to allocate blanket license fees among the many works in its catalog. Although the PROs do not disclose the precise details, certain practices are common. With respect to some licensees, such as music streaming services, the PRO relies on the licensee's actual usage reports. The unique international codes for the sound recording (ISRC) and the musical work (ISWC) help to identify how often each musical work has been streamed.

In the case of films, television shows, and other audiovisual works that are transmitted by television or cable broadcasters, or by audiovisual streaming services, PROs rely on the cue sheets submitted by the producer of the work. (See § 4.2[C] above.) The cue sheet enables the PRO to allocate the proper share of royalties to each composer and publisher whose work was used.

In other cases, such as radio broadcasting, the PRO makes an estimate based on sample surveys taken at various times. Data from one licensee may be used to estimate usage by other licensees for which reliable data is not available (such as music performed in clubs or bars). The actual or estimated usage data for a particular licensee may be assigned a certain "weight" depending on the annual fee paid by the licensee, the nature of the performance, the time of day when the music is performed, and other factors. A PRO may award additional credits or bonuses to songs that are especially popular or hit certain benchmarks.

C. ANTITRUST SCRUTINY

Both ASCAP and BMI are subject to antitrust consent decrees which impose significant constraints on their operations. An understanding of these constraints can be helpful to potential songwriter members as well as potential blanket licensees.

ASCAP, the oldest of the four PROs, was formed in 1914. For many years, ASCAP was the only PRO operating in the United States, controlling 80% of the music played on the radio. In 1939, after broadcasters had become increasingly dissatisfied with ASCAP, the National Association of Broadcasters established BMI as a competing PRO. Shortly after BMI was established, however, the Department of Justice (DOJ) brought antitrust actions against both ASCAP and BMI, arguing that the practice of blanket licensing prevented price competition between the owners of music copyrights, by requiring potential licensees to pay a single price for a PRO's entire music catalog, regardless of how much of that music the licensee wanted to use. In 1941, both suits ended in consent decrees, which have been amended several times over the years.

As a result of the consent decrees, ASCAP and BMI must limit their activities in several ways:

(1) They may not acquire *exclusive* public performance rights from their members, who must be allowed to retain the right to grant direct licenses for public performances of their musical works.

(2) They must accept any songwriter or music publisher that applies for membership, subject to certain minimum criteria.

(3) They must offer alternatives to blanket licenses, such as per-program licenses and blanket licenses with carve-outs for music that a user has licensed directly from the PRO members.

(4) They must not discriminate between similarly situated licensees (that is, licensees within the same business category, such as restaurants) as to the price or other conditions of their licenses.

(5) They must offer licenses at reasonable terms to any users that apply.

(6) Where a local broadcaster's program is supplied by a broadcast network (radio or television), the PRO must offer a "through to the viewer" (or "licensing at the source") license to the network as an alternative to requiring the affiliated station to pay for the music used in that program.

(7) ASCAP may not license any rights other than nondramatic public performance rights in music.[2]

The consent decrees also provide that a party seeking a blanket license from ASCAP or BMI can begin offering nondramatic public performances of the PRO's repertoire immediately upon submitting its application, and need not pay a licensing fee until the parties have concluded their negotiations. If they are unable to agree on a licensing fee, then the dispute will be resolved by the U.S. District Court for the Southern District of New York, which has become known as the "rate court." In rate court proceedings, the burden is on the PRO to prove the reasonableness of its proposed fee, and if it fails to satisfy that

[2] Only ASCAP's consent decree imposed this requirement. However, BMI has thus far refrained from engaging in any other licensing activity.

burden, the court itself will decide what fee is reasonable. (In legislation enacted after the date of the consent decrees, if the suit is initiated by the licensee, the latter is required to pay an interim license fee into an escrow account pending resolution of the dispute. 17 U.S.C. § 513.)

In addition to disputes involving the reasonableness of licensing fees, the Southern District of New York also resolves disputes involving more fundamental questions about the activities of ASCAP and BMI, such as the question whether a particular use constitutes a "public performance" in the first place. For example, the court has determined that neither a digital download nor the transmission of musical ringtones to mobile phone customers constitutes a public performance warranting payment of a licensing fee to ASCAP. *See* United States v. American Society of Composers, Authors and Publishers, 485 F.Supp.2d 438 (S.D.N.Y. 2007), *aff'd,* 627 F.3d 64 (2d Cir. 2010); In re Cellco Partnership, 663 F.Supp.2d 363 (S.D.N.Y. 2009). When ASCAP has sought to impose licensing fees both on local cable television stations and also on the parties that supply their programming (via cable or satellite transmissions), the court has held that ASCAP may not double-dip by collecting two fees for the same broadcast; accordingly, the "through to the viewer" requirements of ASCAP's amended consent decree are not limited to networks that were in existence at the time of the decree. *See* United States v. American Society of Composers, Authors and Publishers (In re Fox Broadcasting), 870 F. Supp. 1211 (S.D.N.Y. 1995); United States v. American

Society of Composers, Authors and Publishers (In re Turner Broadcasting), 782 F.Supp. 778 (S.D.N.Y. 1991).

The DOJ maintains continuing oversight of the activities of ASCAP and BMI, and has periodically reviewed and revised the consent decrees. Although it reviewed the consent decrees most recently in 2016 and 2019, no changes have resulted from these reviews.

The Southern District of New York also rejected an attempt by ASCAP-affiliated music publishers to withhold certain public performance rights from ASCAP. Dissatisfied with the licensing fees they were receiving from digital music services, several major publishers withdrew their digital public performance rights (and *only* those rights) from ASCAP, in order to force digital music services to license those rights directly from the publishers. However, the court held that this attempt at partial withdrawal was ineffective, because the consent decree prohibits ASCAP from denying licenses to any particular subgroup of potential licensees—in this case, digital music services. *See* In re Pandora Media, Inc., 2013 WL 5211927 (S.D.N.Y. Sept. 17, 2013), *aff'd,* 785 F.3d 73 (2d Cir. 2015). Thus, with respect to nondramatic public performance rights in any particular song, a publisher's grant of licensing authority to ASCAP must encompass all potential licensees. The same rule presumably applies to BMI.

Because SESAC and Global Music Rights are not subject to these antitrust consent decrees, they have more freedom with respect to their membership and licensing practices. Their membership is by invitation only, enabling them to curate their catalogs. Because their licensing fees are not subject to court oversight, they are free to pursue more aggressive pricing strategies with licensees, enabling them to entice new members with promises of larger payouts. In addition, their activities are not limited to nondramatic public performance licensing of musical works. Therefore, they may engage in other licensing activities. In 2015, for example, SESAC expanded into mechanical licensing by acquiring the Harry Fox Agency (HFA), which issues mechanical licenses as an agent for music publishers.[3]

Even though they are not bound by consent decrees, the activities of SESAC and Global Music Rights are not immune from antitrust scrutiny. As SESAC has expanded its catalog and its resulting market power, it has been the target of two antitrust suits by radio and television broadcasters. In 2015, both of these suits ended in settlements, under which SESAC agreed to modify its licensing practices in several respects, including submitting royalty disputes to binding arbitration. *See* Meredith Corp. v. SESAC LLC, 87 F.Supp.3d 650, 657–58 (S.D.N.Y. 2015); Radio Music License Comm. v. SESAC, Inc., Case No. 2:12–cv–05807 (E.D.Pa., filed Oct. 11, 2012). In 2022, Global Music Rights settled a similar dispute with radio stations, although the terms of the settlement are not public. *See* Radio Music License Comm. v. Global Music Rights, LLC, 2017 WL

---

[3] The newest PRO, AllTrack, is also not subject to a consent decree, and launched a mechanical rights division in late 2024.

104307 (E.D. Pa. Jan. 5, 2017); Global Music Rights, LLC v. Radio Music License Comm., 2017 WL 3449606 (C.D. Cal. Apr. 7, 2017).[4]

The potential for antitrust complaints therefore gives these organizations a motivation to exercise some restraint in their dealings with actual or potential licensees, rather than to capitalize on the full extent of their market power.[5] In contrast, state laws that obstruct the activities of PROs without an adequate justification under antitrust or unfair competition laws are likely to be unenforceable, because they interfere with enforcing the exclusive rights of copyright owners. For example, in ASCAP v. Pataki, 930 F.Supp. 873 (S.D.N.Y. 1996), a New York state statute required PROs to send venue owners a report, within 72 hours after a representative had visited their establishments, listing the copyrighted works that were performed during the visit. The court held that the state law was preempted by federal copyright law, because it unduly burdened the rights of the copyright owners.

D. FOREIGN PUBLIC PERFORMANCE ROYALTIES

What rights do U.S. songwriters and publishers have when their copyrighted music is publicly performed abroad? Almost every country will

[4] During the litigation, the Department of Justice filed a statement of interest supporting Global Music Rights. Antitrust Division, United States Department of Justice, *Statement of Interest of the United States* (Dec. 5, 2019).

[5] At this time, AllTrack is still too small to have generated antitrust concerns.

recognize their exclusive rights, including the public performance right. Dramatic and grand rights will have to be individually negotiated, as is the case in the U.S. And most foreign countries also have national (or sometimes multinational) PROs that collect blanket licensing royalties for public performances within their respective territories, including those attributable to songs that are represented by PROs in the United States.

When foreign PROs collect their blanket licensing fees, they remit the allocable portion of their royalty collections to the domestic PROs for distribution to their respective songwriters and publishers. Under reciprocity arrangements, domestic PROs do the same for their foreign counterparts. In some cases, a domestic publisher may use a foreign subpublisher, and will direct the foreign PRO to remit the publisher's royalty share directly to the local subpublisher.

CHAPTER 7
PERFORMANCE RIGHTS IN SOUND RECORDINGS

§ 7.1 LIMITED SCOPE

In contrast to the robust public performance right recognized for musical works, federal law does not recognize a general public performance right in the sound recordings that embody them. 17 U.S.C. § 114(a). As a result, when recorded music is played on AM/FM radio or in public venues such as clubs, bars, retail stores, or hotels, the owner of the rights in the sound recording—typically, a record label—is not entitled to receive a royalty. The U.S. is one of very few countries in the world that does not recognize such a right.

Instead, federal law provides a very specific type of public performance right for sound recordings. As delineated in § 106(6), the public performance right for sound recordings is limited to the right to perform a recording publicly by means of a "digital audio transmission." In this context, digital audio transmissions include satellite radio (SiriusXM), music streaming services, cable television music services, and webcasting. However, they do not include any transmissions of audiovisual works. *Id.* § 114(j)(5).

Section 106(6) was enacted in the Digital Performance Right in Sound Recordings Act (DPSR) of 1995. Both before and after the DPSR, there have been numerous proposals to enact a general public performance right in sound recordings, which would align the United States with the rest of the world. However, those proposals have been successfully opposed by broadcasters as well as publishers.

Because the U.S. does not recognize a general public performance right in sound recordings, collecting societies in many countries have declined to remit to U.S. record labels the royalties collected for non-digital public performances of American-made sound recordings in those countries, citing the lack of reciprocity. Due to the popularity of American music overseas, this has resulted in a significant loss of potential revenue for the U.S. recording industry.

In 2020, the Court of Justice of the European Union (CJEU) ruled that all recording artists are entitled to share in the public performance royalties generated by public performances of their sound recordings, regardless of their nationality or the lack of reciprocity in their home countries. *See* Recorded Artists Actors Performers Ltd v. Phonographic Performance (Ireland) Ltd, C–265/19 (Sept. 8, 2020) (known as the *RAAP* ruling). Under this ruling, each country in the EU must send U.S. record labels and recording artists their allocable share of all public performance royalties generated in that country. This will significantly reduce the pool of royalties available to EU artists and labels. The European recording industries are seeking to overturn the CJEU's decision through legislation.

§ 7.2 STREAMING OF SOUND RECORDINGS

As discussed in Chapters 5 and 6, music streaming services obtain blanket mechanical licenses from the MLC and blanket public performance licenses from the various PROs; however, these licenses cover only the underlying musical works. Under § 106(6), streaming services must also obtain performance licenses for the sound recordings that embody these musical works. Depending on the nature of the streaming service, these licenses may be voluntarily negotiated or may be covered by a statutory license under § 114.

The rights granted in § 106(6) apply to both copyrighted sound recordings and those protected by the sui generis right under § 1401 (which applies to sound recordings fixed before February 15, 1972). Throughout this chapter, the term "rights owner" will be used to encompass both copyright owners and the owners of exclusive rights under § 1401.

Section 106(6) was added to copyright law in 1995, at a time when streaming and satellite radio were relatively new technologies. With the explosive growth of streaming since then, however, the digital audio transmission right has become a significant royalty source for the rights owners of sound recordings. In addition, because performances through digital audio transmissions have largely supplanted sales of physical records and permanent downloads, record labels and recording artists now rely on the digital audio transmission royalty to replace the royalties they used to receive from the sales of records and downloads.

The implementation of the § 106(6) right is complex. The details are found in § 114, which distinguishes among three categories of digital audio transmissions—exempt, interactive, and noninteractive. Only the latter two generate a sound recording performance royalty.

If a digital audio transmission is "exempt," no public performance license for the sound recording is required. (However, a license to publicly perform the *musical work* is still required, and obtained typically through blanket licenses from PROs.) Generally speaking, the exemption applies to noninteractive digital transmissions that are either (1) nonsubscription broadcast transmissions from FCC-licensed stations (and certain retransmissions thereof), or (2) music transmitted to or within a business establishment (e.g., background music services). *Id.* § 114(d)(1).

Non-exempt digital audio transmissions—those that require a § 106(6) public performance license—are divided into two categories: *interactive* and *noninteractive* services. The distinction is important, because these two types of services are subject to completely different licensing regimes. While both interactive and noninteractive services need licenses to perform sound recordings, a noninteractive service can qualify for a *statutory* license, while an interactive service must negotiate for a voluntary license from the rights owner of each sound recording. If a transmitting entity offers both types of services, each service will be subject to a different licensing regime.

Congress created two separate licensing regimes because it recognized that interactive streaming services are more likely to displace record sales. If a listener can choose to hear to a particular recording on demand, the listener has less reason to purchase a physical record or download of that recording. In contrast, because noninteractive services are more like traditional AM/FM radio, they are no more likely than radio broadcasts to displace record sales.

§ 7.3 INTERACTIVE AND NONINTERACTIVE SERVICES DISTINGUISHED

To determine which licensing rule applies, § 114 distinguishes between interactive and noninteractive services by applying a specific set of criteria.

An *interactive* streaming service is one that "enables a member of the public to receive a transmission of a program specially created for the recipient, or on request, a transmission of a particular sound recording . . . which is selected by or on behalf of the recipient." *Id.* § 114(j)(7). While it is clear what it means for a user to request "a particular sound recording," it is less clear what constitutes a "program specially created for the recipient." Because the statute does not define this term, it has been left to judicial interpretation.

In Arista Records, LLC v. Launch Media, Inc., 578 F.3d 148 (2d Cir. 2009), the Second Circuit was asked to determine whether the programs offered by a webcasting service were "specially created" for a particular user. LAUNCHcast was an internet radio platform (or "webcasting" service) that enabled users to create "stations" that played songs within a particular genre or similar to a particular artist or song selected by the user. The court held that a program was not "specially created" merely because it reflected some degree of user input. In this case, while LAUNCHcast created playlists unique to each user, it used a complex system to randomize the selections that were included in each user's playlist, and to ensure that users could not select or predict which song would be played, and could not restart or replay any recordings on the playlist. After a detailed analysis of LAUNCHcast's method of creating playlists, the court concluded that the service did not "provide a specially created program within the meaning of § 114(j)(7) because the webcasting service [did] not provide sufficient control to users such that playlists are so predictable that users will choose to listen to the webcast in lieu of purchasing music." 578 F.3d at 162. Accordingly, LAUNCHcast was a not an interactive service under the statute.

As *Launch Media* illustrates, a *noninteractive* streaming service does not enable the user to select, or even predict, which recording will be transmitted at any specific time; in other words, it provides a traditional radio-style listener experience. This is why SiriusXM satellite radio qualifies as a noninteractive digital audio transmission service despite its specialized channels. Even if a digital music service takes user requests for a particular recording to be played for all listeners, it will not be treated as interactive if the programming on each of its channels does not substantially consist of recordings that are performed within one hour of being requested or at a designated time. 17 U.S.C. § 114(j)(7).

For a streaming service to qualify as noninteractive, and thus eligible for the statutory license, it must meet certain criteria. While the rules are somewhat complex, in general a service will be considered noninteractive, and eligible for statutory licensing, only if: (1) to the extent it is technically feasible, the transmissions are accompanied by information encoded by the record label that identifies the title, featured recording artist, underlying musical work, and songwriter(s); (2) the service does not publish its program schedule in advance, and (3) its transmissions do not exceed the "sound recording performance complement." *Id.* § 114(d)(2)(B).

The first of these requirements helps in allocating the statutory royalty accurately among the parties entitled to a share—the record label and the featured and nonfeatured recording artists (see § 7.5 below)—and, by identifying the underlying musical work and its songwriter(s), also helps in allocating the § 106(4) public performance royalty that is collected and distributed by the relevant PRO under a blanket license.[1] The second and third requirements make it

---

1 The embedded data identifying the songwriter(s) also helps when the recording is streamed by an interactive service,

difficult for listeners to predict when a particular recording will be played; this reduces the likelihood that the streaming service will provide a substitute for record sales. While the second requirement is self-explanatory, the "sound recording performance complement" warrants explanation.

The "sound recording performance complement" is a set of specific restrictions on what recordings can be streamed on a particular channel within any 3-hour period. The restrictions are designed to make it difficult to predict which music will be heard within that time period.

To stay within the sound recording performance complement, a streaming service must not transmit on any given channel, within a 3-hour time period, more than:

(A) 3 different selections of sound recordings from any one phonorecord (and no more than 2 consecutively); or

(B) 4 different selections of sound recordings (and no more than three consecutively)—

 (i) by the same featured recording artist; or

 (ii) from any set or compilation of phonorecords lawfully distributed together as a unit for public performance or sale in the U.S.

because it can be used in allocating the blanket mechanical license fee collected by the MLC. See Chapter 5.

Id. § 114(j)(13).

§ 7.4 INTERACTIVE STREAMING LICENSES

Interactive streaming services must obtain their § 106(6) licenses through voluntary negotiation with the rights owners of the sound recordings. While the terms of these negotiated licenses are largely up to the parties, § 114 imposes one restriction: No interactive service can obtain an *exclusive* public performance license for a sound recording for a period greater than 12 months (or 24 months if the licensor owns the rights to 1000 or fewer sound recordings). *Id.* § 114(d)(3)(A). After each such license expires, the licensee must wait 13 months before obtaining another exclusive license for the same recording. *Id.*

This restriction is designed to prevent record labels from exercising too much control over the market for interactive streaming. The restriction does not apply if the label *either* (1) has licenses in force with at least five different interactive services, with each license covering at least 10 percent of the sound recordings that the label has licensed for interactive streaming (and a minimum of 50 recordings), or (2) the exclusive license covers no more than 45 seconds of the recording and is solely to promote the recording. *Id.* § 114(d)(3)(B).

The interactive service must also, of course, have a license to publicly perform the underlying musical work embodied in the sound recording (see Chapter 6) as well as a mechanical license for the musical work (see Chapter 5).Copyright law does not dictate whether or to what extent the record labels must share their interactive streaming royalties with the recording artists who performed on the licensed recordings. In fact, § 114(g)(1) expressly states that this is determined by the record label's contract with the recording artists.

Recording artists, therefore, should bear this in mind when negotiating their recording contracts, and should insist on language guaranteeing them a specific share of the royalties that the record label receives from interactive streaming services. The artist may also negotiate for a share of any advances that the streaming services pay to the record labels. These advances can be substantial.

Although record labels rarely divulge their financial arrangements with these services, a recording artist who negotiated for audit rights in his or her recording contract is entitled to see how his or her streaming royalties were calculated.

The record label's license with an interactive service will require the service to report detailed usage data for each recorded track covered by the license. The label needs this data to determine whether the service has paid the correct amount of royalties for the reporting period. It also enables the label to allocate the royalties among its various recordings. If a particular recording artist is entitled to share in interactive streaming royalties under his or her recording contract, then the artist's payout will depend on the share of royalties allocable to that artist's recordings.[2]

§ 7.5 NON-INTERACTIVE STREAMING LICENSES

A noninteractive music streaming service need not negotiate for § 106(6) licenses from the record labels. Instead, it can use the statutory license authorized under § 114(d)(2).

The rates and terms for § 114 statutory licenses are determined by the Copyright Royalty Judges periodically through rate-setting proceedings, applying a willing buyer/willing seller standard. At these proceedings, the sound recording rights owners and the noninteractive services may present evidence and arguments in support of their proposed rates. However, they also remain free to negotiate voluntary license agreements, in which case the rates and terms of their negotiated licenses will supersede the license terms established by the Copyright Royalty Judges.

By law, the statutory royalty paid by the noninteractive services is not allocated entirely to the rights owner of the sound recording. In fact, only 50% of the royalty goes to the rights owner. Another 45% goes to the featured artist(s) on the recording.[3] The

---

[2] The 2024 federal indictment discussed in § 3.13[E] above illustrates the use of automated bots to manipulate usage data in order to fraudulently divert interactive streaming royalties.

[3] When a specific band, orchestra, or vocal group is featured on the recording, the term "featured recording artist" refers to the

remaining 5% goes to a fund for the nonfeatured ("session") performers who have performed on the sound recordings; 2.5% is allocated to nonfeatured musicians, and 2.5% to nonfeatured vocalists. § 114(g)(2). (Note that this mandatory allocation applies only to the statutory royalty paid by noninteractive services; it does not to apply to the royalties that *interactive* services pay to record labels under their negotiated licenses. These are discussed in § 7.4 above.)

To ensure that the statutory royalties are collected and distributed correctly, Congress authorized the Copyright Royalty Judges to designate a nonprofit collective to collect the statutory royalties from all of the various noninteractive services, to allocate the total amounts collected among the many different rights holders and recording artists whose works had generated the royalties, and to locate and pay all of the parties entitled to receive these payments. Today, that organization is SoundExchange.

SoundExchange is an independent organization that acts on behalf of all parties owning exclusive rights in sound recordings as well as the vocalists and musicians who performed on the recordings. It is governed by a Board of Directors, on which rights owners and recording artists are equally represented.

Unlike the PROs for songwriters and publishers, SoundExchange is not a voluntary membership

---

entire band, orchestra, or group. However, it does not include session musicians.

organization; it acts on behalf of *all* persons entitled to receive a share of the statutory royalties under § 114. Because it is the only organization authorized to collect and distribute those royalties, it is crucial for rights owners and featured recording artists to register with SoundExchange, and maintain their registrations with updated contact information, in order to receive their shares of the statutory royalties. Registration is free. SoundExchange, in turn, is required to use its best efforts to identify and locate rights owners and featured recording artists who have not yet registered.

Statutory licensees under § 114 must pay their royalties to SoundExchange on a monthly basis. Each payment must be accompanied by a usage report disclosing which recordings were streamed and how often. 37 C.F.R. § 370.4(d)(2)–(3). SoundExchange must retain these reports for three years, making them available for inspection by sound recording rights owners. *Id.* § 370.5(d).

SoundExchange maintains a searchable public database that matches the title of each sound recording (specifically, each track) with its International Standard Recording Code (ISRC) and its rights owner, and identifies the recording artists featured on the recording. Rights owners and recording artists can search the database to verify its accuracy, and can submit updated information as needed.

When particular rights owners or featured performers have not yet registered with SoundExchange, the organization must retain their unclaimed royalties for three years, after which it is allowed to use the unclaimed funds to offset administrative expenses. *Id.* § 380.4(b). In practice, however, SoundExchange has held unclaimed funds for more than three years, in order to give eligible claimants additional time to register and file their claims.

Prior to distributing any § 114 royalties, SoundExchange is entitled to deduct its reasonable administrative costs, including the cost of settling disputes. 17 U.S.C. § 114(g)(3)(A)–(B). SoundExchange is required to publish (online) an Annual Report explaining how it operates and how it collects and distributes royalties, and reporting its administrative expenses for the fiscal year. 37 C.F.R. § 370.5(c).

Some featured recording artists choose to share some of their statutory royalties with other individuals who made creative contributions to the sound recording but who are not automatically entitled to claim a portion of the statutory royalty under section 114. Featured artists can redirect a portion of their 45% share by giving SoundExchange a Letter of Direction instructing it to distribute a specific share of the artist's royalty to the designated party. Generally speaking, SoundExchange must honor Letters of Direction that designate producers, mixers, and sound engineers. 17 U.S.C. § 114(g)(5)(A). Acceptance of Letters of Direction in favor of other parties is left to SoundExchange's discretion. *Id.* § 114(g)(5)(C).

There are some Letters of Direction that SoundExchange will not honor. Because SoundExchange does not distribute any royalties directly to the nonfeatured vocalists or musicians on the recording (but rather sends their shares to a separate fund administered by the relevant labor unions), it will not honor Letters of Direction instructing it to send royalties to nonfeatured performers. Where a sound recording is a collaboration among several featured artists, Letters of Direction cannot be used to allocate the featured artists' 45% royalty share among the collaborators; SoundExchange will allocate the royalties equally among them, unless they inform SoundExchange that they want a different allocation. Featured artists may not use Letters of Direction to allocate any of their royalties to parties that did not make creative contributions to the recording; according to SoundExchange, such parties include record labels, lenders, or companies that provided the artists with royalty advances.

With respect to sound recordings created before § 106(6) was enacted in 1995, SoundExchange may be required to distribute 2% of a recording's statutory royalty to a producer, mixer, or sound engineer who can prove a contractual entitlement, deducting this amount from the featured artist's share, unless the featured artist objects. *Id.* § 114(g)(6).

Although SoundExchange must make direct payments to the rights owners of the sound recordings (50%) as well as the featured recording artists (45%), it must pay the 5% share for nonfeatured musicians and vocalists into the AFM & SAG-AFTRA Intellectual Property Rights Distribution Fund (the "Fund"). *Id.* § 114(g)(2)(B)–(C). The Fund is a nonprofit trust that is jointly administered by two labor unions—the American Federation of Musicians (AFM), which represents musicians, and SAG-AFTRA, which represents vocalists. The Fund, in turn, maintains separate subfunds for musicians and for vocalists; these are known as the Musicians' DPRA Subfund and the Vocalists' DPRA Subfund. Payments are allocated to individual performers based on usage data from SoundExchange.

However, due to the large number of sound recordings that are streamed and the relatively small royalty share allocated to nonfeatured performers, in order to avoid distributing de minimis payments the Fund considers only the top 25,000–50,000 unique sound recordings during the calendar year. The royalties in each subfund are allocated to each of these recordings based on its relative market share, and are then divided equally among all of the nonfeatured performers (musicians or vocalists, respectively) on that recording. Distributions are made at least once per year, and performers need not be members of AFM or SAG-AFTRA in order to receive their royalty shares. *Id.* § 114(g)(2)(B)–(C).

The Fund publishes a list of sound recordings (the "Covered Recordings" list) for which it has funds available for distribution. To account for nonfeatured performers who have not yet been identified at the time of the distribution, the Fund withholds up to

1.5% of the total distributable amount, depositing it into an Omissions Fund for future distribution as these claimants come forward. A performer must submit his or her claim within three years of a recording's inclusion in the Covered Recordings list, or the claim will be extinguished and the funds distributed to other performers.

§ 7.6 EPHEMERAL RECORDINGS

Digital audio transmissions of sound recordings involve not only public performances, but also the making of temporary "server" copies, also known as ephemeral recordings. Digital music services must pay an additional non-negotiable royalty to compensate sound recording rights owners for making these copies (technically, "phonorecords").

Section 112(e), enacted in the 1998 DMCA, created a statutory license that allows digital music services to make ephemeral recordings of sound recordings that are transmitted either under a § 114(f) statutory license or in a transmission that is exempt from the § 106(6) performance right because it is a transmission to a business establishment in the ordinary course of its business that meets the requirements of § 114(d)(1)(C)(iv).

SoundExchange is the sole entity authorized by the Copyright Office to collect and distribute the statutory royalty for ephemeral recordings used in digital public performances of sound recordings. 37 C.F.R. § 380.4(d)(1). The rates for the § 112(e) royalty are determined in proceedings conducted by the Copyright Royalty Judges, based on information provided by the sound recording rights owners and the transmitting organizations, and are based on a willing buyer/willing seller standard. 17 U.S.C. § 112(e)(3)–(4). A licensee under § 112(e) must deliver its statutory royalty payment and a usage report on a monthly basis to SoundExchange, which distributes the royalties to the rights owners of the recordings based on the usage report. 37 C.F.R. §§ 370.4(d), 384.4. SoundExchange may conduct an annual audit of each § 112(e) licensee, and the rights owners, in turn, may conduct annual audits of SoundExchange. 37 C.F.R. §§ 384.6, 384.7. SoundExchange must retain any unclaimed royalties for three years, after which it can apply them to its expenses related to its § 112(e) activities. *Id.* § 384.8.

CHAPTER 8
TRADEMARKS

§ 8.1 INTRODUCTION

Trademarks (or "marks" for short) play a valuable role in the music industry. Therefore, it is useful to know a few basic rules of trademark law.

At the initial stage of selecting a trademark—for example, coming up with a name for a newly formed band—many artists do not think about trademark law. However, this can lead to problems later on, especially if it turns out that someone else is already using the same mark, or one that is confusingly similar. In this situation, the artist could be forced to abandon the trademark and start over with a new one, potentially losing the fan following and all of the reputational benefits that have accrued to the original mark. Therefore, it is wise to think about trademark protection from the very start of new enterprise.

Although trademark law exists at both the state and federal levels, the rules at both levels are generally similar. Because the business activities of the music industry cross state boundaries, claims arising from these activities are typically brought under federal trademark law. For these reasons, this chapter focuses on federal law.

The federal trademark rules are in Title 15 of the U.S. Code, and are known as the "Lanham Act." Therefore, all of the statutory references in this chapter can be found in Title 15 (15 U.S.C. §§ 1051 et seq.).

§ 8.2 WHAT IS A TRADEMARK?

First, what is a trademark? It is simply a source identifier: It helps the consumer to identify who is responsible for the goods or services the consumer has encountered.[1] If a consumer's experience with a particular source was favorable, the trademark helps that consumer to choose future goods and services from the same source. A trademark can be the name that a business uses for various goods or services, the name of a musical group, or even the stage name of an individual artist.

A trademark can be a source indicator even if consumers cannot name the actual owner of the mark. It is enough that consumers perceive all goods and services bearing the mark as coming from (or having some connection with) a common source. For example, when people see the word "Batman" in the titles of movies or television shows, or on various kinds of merchandise, they assume that these are all produced or licensed by the same source, even if they cannot name the source (which happens to be DC Comics).

In the music context, a trademark identifies the source of goods, such as musical works, sound recordings, and merchandise, as well as services

---

[1] Technically, a mark used for services is called a "service mark," but this degree of linguistic precision is rarely necessary in general discussions of trademark law.

(including not only a specific artist's entertainment services, but also many music-related services, such as streaming, broadcasting, publishing, recording, distribution, tour promotion, ticketing, management, royalty collection, website design, and even accounting). The names "Beyoncé" and "The Black-Eyed Peas" are trademarks, because they enable fans of these artists to identify and select the goods and services of these artists, whether for record purchases, merchandise, live performance, or streaming. The name "Spotify" is a trademark, because it enables consumers to distinguish this streaming service from the many others that are available. "Big Machine" is a trademark, because it identifies one record label and distinguishes it from others.

Many things can qualify as trademarks. The examples given above are word marks. But trademarks can also take other forms, such as symbols, copyrighted works, and sounds. A musical work or sound recording can serve as a trademark—for example, where it is used as an advertising jingle, or as the theme music for a television series. Even a recording of a single sound can be a trademark—for example, the MGM lion's distinctive roar. In some cases, a trademark is not a distinct word, sound, or emblem; it can be the overall appearance of a product or its packaging. In such cases, it is referred to as "trade dress." In the case of entertainers, trade dress can include distinctive hairstyles, make-up, props, or costuming. *See, e.g.,* MGA Entertainment, Inc. v. Harris, 2023 WL 6194387 (C.D. Cal. Sept. 15, 2023) (applying trade dress protection to hairstyles and wardrobe of *OMG Girlz* musical group).

When a copyrighted work (such as a musical jingle, a cartoon character, or a graphic design) is also used as a trademark, this does not undermine its copyright protection. A work can be protected by both trademark and copyright law at the same time. Thus, for example, a musical work that is used as an advertising jingle is still a copyrighted work, but once consumers begin to associate it with the product being advertised, it becomes a trademark as well.

Sometimes an individual element of a larger creative work emerges as a trademark. For example, if a film is very successful, the film studio may re-use the title, the name or image of a character, a character's catch-phrase, or other memorable elements of the film in sequels, prequels, spin-offs, soundtrack recordings or licensed merchandise. If the re-used creative element causes consumers to associate these new products with the original film, then the element is functioning as a trademark. *See, e.g.,* DC Comics v. Kryptonite Corp., 336 F.Supp.2d 324 (S.D.N.Y. 2004) (name of fictional element "Kryptonite" in *Superman* works had become a trademark for goods and services authorized by DC Comics); DC Comics, Inc. v. Powers, 465 F.Supp. 843 (S.D.N.Y. 1978) (similar ruling for "The Daily Planet"). In these circumstances, the creative element is said to have acquired "secondary meaning," because consumers have learned that it is a source indicator. A classic example would be Disney character Mickey Mouse. Mickey began as a cartoon character, but developed secondary meaning when Disney used his name and image in numerous films and television shows as well as on licensed merchandise. Today, Mickey's name and image—even just Mickey's ears—are powerful trademarks.

Aspects of a performer's stage persona may also emerge as trademarks. For example, a court found that comedian Jeff Foxworthy's catch-phrase "You might be a redneck . . ." had acquired secondary meaning and therefore functioned as a trademark for his entertainment services. Foxworthy v. Custom Tees, Inc., 879 F.Supp. 1200 (N.D. Ga. 1995).

A trademark is meaningless in the abstract. It has meaning—and legal protection—only if the relevant consumers associate it with a specific source of goods or services. And typically the owner of the mark can protect it only with respect to the goods or services on which it is being used, or closely related goods or services. For example, the owner of the "Def Jam" mark for sound recordings could certainly stop someone else from using "Def Jam" as a mark for sound recordings, and probably also for music streaming or concert ticketing services; even if the owner of the Def Jam mark is not currently using it for those services, they are so closely related to the business of making and distributing sound recordings that consumers would readily believe that the services came from the same source as the recordings. This would create an actionable "likelihood of confusion," allowing Def Jam to bring a claim for trademark infringement. While courts take many factors into consideration in determining a likelihood of confusion (see § 8.5 [A] below), the similarity of the marks and the similarity of the goods and services are two of the most important factors.

§ 8.3 ESTABLISHING TRADEMARK RIGHTS

In the U.S., trademark registration is optional. As discussed below, a trademark can receive strong protection under the Lanham Act (and under the laws of most states) even if it is never registered. However, there are significant benefits to federal registration.

A. COMMON LAW PROTECTION

An unregistered trademark is called a common law mark. A word, phrase, symbol, color, design, image, musical work, or sound—or any combination thereof—can become a common law mark if (1) it is used in connection with goods or services, and (2) consumers recognize it as a source identifier for those goods or services. If two parties have adopted similar marks for similar goods or services within the same general territory, in most cases the first adopter (the "senior user") will own the trademark, and will therefore have the legal right to prevent the junior user from infringing.

In the U.S., many trademarks begin as common law marks, even if they are subsequently registered. This is especially true of marks that begin as elements of creative works, such as the Kryptonite and Mickey Mouse trademarks discussed in § 8.2

above. These elements acquire a second life as source indicators when they achieve secondary meaning in the minds of the public. In these cases, the person that created the mark may not have originally envisioned it as a mark, but its appeal to consumers leads the creator to use it on additional goods or services, or additional creative works, at which point it may begin to function as a source indicator. Once that happens, it can be protected as a common law mark.

Infringement claims involving common law marks are brought as "false designation of origin" (alternatively, "false endorsement" or "unfair competition") claims under the federal unfair competition statute, 15 U.S.C. § 1125(a).

The owner of a common law mark has exclusive rights in the mark only in the territories where the mark is actually being used. It is possible, then, that someone else could be using the same mark in a different territory, and could thereby become the owner of that mark in the other territory. This is one of the risks of relying on common law protection: Two businesses in different parts of the United States could be using similar marks with no problem until one or both of them decide to expand their territorial reach. At that point, there could be a likelihood of confusion if both are using similar trademarks within the same territory. The use of social media and other Internet platforms as tools for promotion and sales makes confusion even more likely to occur.

Confusion could easily happen with two bands with similar names. The bands might start out performing locally in different parts of the U.S., but if either of them achieves success and begins to tour, the similarity of their names could create confusion if they are both performing in the same city.

For this reason, owners of common law marks often decide that it is in their best interest to increase their level of trademark protection by obtaining federal registration for their marks.

B. FEDERAL REGISTRATION

Even if a mark has acquired strong common law protection, registration on the *principal register* of the U.S. Trademark Office offers significant advantages in protecting the trademark. Among other things, federal registration can enable a business to protect its trademarks even in parts of the country where it is not yet using the marks. This enables a business that starts in one location to keep using its valuable trademarks as it expands into other locations, even nationwide.

For example, Simon Tam of the Portland-based Chinese-American dance band "The Slants" fought a multi-year battle to federally register the band's name (which the Trademark Office deemed racially "disparaging"), in order to establish nationwide ownership of the name even in parts of the U.S. where the band had not yet performed. He took his case all the way to the U.S. Supreme Court, where he won (by overturning the statute that banned registration of disparaging marks). Matal v. Tam, 582 U.S. 218 (2017).

Sometimes people begin using similar trademarks in different parts of the country without even knowing about one another. For example, Simon Tam's discovery that some new bands in other states were already calling themselves "The Slants" is what prompted him to register his band's name. As those bands began to promote themselves through social media, and book tour dates around the country, there was a serious risk that consumers would be confused about which band they were buying tickets for. (Alternatively, if one of those bands engaged in activities that provoked consumer backlash, such as not showing up for their concerts, consumers hearing these reports might mistakenly attribute this to Simon Tam's band.) Because he was able to prove that his band was the first to adopt the name, and he succeeded in getting it registered, Tam's federal registration gave his band superior rights nationwide over any other bands that tried to adopt the same name *after* he applied for registration. Those who were already using the name before his application date could continue to use it within their already-established locales, but could not expand their use geographically. Thus, the likelihood of confusion was reduced, but not completely eliminated,

Unlike The Slants, most applicants for federal trademark registration do not have to fight for their rights in court. However, they must still follow the application process. To begin, they file an application, which is then reviewed by the U.S. Trademark Office to determine if the mark is eligible for registration on the principal register. The Trademark Office also publishes a notice of the pending registration, so that owners of similar trademarks have the opportunity to raise objections.

To be eligible for the principal register, a mark must meet certain legal requirements. In most cases, the applicant must already be using the mark in interstate commerce somewhere in the U.S.[2] (In other words, it must already be a common law mark, and its use must cross at least one state line.) 15 U.S.C. § 1051(a)(1). Also, the mark must not be confusingly similar to one that is already registered, or already in use as a common law mark anywhere it the U.S. *Id.* § 1052(d).

Another registration bar is especially relevant to entertainers: No one can register the name or likeness of a living person without that person's written consent. *Id.* § 1052(c). In 2024, the Supreme Court upheld this registration bar against a First Amendment challenge brought by a party that wanted to register TRUMP TOO SMALL. *See* Vidal v. Elster, 602 U.S. 286 (2024).

Once the Trademark Office publishes notice of a pending registration, any party believing that it has a superior claim to the trademark, or that it might be harmed by the registration, may express its objections by filing an opposition to the pending registration. *Id.* § 1063. (For example, other bands already calling themselves "The Slants" could have opposed Simon Tam's application, but apparently

---

[2] As a result of international agreements, there is an exception for trademarks that are already registered in certain foreign countries.

none of them did.) The Trademark Office will consider the arguments of the applicant and the opposer, and will decide whether to grant the application. Because any mark that is registered on the principal register has survived this examination process, it is rebuttably presumed to be valid in any subsequent litigation. *Id.* § 1115(a).

An applicant can actually start the federal registration process even before beginning to use the mark, by filing an "intent to use" application ("ITU"). After filing the ITU, the applicant must begin using the mark within a period of time set by statute (six months, or up to three years if extensions are granted). Only then can the registration be finalized. Once the mark is registered, however, the applicant's right of priority over others adopting similar marks dates back to the date on which the ITU was filed. *Id.* §§ 1051(b)–(d), 1057(c).

In some cases where two or more persons are using similar trademarks, it may be difficult or impossible to establish that one of them clearly has superior rights compared to the others. Under these circumstances, the parties may decide against litigation. They may decide that they can both continue to use their marks, taking steps to minimize the degree of confusion, or one party may buy out the other's rights.

For example, the "Apple" word mark was the subject of a long series of disputes between Apple, Inc., and Apple Corps. When Apple, Inc., first started in 1976, it was just a computer company. At that time, the "Apple" mark was already being used by

Apple Corps, a multimedia entertainment company formed by the Beatles in 1968. Because the two companies' different businesses did not overlap at that time, there was no likelihood of confusion. However, as Apple expanded into the music business, and then more widely into other entertainment services, the companies' marks increasingly came into conflict. They initially entered settlement agreements to set boundaries for each parties' respective use of the conflicting marks. However, as Apple kept expanding, it crossed those boundaries, leading to new conflicts and new settlement agreements. Eventually, in 2007, Apple Corps sold the "Apple" mark to Apple, Inc., which in turn granted Apple Corps an exclusive license to use the mark under specified conditions.

A similar problem arose in connection with DC Comics' "Kryptonite" mark. Although DC Comics had been featuring Kryptonite in the Superman franchise since the 1940s, in 1972 the unrelated Kryptonite Corporation began using the same word as a trademark for its bike locks and related products. The parties reached an agreement in 1983 which allowed both parties to hold concurrent federal registrations for the mark, subject to specific restrictions on how each party could use the mark in order to minimize any likelihood of confusion. When Kryptonite Corporation flagrantly violated these restrictions in the 1990s, DC Comics successfully sued for trademark infringement. DC Comics v. Kryptonite Corp., 336 F.Supp.2d 324 (S.D.N.Y. 2004).

Another dispute involved the stage names of two performers. In 2020, the country pop band widely known as Lady Antebellum changed its name to "Lady A." It did so in order to disassociate itself from the Civil War Confederacy. It was apparently unaware that blues singer Anita White had already been using the stage name "Lady A" for several decades. Although she was less well-known, and had never registered her mark, she was still in a strong position to assert superior rights based on long-term use. (There was some evidence, however, that Lady Antebellum had occasionally used the "Lady A" mark during the same time period.) After filing lawsuits against one another, the parties avoided what was likely to be lengthy and costly litigation (and bad publicity for the alleged usurper) by reaching a settlement. Today, both parties continue to perform as "Lady A." Is there some likelihood of confusion? Yes: Both parties offer similar goods and services (musical recordings, live performances, and merchandise), and both of them take their shows on tour. However, their genres and target audiences are different, they are each well known to their loyal fans, and both seem willing to tolerate some low level of confusion in order to keep their names and the reputations (called "goodwill" in trademark law) that are attached to those names.

As this discussion reveals, it is important to think about trademark law even at the initial stage of selecting a name for a band, or for any other kind of business. There are specialists who can perform rigorous trademark searches for a fee (searching for both registered and common law marks). However, anyone can search the principal register at no cost to see if a particular mark has already been registered, or even if there is an application pending. The website of the Trademark Office, uspto.gov, enables searches of the entire registration database.

C. TRADEMARK PROTECTION ABROAD

Trademark protection is territorial; generally speaking, a trademark is protected only in the country where it is used or registered. Therefore, if a trademark owner uses a particular mark only in the U.S., they may not have rights in that mark outside of the U.S. (and vice versa). Indeed, in another country someone else may have already established superior rights by using or registering a similar mark in that country.

In many countries, trademark registration is much more important than it is in the U.S. In some nations, a person can register a trademark without ever having used it, and as the registered owner of the mark that person can prevent all others from using it within that country. Thus, even if a person has used and registered a mark in the U.S., another person who is not even using the mark may have already established superior rights in another country through registration. It is sometimes possible to overcome those rights, but it can be a difficult process, and is governed by the laws of the foreign country. Musical acts that tour internationally could conceivably encounter such trademark conflicts, involving the band's name or any commercial sponsors of the tour who will display their marks at the venue or in promotional activities. The artist's tour promoter, record label, and/or band manager should try to anticipate such problems by checking for similar trademark registrations in the countries where the artist will tour, and retaining local attorneys to take the necessary steps to ward off unpleasant surprises (such as last-minute injunctions preventing the performance).

Sometimes a U.S. trademark owner will discover that someone else is using the same mark in an infringing manner in another country. For example, Les Ballets Trockadero de Monte Carlo, a satirical all-male ballet troupe, discovered that a former member of the company had begun operating a competing ballet troupe in Japan under a confusingly similar name. The company successfully sued for infringement under the Lanham Act. Les Ballets Trockadero de Monte Carlo, Inc. v. Trevino, 945 F.Supp. 563 (S.D.N.Y. 1996). However, as discussed below, it has recently become more difficult to bring Lanham Act claims against overseas infringers.

The Supreme Court ruled in 2023 that the Lanham Act does not apply to infringing conduct taking place outside the U.S., overturning years of contrary precedents. *See* Abitron Austria GmbH v. Hetronic Int'l, Inc., 600 U.S. 412 (2023). As a result, if the owner of a mark protected in the U.S. believes that its mark is being infringed in another country, but none of the infringing conduct occurs in the United States, the owner must sue under the trademark laws of that country. In most cases, the trademark owner will have to pursue those claims in the courts and/or administrative agencies of that country rather than in a U.S. court. Therefore, it will be necessary to retain local counsel in the country where the dispute arises. However, since *Abitron* is a relatively recent decision, it is possible that there will be further developments as it is interpreted and applied by lower courts.

§ 8.4 NAMES OF MUSICAL GROUPS

Generally speaking, in the U.S. a trademark is owned by the party that uses the mark in connection with offering goods or services to the public. Typically, the trademark owner is an individual or a business entity. (If the mark is registered, the owner will be identified in the registration record.) Ownership can be more complicated, however, if a group of individuals—such as a band—begin using a mark without addressing ownership rights through some sort of formal business arrangement.

Band names can present difficult questions of trademark ownership. When a group of artists forms a band, their collaboration is often informal—at least at the start of their career, before they formalize their relationship through a partnership or contractual agreement that addresses matters like copyright and trademark ownership. Therefore, in the beginning, they are unlikely to think about who owns the name of the band (and any other trademarks that the band uses).

However, band membership does not always remain static. Old members may leave, and new members may join. At some point, the band may break up. What, if any, ownership claims can departing members assert with respect to the band's name? And what rights, if any, can the band's manager, promoter, or record label claim?

In the absence of written agreements, the general rule is that the band as a whole owns the band name. This normally means that, if a member departs, the name belongs to the remaining band members. *See* Kingsmen v. K-Tel Int'l, Ltd., 557 F.Supp. 178 (S.D.N.Y. 1983); HEC Enters., Ltd. v. Deep Purple, Inc., 213 U.S.P.Q. 991 (C.D.Cal. 1980). However, the general rule becomes difficult to apply when a group continues to perform over an extended period, during which time multiple members come and go, sometimes rejoining after their initial departures. A classic example is The Platters, a singing group that was formed in 1952 and continues to perform today. During these many decades, their membership changed frequently, and some departing members formed new groups calling themselves The Platters. As a result, from the 1980s through at least 2014, there were numerous lawsuits involving ownership of the group's name. *See, e.g,* Robi v. Reed, 173 F.3d 736 (9th Cir. 1999). The ultimate victor in these lawsuits (a limited liability company) today holds a federal registration for the name.

In some circumstances, a band's name might belong to a manager, promoter, producer, or record label. This could be the result of a contract. In the absence of a contract, courts have held that a musical group's name belongs to the person who controls the qualities or characteristics that the public associates with the group. *See* Rick v. Buchansky, 609 F.Supp. 1522 (S.D.N.Y. 1985). While in most cases this is likely to be the group itself, there are some situations in which the organizer of a band begins by developing a "concept" for a group, auditions performers and "casts" only those who fit the concept, replacing them as needed.

This approach is exemplified by the phenomenon of "boy bands," groups of young pop singers selected not only for their singing talent but also for their youthful appearance. For example, the boy band Menudo was created by music producer Edgardo Diaz. Band members were selected by audition, typically joined the group at age 9–14, and typically left at age 15–19 as they "aged out" of the group's youthful concept, leading to another round of auditions and casting for their replacements. Menudo usually had five members at any given time, but due to the group's continuing popularity and the need to maintain its youthful image, about 30 different performers rotated through the group between 1977 and 1997. (Of course, not all concept bands share Menudo's longevity and the resulting need for continuing replacements.) If a group fits the "concept band" model, then typically the person who creates the concept, casts the performers, and maintains the band's characteristics has the strongest claim for ownership of the band's name. *See* Bell v. Streetwise Records, Ltd., 640 F.Supp. 575 (D.Mass. 1986) (finding that 1980s boy band New Edition was not a concept band).

§ 8.5 UNAUTHORIZED USE OF TRADEMARKS

A. INFRINGEMENT AND DILUTION CLAIMS

Unauthorized use of another's trademark in a way that is likely to create confusion as to the source or sponsorship of goods or services can lead to liability for trademark infringement. Claims may be brought for infringement of registered marks (15 U.S.C. § 1114) or unregistered marks (*id.* § 1125(a)). The latter claim is referred to variously as a § 43(a) claim or as an unfair competition, false designation of origin, or false endorsement claim, but the analysis is similar to infringement of registered marks. If a court finds that confusion is likely, then it will typically order the infringer to stop the infringing activity, and may award substantial damages to the trademark owner.

To evaluate the likelihood of confusion, courts consider a number of factors, such as the strength of the plaintiff's mark, the similarity of the marks, the similarity of the parties' goods or services, the degree of care that consumers exercise in purchasing goods or services of this type, the defendant's good or bad faith, the sales and marketing channels used by each party, and any evidence of actual confusion. The precise factors vary by jurisdiction, but the overall inquiry is the same. *See, e.g.,* DC Comics v. Kryptonite Corp., 336 F.Supp.2d 324, 333 (S.D.N.Y. 2004) (listing Second Circuit factors); AMF Inc. v. Sleekcraft Boats, 599 F.2d 341, 348–49 (9th Cir. 1979) (listing Ninth Circuit factors).

The ultimate question in these cases is whether the continued use of both marks is likely to cause confusion for "an appreciable number of ordinarily prudent consumers." CBS, Inc. v. Liederman, 866 F.Supp. 763, 766 (S.D.N.Y. 1994). The confusion may involve consumers' belief that the trademark owner is actually the source of the infringer's goods or services, or that the trademark owner somehow sponsors, endorses, or is affiliated with those goods or services. *See, e.g.*, Foxworthy v. Custom Tees, Inc., 879 F.Supp. 1200 (N.D. Ga. 1995) (holding that use of comedian's catch-phrase on unauthorized merchandise was likely to make consumers believe that he endorsed or was somehow affiliated with the products).

In addition to claims based on a likelihood of confusion, using an especially *famous* mark without the consent of its owner can sometimes lead to liability even when there is no likelihood of confusion. This is the concept of trademark "dilution." Dilution claims are recognized under federal law (15 U.S.C. § 1125(c)) as well as the laws of many states. State laws can differ slightly from the federal law.

The underlying theory of dilution is that even a non-confusing use of a famous mark can weaken or tarnish the mark's reputation. Names such as "The Beatles" and the "Rolling Stones" easily qualify as famous marks eligible for dilution protection, because they are so well known nationwide. Although both of these marks are registered, marks can be famous for dilution purposes even if they are not registered.

In a case involving the unauthorized commercial use of an artist's name or likeness, the artist may be able to bring a claim not only under trademark or unfair competition laws, but also under state laws protecting an individual's "right of publicity," which is the subject of Chapter 9. Specifically, the potential for dual claims is discussed in § 9.7.

B. TRADEMARK CLAIMS AGAINST CREATIVE WORKS

The concepts of both infringement and dilution were developed largely in the context of traditional goods and services, where the unauthorized use of another's mark could confuse consumers into purchasing from the wrong merchant. However, some trademark owners have pursued infringement and dilution claims against unauthorized uses that involve creative expression rather than traditional goods and services. Both Congress and the courts have attempted to curb overreaching trademark claims that threaten creative expression, but there are still many instances where the lines are not clearly drawn.

One well-known case involved the song *Barbie Girl*, written and recorded by the musical group Aqua. The song clearly poked fun at Barbie's status as a cultural icon. (This was long before the *Barbie* movie.) Thus, it qualified as criticism, commentary or parody—types of expression that receive a high degree of protection under the First Amendment. However, because Aqua released its song on a commercial recording, it was offering its goods for sale to the public, using Mattel's "Barbie" trademark in the title (as well as the lyrics). Therefore, Mattel argued that the title used its trademark in a way that both infringed and diluted its mark (which was undeniably famous enough to qualify for dilution protection under federal law). Mattel, Inc. v. MCA Records, Inc., 296 F.3d 894 (9th Cir. 2002).

With respect to dilution claims, the current federal dilution statute includes specific exceptions designed to protect First Amendment rights. Of particular relevance to works of creative expression are the exceptions for the "fair use"[3] of someone's trademark in "parodying, criticizing, or commenting upon the famous mark owner or the goods and services of the famous mark owner" as well as "any noncommercial use" of the famous mark. 15 U.S.C. § 1125(c)(3). The *Barbie Girl* song today would qualify for both exceptions. First, judging by the song's lyrics, it was clearly a parody, criticism, and/or commentary on the cultural significance of Barbie. Second, even though the song was a commercial release, works of artistic expression (including not only visual artwork but books, music, films, television shows, and even videogames) are generally considered "noncommercial" in the First Amendment analysis unless they are nothing more than advertising or marketing materials (which could be the case if the

---

[3] The precise meaning of "fair use" in the context of the federal dilution exceptions remains unsettled. Generally speaking, however, the unauthorized use of a mark is "fair" in trademark law if the defendant does not make it seem like a source indicator for the defendant's own goods or services, because that could create a significant likelihood of confusion or dilution.

song were a commercial jingle). In the actual *Barbie Girl* case, the court applied only the noncommercial use exception because, at that time, the federal dilution statute did not yet include an express exception for parody, criticism, and commentary. Mattel, Inc. v. MCA Records, Inc., 296 F.3d 894 (9th Cir. 2002). However, were a similar case to arise under today's version of the statute, both exceptions would apply.

State dilution laws do not necessarily include the exceptions that exist in the federal dilution statute. However, the First Amendment would still provide a strong defense. In a situation like the *Barbie Girl* case, if the owner of a famous trademark brought a dilution claim under a state law which had no exceptions for creative expression or commentary, a defendant would invoke the First Amendment directly, arguing that a judgment in favor of the trademark owner would unduly interfere with free expression. This approach was successful for a defendant that produced a literary parody of the L.L. Bean catalog in L.L. Bean, Inc. v. Drake Publishers, Inc., 811 F.2d 26 (1st Cir. 1987).

Some courts have rejected dilution claims against works of creative expression without applying either the statutory exceptions or the First Amendment. Where a creative work of obvious fiction parodies the mark or otherwise uses it in a humorous context, these courts have found it unlikely that the challenged use of the mark would dilute its reputation, because (1) a mark that is famous enough to become an object of parody or humor is probably strong enough to survive being targeted in this way, and (2) if a work is obviously fictional, audiences are unlikely to take its depictions of the trademark seriously. For an example of this approach, see Caterpillar, Inc. v. Walt Disney Co., 287 F.Supp.2d 913 (C.D. Ill. 2003) (noting that "even the most credulous viewer or child" would understand the "fantastic nature" of the movie rather than attribute evil intentions to the Caterpillar bulldozers operated by the movie's villains). In contrast, where a court believes that a creative work might actually alter the public's perception of another's trademark—which was the situation in the *Barbie Girl* case—the statutory exceptions or First Amendment defense will be crucial to the defense.

Even if a mark is not famous enough for a *dilution* claim, its owner might bring a claim of *trademark infringement* or *false designation of origin*, based on a likelihood of confusion, against a defendant that references the trademark in a work of creative expression, including the title and/or lyrics of a song. Unlike the federal dilution statute, the infringement and false designation provisions of the Lanham Act (15 U.S.C. §§ 1114 and 1125(a)) do not include any exceptions for creative expression. Therefore, the most likely defenses against such claims are: (1) there is no likelihood of confusion, because consumers are not likely to believe that the trademark owner produced or authorized the creative work, and/or (2) the work is creative expression that incorporates the trademark in a manner protected by the First Amendment. As discussed below, neither of these defenses involves clear line-drawing; both require courts to consider, on a case-by-case basis, a variety of circumstances unique to the work in question.

1. No Likelihood of Confusion

Courts assessing whether the unauthorized use of a trademark is likely to confuse consumers about the source or sponsorship of goods or services consider a variety of factors in order to answer this ultimate question. While these factors vary by jurisdiction, they typically include the strength of the plaintiff's trademark, the similarity between the plaintiff's mark and the mark used by the defendant, the similarity of the goods or services offered by the parties, any evidence of actual confusion, whether the defendant intended to take advantage of the mark's reputation, and any other facts that elucidate the context in which consumers experience the defendant's use of the mark. When the unauthorized use occurs in a creative work, this is typically a very different context from garden-variety trademark infringement, where the consumer encounters the mark while shopping for traditional goods or services.

The fact that the alleged infringement occurs in a work of creative expression will frequently work in the defendant's favor. For example, Disney's comic film *George of the Jungle 2* includes a scene in which the villain's evil henchmen use Caterpillar bulldozers in an attempt to destroy the hero's jungle home. When Caterpillar sued to stop the film's release on trademark infringement grounds, the court applied the likelihood-of-confusion factors even though it acknowledged that they are not well-suited to evaluating works of creative expression. Based on these factors, the court expressed "substantial misgivings" on the merits of the plaintiff's claim, and refused to grant a restraining order against Disney, noting: "[I]t appears unlikely to the Court . . . that any consumer would be more likely to buy or watch *George 2* because of any mistaken belief that Caterpillar sponsored this movie." Caterpillar, Inc. v. Walt Disney Co., 287 F.Supp.2d 913, 920 (C.D. Ill. 2003).

Similarly, in Hormel Foods Corp. v. Jim Henson Prods., 73 F.3d 497 (2d Cir. 1996), the maker of the canned meat product SPAM sued the producer of the film *Muppet Treasure Island* for trademark infringement because the film featured a wild boar character named "Spa'am," who also appeared on merchandise related to the film. Applying the likelihood-of-confusion factors, the court ruled in the defendant's favor. The court gave particular weight to the humorous context and the obvious joke.

In cases where a trademark is used too prominently or pervasively in a creative work, this can lead consumers to believe that the trademark owner produced, sponsored, or approved the work in some way. For example, in the 1978 pornographic film *Debbie Does Dallas,* the not-so-wholesome cheerleader characters wore uniforms strikingly similar to the distinctive uniforms of the Dallas Cowboys Cheerleaders organization, which won a false designation of origin suit (based on trade dress) against a movie theatre that was exhibiting the film. Dallas Cowboys Cheerleaders, Inc. v. Pussycat Cinema, Ltd., 604 F.2d 200 (2d Cir. 1979).

It is worth noting, however, that music is quite different from movies and television shows. The public knows that many films are in fact sponsored or endorsed by the trademark owners whose marks are prominently feature in those films, which is not typically the case with music (although it is often the case with concert tours). Therefore, the likelihood of confusion is arguably greater in the context of films than music.

Another case that analyzed the likelihood of confusion without ever considering a First Amendment defense is Sullivan v. CBS Corp., 385 F.3d 772 (7th Cir. 2004). In that case, Frank Sullivan, the last remaining member of the band Survivor, owned the federal registration for the band's name. Even though Survivor had not produced any new music since 1993, its music was still licensed and performed on radio and television, its CDs were still being sold, and Sullivan continued to perform live concerts and sell merchandise under the band's name. In 2000, CBS began broadcasting a "reality" television series called *Survivor*. The series was successful, and CBS released two music CDs as well as a variety of other merchandise displaying the series name and logo. Sullivan sued for trademark infringement. In analyzing the likelihood of confusion factors, however, the court found Sullivan's evidence unconvincing, and ruled in favor of CBS.

2. First Amendment Protection

While the First Amendment does not completely immunize creative works from trademark infringement and false designation of origin claims, it can provide heightened protection. Because courts take a variety of approaches, and this area of the law is rapidly evolving (especially since 2023), research will be necessary to predict how the courts in a particular jurisdiction will analyze a specific case.

According to a 2023 decision by the Supreme Court, courts should reject a First Amendment defense if the accused infringer is using the trademark as a source indicator for its own goods or services. Jack Daniels Props. v. VIP Prods. LLC, 599 U.S. 140 (2023). However, in the context of creative expression, it is not always easy to determine whether a mark is functioning as an indication of source or sponsorship for the defendant's creative work, or simply as a creative element or object of commentary within that work—for example, where the trademark appears in the title of work, such as *Barbie Girl,* or where it is featured prominently throughout a work, as in *Debbie Does Dallas*.

With respect to the *titles* of creative works, under the currently prevailing view the First Amendment permits the unauthorized use of trademarks in titles if the mark (1) has at least some artistic relevance to the content of the work (and this is a low standard), and (2) does not explicitly mislead as to the source or content of the work. (Most courts say that the mere *presence* of the mark in a work's title is not enough to make it explicitly misleading.) This test is derived from a Second Circuit case involving the Fellini film *Ginger and Fred*, in which the main characters were nicknamed after Ginger Rogers and Fred Astaire. Rogers v. Grimaldi, 875 F.2d 994 (2d Cir. 1989). (The same court had taken a much narrower approach to the First Amendment defense in the *Dallas Cowboys Cheerleaders* case ten years earlier.)

For example, the *Rogers* test was applied to a song title in the *Barbie Girl* case. The court ruled that the use of Mattel's trademark in the title of *Barbie Girl* was non-infringing, because the "Barbie" mark was artistically relevant to the song's content, and nothing about the song explicitly indicated endorsement by Mattel. *Mattel,* 296 F.3d at 902.

The *Rogers* test was also applied when the late civil rights icon Rosa Parks sued for the unauthorized use of her name in the title of OutKast's *Rosa Parks*, a song that was not about her at all. (Technically, she described her claim as one for "false advertising," but the court analyzed it—appropriately—as a claim for false designation of origin.) She argued that the title would mislead the public into believing that the song was about her, that she sponsored or approved the song, or that she was affiliated with the defendants, and that the potential for confusion was enhanced by the fact that her authorized *Tribute* album was competing in the same market. Although the court found that the title was not "explicitly misleading," it also found the artistic relevance of the title to be "highly questionable," and remanded the latter issue for additional fact-finding. Parks v. LaFace Records, 329 F.3d 437, 459 (6th Cir. 2003).

Increasingly, courts have applied the *Rogers* test not only to titles but also to the *content* of creative works. For example, courts have applied the test to reject false designation of origin claims arising from the content of artwork, motion pictures, and videogames. *See, e.g.,* University of Alabama Board of Trustees v. New Life Art, Inc., 683 F.3d 1266 (11th Cir. 2012); E.S.S. Entertainment 2000, Inc. v. Rock Star Videos, Inc., 547 F.3d 1095 (9th Cir. 2008); ETW Corp. v. Jireh Publishing, Inc., 332 F.3d 915 (6th Cir. 2003); Louis Vuitton Malletier S.A. v. Warner Bros. Ent't, Inc., 868 F.Supp. 2d 172 (S.D.N.Y. 2012).

In a particularly expansive application of the *Rogers* test, one court permitted Fox Television to use the name "Empire" as the name of a fictional New York hip hop record label in a television series, and also as the title of the series, even though "Empire" is the name of an actual hip hop record label in New York. The court even allowed Fox to use the "Empire" name on promotional merchandise, soundtrack albums, radio play, and live concerts, thus creating a situation in which two parties were allowed to use the same trademark on similar goods and services potentially offered to the same customers. Twentieth Century Fox Television v. Empire Distribution, Inc., 875 F.3d 1192 (9th Cir. 2017). While a court would ordinarily look at all the facts and circumstances to determine whether this would create a likelihood of confusion, the *Rogers* test foreclosed this line of inquiry.

After the Supreme Court's 2023 decision in *Jack Daniels*, it may become more difficult to assert the

Rogers defense with respect to the unauthorized use of a trademark in the *title* of a creative work. This is because a title might also be perceived as a source indicator for the creative work. *See, e.g.*, Homevestors v. Warner Bros. Discovery, Inc., 2023 WL 8826729, *1 (D. Del. Dec. 21, 2023).

In the *Empire* scenario described above, *Jack Daniels* could also change the analysis with respect to the spin-off merchandise. In MGA Entertainment, Inc. v. Harris, 2023 WL 6194387 (C.D. Cal. Sept. 15, 2023), the court ordered a new trial, in light of *Jack Daniels*, after its previous decision had instructed the jury to apply *Rogers* to dolls whose appearance imitated the trade dress (specifically, the hairstyles and costuming) of the OMG Girlz musical group.

Some courts have approached the First Amendment analysis quite differently. Under the most restrictive (and, these days, the least commonly used) approach, an expressive work's unauthorized use of a trademark is not protected by the First Amendment if there were other "alternative avenues" the creator could have used to express the idea. *See, e.g.*, Mutual of Omaha Ins. Co. v. Novak, 836 F.2d 397 (8th Cir. 1987); American Dairy Queen Corp. v. New Line Productions, Inc., 35 F.Supp.2d 727 (D. Minn. 1998).

One court that rejects *Rogers* has adopted an alternative test that is relatively artist-friendly. This test asks whether the defendant had a "genuine artistic motive" for using the plaintiff's trademark. Stouffer v. National Geographic Partners, LLC, 400 F.Supp.3d 1161 (D. Colo. 2019) (listing subsidiary questions aimed at discerning the defendant's motives), *later proceeding,* 460 F.Supp.3d 1133 (D. Colo. 2020) (applying the test to rule in defendant's favor).

Another artist-friendly defense is nominative fair use, which permits the use of another party's trademark to the extent necessary to identify that party's goods or services, as long as the use is not excessive or affirmatively misleading as to the source or sponsorship of the defendant's goods. Although this judge-made defense was not developed specifically for creative works, and does not directly invoke the First Amendment, when it is applied to creative works it can protect the First Amendment right to engage in parody, criticism, or commentary. *See* Mattel v. Walking Mountain Productions, 353 F.3d 792 (9th Cir. 2003) (applying the defense to artist's Food Chain Barbie photo series depicting Barbie dolls endangered by vintage kitchen appliances).

§ 8.6 CYBERSQUATTING

The unauthorized use of a trademark in a domain name may be actionable under the federal anti-cybersquatting statute if it is confusingly similar to the trademark or if it is likely to dilute a famous trademark, but only if the party using the domain name has a "bad faith intent to profit" from the mark. 15 U.S.C. § 1125(d).

The statute provides a nonexhaustive list of factors for a court to consider in determining whether the defendant has a "bad faith intent to profit." One factor asks whether the defendant's use of the mark was a "bona fide noncommercial or fair use of the mark." *Id.* § 1125(d)(1)(B)(i)(IV). Based on this factor, as well as First Amendment considerations, a cybersquatting claim should not succeed against a domain name that is used for a website devoted to expressing information or opinions about the owner of the mark, or the owner's goods or services. For example, neither a "fan site" devoted to news and opinions about an entertainer nor a site devoted to negative commentary about the entertainer (no matter how spiteful) is likely to be considered actionable. However, if the expression of news and opinions is merely a pretext, and the true purpose of the website is to sell goods or services, to host advertising, to divert consumers to another website, or to extort money from the entertainer (by inducing him or her to purchase the domain name), then there is a greater chance a court would find a bad faith intent to profit.

As an alternative to litigation against cybersquatters, trademark owners can often achieve cheaper and faster results through the arbitration procedure provided under the Uniform Domain Name Dispute Resolution (UDRP) Policy of the Internet Corporation for Assigned Names and Numbers (ICANN). If the arbitrators rule that the domain name uses the trademark in bad faith (under UDRP's own set of bad faith factors), they can order the cancellation of the domain name registration or the transfer of the registration to the trademark owner.

§ 8.7 TRUTH IN MUSIC LAWS

Band names, like other source indicators, are protected by trademark infringement, false designation of origin, and dilution laws. It should be clear from this chapter, however, that the analysis of these claims is highly fact-specific, making it difficult to predict whether a particular unauthorized use of a band name will be actionable. Problems can arise, for example, when a particular band has splintered or has not performed live together for a lengthy period. "Tribute" bands present challenging legal questions as well. For a band to enforce its trademark can be costly and time-consuming, especially where there are multiple unauthorized users.

To increase protection for at least some band names, a majority of states have enacted laws that enable the state itself to prosecute the unauthorized user of a band's name. Known as "Truth in Music" (alternatively, "Truth in Music Advertising") laws, these statutes protect the names of bands that have previously released at least one commercial recording (referred to as "recording groups" in the statutes). These laws prohibit certain uses of a recording group's names regardless of whether those uses are also actionable under generally-applicable trademark laws. Truth in Music statutes also include exceptions, describing specific circumstances under which they do not proscribe the use of a band name. However, these exceptions insulate potential defendants only from claims that arise under the Truth in Music laws. They do not protect against claims arising under generally applicable trademark and unfair competition laws (state or federal).

While the specifics of Truth in Music laws may vary from state to state, as a general principle they prohibit advertising or producing a live musical performance in a manner that creates a false or misleading association between the performing group and a recording group, unless *any* of the following exceptions applies: (1) The performing group owns a federally registered mark in its name;[4] (2) At least one member of the performing group was also a member of the recording group and has a legal right to use the name; (3) All advertising and promotion identifies the live performance as a salute or tribute, and the performing group's name is not so similar or related to that of the recording group as to cause confusion; (4) The advertising pertains to an out-of-state performance; or (5) The recording group has expressly authorized the performance. Thus, for example, the statute allows live performances by a tribute band that imitates The Beatles, but unless the owners of "The Beatles" mark have granted them a license, the band must be clearly advertised as a tribute band, and must adopt a name other than "The Beatles," "The Fab Four," or any other name closely

---

[4] A federal court interpreting New Jersey's Truth in Music law, N.J. Stat. § 2A:32B–2(a) (2003), questioned the statute's distinction between registered and unregistered marks, and the state ultimately conceded that a defendant holding a valid unregistered mark in the disputed name was entitled to invoke the exception. Singer Mgt. Consultants v. Milgram, 650 F.3d 223 (3d Cir. 2011). Despite this, the language of New Jersey's statute has not been amended.

associated with The Beatles. Penalties for violating Truth in Music laws include fines and injunctions.

The Truth in Music laws do not create a private right of action; only the state can bring a complaint. Regardless of whether the state takes action, however, bands remain free to bring claims under state or federal trademark and false designation of origin laws, as well as state right of publicity laws (see Chapter 9).

§ 8.8 LICENSING AND MERCHANDISE

Successful artists in the music industry typically have the opportunity to generate additional income through licensing their names and/or other trademarks for use on various kinds of merchandise, which may be sold at their concert venues, on their official websites, or through other online platforms. Since the artists themselves do not manufacture or sell the merchandise, they enter merchandising deals with third parties who operate such businesses. These deals involve trademark licenses. To ensure that the merchandising efforts will benefit the artist financially while also protecting the artist's reputation, the artist's manager and attorney should review the terms of such licensing agreements with care.

CHAPTER 9

NAME, LIKENESS, AND VOICE PROTECTIONS

§ 9.1 THE IMPACT OF UNAUTHORIZED APPROPRIATION

An artist's identity may have significant commercial value. For example, the performer (as an individual and/or as a member of a band) may derive income from merchandising his or her name and/or likeness through the sale of T-shirts, posters, or other items at concerts or through a website. The performer may license his or her name, likeness, and/or voice for use in video games or other audiovisual works. The performer's name, likeness, and voice will also be needed to promote his or her records, concerts, videos, and appearances on film and television. That is why recording contracts typically include a clause permitting the record label to use the artist's identity in order to promote his or her recordings. Whenever an artist authorizes commercial uses of his or her identity, there should be a written licensing agreement that clearly spells out the terms, conditions, and duration of the authorized use, as well as the circumstances under which the artist can terminate the agreement.

It is not unusual, unfortunately, for unauthorized parties to capitalize on the value of an artist's identity by misappropriating the artist's name, likeness, voice, or other aspects of the artist's identity. This may be as simple as the sale of unauthorized merchandise bearing the artist's name or likeness. *See, e.g.*, Bi-Rite Enterprises, Inc. v. Bruce Miner Co., 757 F.2d 440 (1st Cir. 1985) (applying state right of publicity laws to unauthorized posters of pop musicians). Unauthorized audio or audiovisual recordings of a musician's live performance ("bootlegs") may find their way into the marketplace and compete with the musician's licensed recordings. With the growth of artificial intelligence, more sophisticated modes of misappropriation are now possible. The voice and/or appearance of a performer (living or dead) may be reproduced and manipulated to create sound recordings or audiovisual works in which the performer did not actually participate.

Such unauthorized uses of an artist's identity undermine the artist's ability to control the commercial uses of his or her identity and to capture the resulting revenue streams. They can also be detrimental to the artist's reputation and relationship with fans—for example, if the unauthorized goods are low in quality or the unauthorized use makes it appear that the artist willingly participated in an activity that conflicts with his or her public image or values. In some cases, these acts of misappropriation can cause emotional distress to the artist or the artist's family.

Several sources of law offer protection against the unauthorized appropriation of an artist's identity or live performance. Most states have laws protecting an individual's rights of privacy and publicity. Federal law includes a very specific anti-bootlegging statute. Both state and federal trademark and unfair competition laws also come into play. Each of these sources of law is addressed below.

§ 9.2 RIGHTS OF PRIVACY AND PUBLICITY

A. SCOPE OF PROTECTION

In most states, individuals can bring a cause of action for the unauthorized commercial use of certain aspects of their personal identity. In many states, these are called "right of publicity" laws, while in others, such as New York, they may be subsumed under privacy or civil rights laws. Some states offer statutory protection, while others rely on common law, and some, such as California, offer both.

There is wide variation in the specifics of these laws, although, at a minimum, they apply to a person's name and visual likeness. Laws differ, however, in what else may qualify as an appropriation of a person's identity. Must there be a clearly identifiable image of the person's face? Or does the law include other identifying characteristics that are merely suggestive of identity, such as hairstyle, silhouette, gestures, posture, clothing, or anything else that is closely associated with the person? *See, e.g.*, White v. Samsung Elecs. America, Inc., 971 F.2d 1395 (9th Cir. 1992) (television commercial featuring robot in evening gown and blond wig on Wheel of Fortune set could be actionable appropriation of Vanna White's identity); Motschenbacher v. R.J. Reynolds Tobacco Co., 498

F.2d 821 (9th Cir. 1974) (distinctive markings of professional driver's racing car sufficiently identified driver).

Some right of publicity laws protect a person's actual voice, while others also encompass vocal imitations. *See* Midler v. Ford Motor Co., 849 F.2d 460 (9th Cir. 1988) (imitation of singer's distinctive voice was actionable under common law but not statutory right of publicity); Waits v. Frito-Lay, Inc., 978 F.2d 1093 (9th Cir. 1992) (applying *Midler,* and upholding damages award for imitation of singer's distinctive voice in radio commercial). While at one time the laws of New York and Tennessee did not apply to the appropriation of voices, today both of them do. *See* N.Y. Civ. Rts. § 51; Tenn. Code Ann. §§ 47–25–1101–1107.

An emerging issue is whether, under the general right of publicity laws existing in most states, a person can bring suit over the use of a voice manufactured by an artificial intelligence system that has been "trained" on the real performer's voice. *See* Lehrman et al. v. Lovo, Inc., Docket No. 1:24–cv–03770 (S.D.N.Y. filed May 16, 2024). As discussed in § 9.5 below, the unauthorized use of artificial intelligence to replicate an individual's voice or likeness has only begun to be addressed through new legislation.

B. POSTMORTEM RIGHTS

In a number of states, the right of publicity persists even after the individual's death. It becomes part of the estate that passes to the individual's heirs, unless it has already been assigned during the individual's lifetime—for example, to a corporation. (See § 9.5 below for a discussion of such assignments.) In states where there is no postmortem right, however, the deceased individual's name, likeness, voice, and other identifying characteristics become available for others to exploit, except to the extent that their use may create a likelihood of confusion that is actionable under trademark and unfair competition laws. (See § 9.7 below.)

States that recognize the postmortem right typically subject it to certain limitations. For example, the right may be subject to a time limit, lasting for only a fixed number of years (e.g., 25, 50, or 70) after the individual's death. The postmortem right may also expire if there is an extended period of non-use. State law may require proof that the individual exploited the commercial value of his or her identity while still living; in the case of professional entertainers, of course, this condition is easily satisfied. In some states, parties claiming ownership of postmortem rights are required to register their claims with a state agency before they can enforce them in court.

§ 9.3 LICENSES AND ASSIGNMENTS

A person's right of publicity may be licensed. For example, performers may license their name, likeness, and voice to a record label for use in advertising, promoting, and selling their recordings, to concert promoters for the purpose of promoting their concerts, and to merchandising companies that will use their names and likenesses to produce goods such as T-shirts and posters. Each license is unique, and artists should always have an attorney review their license agreements before signing.

In most states, a person can also assign his or her right of publicity. Generally speaking, however, assignments should be avoided, since an assignment gives someone other than the artist complete and perpetual control over the use of the performer's identity. The only exception would be an assignment to an entity that is 100% owned and controlled by the artist, such as a single-member LLC or a personal service ("loanout") corporation. If the artist assigns his or her right of publicity to an entity that the artist does not 100% own, then the artist could lose control over these rights for the remainder of his or lifetime, and/or lose the ability to choose who inherits the postmortem right (if the jurisdiction recognizes such a right). For example, the famous television painter Bob Ross assigned his right of publicity to a corporation he had formed with several friends. Upon his death, pursuant to the rules of the corporation, his ownership share passed automatically to the surviving shareholders rather than to his estate. As a result, his son inherited neither his right of publicity nor his ownership share in the corporation. *See* RSR Art, LLC v. Bob Ross, Inc., 380 F.Supp.3d 510 (E.D. Va. 2019). Ross probably did not intend to disinherit his son. He simply failed to understand the legal impact of assigning his rights to the corporation.

§ 9.4 FIRST AMENDMENT CONSIDERATIONS

Not every unauthorized commercial use of a person's identity necessarily infringes the right of publicity. The classic right of publicity infringement arises when the use is entirely commercial—for example, the use of a celebrity's name, voice, or likeness in commercial advertising. (This is quintessential "commercial speech," receiving a low degree of First Amendment protection.) In contrast, purely noncommercial uses—such as comments and pictures posted by fans or critics on various websites—fall outside the scope of these laws.

It is not always clear whether a particular state's right of publicity law is limited to commercial advertising and sales or whether, and to what extent, it might also prohibit the use of an individual's identity in creative works of expression, where the work itself is the object of the sale. In the latter situation, overly broad enforcement can run afoul of the First Amendment, which protects the right of free expression.

Under the First Amendment, an unauthorized use of a person's identity may be permissible even though it is partially commercial in nature. Typically, these situations involve expressive works such as news and sports reporting and commentary, biographical works, documentaries and docudramas, criticism and commentary, works of art, and works of entertainment such as books, plays, musical works, motion pictures, television shows, TikTok or YouTube videos, and video games. Because these works are creative and expressive, and are not purely commercial in nature (in contrast to commercial speech such as advertising), they typically receive strong protection under the First Amendment. As a result, a right of publicity claim against such a work may fail.

In some states, right of publicity statutes include express exceptions for specific activities, typically (though not always) corresponding to various types of noncommercial speech. Some exceptions may reflect the importance of certain industries within the state: Nevada, for example, exempts live performances by celebrity impersonators as well as government efforts to promote tourism. NRS § 597.790(2)(b), (g). There is wide variation in state laws with respect to the unauthorized use of a person's identity in plays, live musical performances, sound recordings, and audiovisual works such as motion pictures, television shows, and video games. Many state laws are simply silent on these uses, leaving them for the courts to decide.

Even where no express statutory exception applies, courts will give significant weight to the First Amendment implications of enforcing a right of publicity against expressive works that are not purely commercial speech. There is no universal test for determining when the First Amendment outweighs an individual's right of publicity. Instead, courts in different jurisdictions have evolved different approaches.

One influential case exploring these issues involved the BIG EL SHOW, a live performance that essentially imitated an Elvis Presley concert, complete with an Elvis impersonator. The defendant advertised the show as a "tribute" to Presley, and did not argue that it was a parody, burlesque, or other type of commentary. While acknowledging that the production contained "an informational and entertainment element," and thus merited more First Amendment protection than a purely commercial activity such as advertising, the court found that the show served "primarily to commercially exploit the likeness of Elvis Presley without contributing anything of substantial value to society." Accordingly, it held that Elvis's postmortem right of publicity was infringed. Estate of Presley v. Russen, 513 F. Supp. 1339, 1359 (D.N.J. 1981). The court contrasted works that offered more biographical or historical content: "[I]n comparison to a biographical film or play of Elvis Presley or a production tracing the role of Elvis Presley in the development of rock 'n roll, the information about Presley which the BIG EL SHOW provides is of limited value." *Id.* at 1360.

Even a news broadcast—the kind of speech that receives especially strong First Amendment protection—may be found to infringe a person's right of publicity, although such cases have been rare. In Zacchini v. Scripps-Howard Broadcasting Co., 433 U.S. 562 (1977), the Supreme Court held a television news program liable for broadcasting a 15-second clip of the plaintiff's "human cannonball act," in which the plaintiff was shot out of a cannon at a local fair. The Court emphasized that the clip showed the plaintiff's entire performance, which not only damaged his ability to make a living, but also exceeded what was necessary in order to provide a news report about his performance. *Id.* at 574–76. The same reasoning would apply to a musical performance captured by a news crew: If, without obtaining the band's consent, the news program were to broadcast more than a brief clip of the performance, it could be held liable for infringing the band's right of publicity. If it also made the performance audible, it could be liable for violating the performers' rights under the federal anti-bootlegging statute (see § 9.6 below) and for infringing the copyright in the music being performed.

While there is no uniform test for evaluating First Amendment interests in right of publicity cases, California has developed a substantial body of case law that focuses on whether the use of a person's identity in an expressive work is "transformative." Generally speaking, a use is transformative if it does not merely exploit the commercial appeal of the celebrity's identify, but instead adds significant artistic expression. As expressed by the Supreme Court of California:

> When artistic expression takes the form of a literal depiction or imitation of a celebrity for commercial gain, directly trespassing on the right of publicity without adding significant expression beyond that trespass, the state law interest in protecting the fruits of artistic labor outweighs the expressive interests of the imitative artist.

Comedy III Productions, Inc. v. Gary Saderup, Inc., 25 Cal.4th 38, 405, 106 Cal. Rptr.2d 126, 21 P.3d 797 (2001). The Ninth Circuit and the Third Circuit have both adopted the transformative use test.

Several cases applying this test have involved musical performers:

In Winter v. DC Comics, 30 Cal.4th 881, 69 P.3d 473 (2003), recording artists Johnny and Edgar Winter sued DC Comics for publishing a comic book featuring two depraved half-worm, half-human characters called Johnny and Edgar Autumn. In addition to their names, the comic book characters bore some physical resemblance to the Winter brothers. Despite this resemblance, the court found that the comic book was not a literal depiction of the brothers; rather, it distorted their images for the purpose of "lampoon, parody, or caricature." 69 P.3d at 479. The characters were only part of a larger story that contained "significant expressive content" other than their likenesses. *Id.* Accordingly, the comic book was transformative and therefore non-infringing.

In Kirby v. Sega of America, 144 Cal. App.4th 47, 50 Cal. Rptr.3d 607 (2006), singer Kierin Kirby alleged that her right of publicity was infringed by a video game featuring a character who bore some physical resemblance to Kirby, wore clothing styles similar to Kirby's, used some similar verbal expressions, and whose name—"Ulala"—resembled Kirby's signature lyrical expression, "Ooh la la." However, there were also significant differences. In the end, the court found that, far from being "a mere likeness or literal depiction of Kirby," the Ulala character contained sufficient original expression to be transformative. The court therefore rejected Kirby's claim.

In another video game case, No Doubt v. Activision Publishing, Inc., 192 Cal.App.4th 1018, 122 Cal. Rptr.3d 397 (2011), the rock band No Doubt brought a right of publicity claim against the publisher of the *Band Hero* video game, which featured detailed avatars that closely resembled the band members. Although the band had granted Activision a license to use their images, they contended that Activision had infringed their right of publicity by exceeding the scope of that license. Specifically, they objected to the game's "unlocking" feature, which enabled the game's players to make the No Doubt band members' avatars appear to perform songs by other songwriters in addition to the songs No Doubt had licensed to Activision. The court therefore analyzed whether the depiction of the avatars singing the unauthorized songs was transformative or simply "pure mimicry" that did nothing more than exploit the value of their celebrity. 122 Cal. Rptr.3d at 410. In the court's view, the many creative elements of the game failed to outweigh its exploitative use of the band members' images. Therefore, the game's use of their images was not transformative, and infringed their right of publicity.

Jurisdictions that have not adopted the transformative use test nevertheless tend to take comparable approaches that weigh the degree of exploitativeness against the degree of creative expression in a particular expressive work that uses a person's name or likeness. For example, in Doe v. TCI Cablevision, 110 S.W.3d 363 (Mo. 2003), hockey player Anthony "Tony" Twist sued the publisher of a comic book that featured an evil character named Anthony "Tony Twist" Twistelli. While the character did not physically resemble the plaintiff, they shared nicknames as well as "tough guy" personas. The facts sufficiently established a valid right of publicity claim, and the court rejected the First Amendment defense, because "the use was not a parody or other expressive comment or a fictionalized account of the real Twist," and "the use and identity of Twist's name ha[d] become predominantly a ploy to sell comic books and related products rather than an artistic or literary expression." *TCI Cablevision,* 110 S.W.3d at 374.

§ 9.5 ARTIFICIAL INTELLIGENCE

Recent events have illustrated the ability of artificial intelligence systems to generate replicas of individual's images and voices. In 2023, an anonymous user posted a TikTok video that cloned the voices of Drake and The Weeknd, and an AI-generated replica of Tom Hanks was used in an advertisement without his consent. Voice actors filed suit over the digital replication of their voices in Lehrman et al. v. Lovo, Inc., Docket No. 1:24–cv–03770 (S.D.N.Y. filed May 16, 2024). These and similar incidents have led to calls for new state and federal laws that specifically address the use of computer technology, including artificial intelligence, to replicate a person's image and/or voice.

Thus far, statutes that specifically address digital replicas have been enacted, or introduced, in only a handful of states. However, legislation is also being considered at the federal level.

In 2020, New York created a narrowly circumscribed cause of action for the unauthorized use of a digital replica (defined as a newly created computer-generated "performance") of a deceased performer in a "scripted audiovisual work as a fictional character" or "a live performance of a musical work." However, the law has limited utility. It applies only if the use is likely to deceive the public into thinking that the use was authorized. In addition, in the case of a scripted audiovisual work, there is no liability if the person using the replica provides a "conspicuous disclaimer" stating that the use was unauthorized. N.Y. Civ. Rts. § 50–f. Furthermore, the statute does not encompass the unauthorized use of digital replicas in sound recordings. Because the new law applies only to deceased individuals, it does not assist performers who are still living. Instead, they would have to rely on New York's other right of publicity statute, N.Y. Civ. Rts. § 51, the same one that is currently at issue in the voice actors' lawsuit in Lehrman et al. v. Lovo, Inc., Docket No. 1:24–cv–03770 (S.D.N.Y. filed May 16, 2024). Courts have not yet determined, however, whether § 51 covers digital replicas.

In March of 2024, Tennessee enacted the Ensuring Likeness Voice and Image Security (ELVIS) Act, which updates the state's existing right of publicity statute to expressly encompass voices, a term that includes "simulations" thereof. Protection applies to both living and deceased performers. Civil liability and, in some cases, criminal penalties, will apply to anyone who, for a commercial purpose, makes an individual's voice or likeness available to the public, or who makes available any technology or service for replicating that person's voice or likeness, knowing that such use was unauthorized. Tenn. Code Ann. §§ 47–25–1101–1107. The statute includes a number of exceptions designed to protect First Amendment interests. Most notably, it exempts a "representation of the individual as the individual's self in an audiovisual work" unless the audiovisual work "is intended to create, and does create, the false impression that the work is an authentic recording in which the individual participated." *Id.* §§ 47–25 1107(a).

California followed a few months later, amending its right of publicity statute, Cal. Civ. Code § 3344.1, to prohibit the unauthorized use of digital replicas in audiovisual works and sound recordings. However, this protection applies only to deceased persons. Living individuals are protected by California's general right of publicity statute as well as common law, as discussed in § 9.2[A] above.

Also in 2024, federal legislation was proposed to address digital replicas at the national level. The Nurture Originals, Foster Art, and Keep Entertainment Safe (NO FAKES) Act would provide broad protection against the use of nonconsensual computer-generated replicas of a *living or deceased* individual's voice or visual likeness. As of September

2024, the proposed statute would enable plaintiffs to bring suit against any individual or entity that:

(1) produces an unauthorized digital replica of an individual, living or deceased; or

(2) distributes, publishes, transmits, or otherwise makes available to the public an unauthorized digital replica, knowing that it was unauthorized.

However, it would exempt the types of activities that are typically protected by the First Amendment, such as news reporting, documentaries, scholarship, parodies, and commentaries.

Parties eligible to bring suit under the NO FAKES Act include (1) the individual depicted, (2) anyone who owns or controls the rights to the individual's image, voice, or visual likeness, such as a loanout or exclusive licensee, and (3) in the case of recording artists, anyone who has a contract for the artist's exclusive personal services as a recording artist (such as the artist's record label).

Remedies include injunctive relief, damages, and attorney's fees.

If enacted, the NO FAKES Act will have nationwide effect, thus allowing plaintiffs to pursue their claims even in states that do not offer comparable protection.

§ 9.6 FEDERAL ANTI-BOOTLEGGING STATUTE

The federal anti-bootlegging statute protects musical performers against bootlegging of their live performances. Section 1101 allows a performer to bring a civil cause of action against any person who, without the performer's consent, does any of the following:

(1) Records the sounds, or sounds and images, of a live musical performance;

(2) Reproduces any such unauthorized recording;

(3) Transmits to the public the sounds, or sounds and images, of a live musical performance; or

(4) Distributes or offers to distribute by sale or rental, or traffics in, an unauthorized recording of a live musical performance.

17 U.S.C. § 1101(a). Potential remedies include injunctions, damages, attorney's fees, and seizure of any infringing goods. *Id.* Criminal prosecution is possible as well, under 18 U.S.C. § 2319A.

Although the protection provided by § 1101 resembles that provided by the right of publicity at the state level, it applies only to performers engaged in a live musical performance. Thus, its scope is much narrower than the state laws discussed in § 9.2 above.

Because there is little case law interpreting § 1101, many questions remain unanswered. For example, what is a "live musical performance"? Must the live performers be performing live music? What about a live dance performance that uses recorded music, or actors performing a live stage play during which recorded music is occasionally played? Also, while § 1101 does not mention any exceptions, certain unauthorized uses (such as brief clips for news reporting, documentaries, or criticism) might be eligible for First Amendment protection.

Congress enacted § 1101 in 1994 in order to comply with its obligations under a new international treaty. Because the Patent and Copyright Clause of the Constitution does not authorize Congress to protect unfixed works such as live performances (which are not considered "writings" under the Constitution), Congress relied on its Commerce Clause power instead. Although courts have not addressed the constitutionality of § 1101, thus far they have upheld the corresponding criminal provisions in 18 U.S.C. § 2319A as a lawful exercise of Congress's powers under the Commerce Clause. *See* United States v. Martignon, 492 F.3d 140 (2d Cir. 2007); United States v. Moghadam, 175 F.3d 1269 (11th Cir. 1999). It is likely that the same analysis would support § 1101 as well.

§ 9.7 TRADEMARK AND UNFAIR COMPETITION LAWS

Individual artists as well as musical groups do not have to rely only on the protections discussed in this chapter, because their stage names are likely to be protected by trademark and unfair competition laws as well. In most cases, their stage names are automatically eligible for common law protection, and in many cases they are eligible for federal trademark registration as well. For details on trademark and unfair competition laws, see Chapter 8.

The scope of protection for names, likenesses, and voices, and the available defenses and remedies in the event of infringement, are different under trademark and unfair competition laws. For example, there can be a difference in how the court analyzes a First Amendment defense for the unauthorized use of an artist's name, likeness, or voice in expressive works such as video games.

Therefore, to maximize their chance of success (and the range of potential remedies), it is not unusual for artists to sue infringers under both theories. For example, when a radio commercial for Doritos imitated Tom Waits' distinctive voice in a parody of one of his songs, he brought claims for infringement of his right of publicity under California common law as well as false endorsement under § 43(a) of the Lanham Act (the federal unfair competition statute, 15 U.S.C. § 1125(a)). Waits prevailed under both theories. *See* Waits v. Frito-Lay, Inc., 978 F.2d 1093 (9th Cir. 1992).

In contrast, in two Ninth Circuit cases involving the unauthorized use of athletes' identities in video games, the right of publicity claim succeeded but the false endorsement claim failed. The facts of the cases were similar, the decisions were issued by the same panel of judges on the same day, and they were even written by the same judge. Why the different outcomes? Even though video games are creative expression that receives a high degree of First Amendment protection, the Ninth Circuit uses different tests for assessing First Amendment defenses against right of publicity claims versus false endorsement claims. *See* Brown v. Electronic Arts, Inc., 724 F.3d 1235 (9th Cir. 2013) (holding that First Amendment precluded false endorsement claim); In re NCAA Student-Athlete Name & Likeness Licensing Litigation, 724 F.3d 1268 (9th Cir. 2013) (holding that First Amendment did not preclude right of publicity claim).

§ 9.8 CYBERSQUATTING

As discussed in Chapter 8, the federal anti-cybersquatting statute, 15 U.S.C. § 1125(d), creates a cause of action for the unauthorized use of another party's trademark in a domain name, if the user has a "bad faith intent to profit" from using the mark. This cause of action would therefore be available to an artist whose name (if it is qualifies for protection as a common law mark or as a registered mark) has been used in a domain name without his or her consent. For a full discussion, see § 8.6 above.

However, there is also an anti-cybersquatting statute that specifically protects the names of living individuals, even if their names do not qualify as trademarks. *See* 15 U.S.C. § 8131. This could be useful if a domain name appropriates the real name of an artist who is better known by a stage name, because the artist's real name might not qualify for trademark protection, even at common law. It could also be useful for songwriters and other creators whose names might not be well enough known to receive common law trademark protection. The scope of protection under this statute, however, is narrower than the protection for names protected as trademarks. The person whose real name has been used can prevail only if the defendant registered the domain name with the specific intent of selling it for financial gain. If the plaintiff wins, the court will order the domain name to be cancelled or transferred to the plaintiff.

CHAPTER 10
RECORDING CONTRACTS

§ 10.1 APPROACHING THE NEGOTIATION

Musical performers interested in becoming recording artists have two options. They can finance and create their own recordings and use a distributor to get them into the market, or they can sign a recording contract with a record label.

A recording contract establishes the rights and obligations of the recording artist and the record label with respect to one another. The main concerns of artists will be the amount and manner of their compensation, the promotional and other support that the label will provide, how much creative freedom they will retain, and how much control the label will exercise over their professional pursuits. The record label's main concerns will be whether the artist will deliver commercially successful recordings within reasonable time frames and cooperate in promoting those recordings—e.g., by touring. Both parties have an interest in maintaining some degree of creative control over the recordings.

Because a recording contract is a complex legal document, and musicians typically lack the training necessary to understand and negotiate its provisions, before signing such an agreement musicians should have it reviewed by their own legal counsel. Better yet, they should involve their legal counsel in the negotiations. Performers signing their first recording contract often fail to realize that the contract presented to them is not a "take it or leave it" affair; most of its provisions are negotiable. While experienced managers can provide some insight, they are not legal experts, and they do not have a fiduciary duty to look out for the artist's best interests. Only a knowledgeable music attorney can fully understand the language of a recording contract, explain it to the artist, and negotiate for better terms.

Note that if an artist uses a loanout or LLC, then the loanout or LLC rather than the individual artist will be the party to the recording contract. The record label, however, may require the artist to sign a letter of inducement, which may (depending on how it is drafted) include a personal guarantee of the artist's services. (See Chapter 2.)

This chapter examines the key components of a recording contract. Because the recording business is constantly in flux, however, provisions that are standard today may be different a few years from now. And while the provisions described here are typical, they are also negotiable.

§ 10.2 TERM AND EXCLUSIVITY

The term of a recording contract consists of an initial contract period, plus a series of renewal terms (each of which may be one year or multi-year) at the sole option of the record label. This structure enables the record label to evaluate whether the artist's recordings are successful enough to continue the relationship. If at any point the label determines that they are not, it can simply decline to exercise its next renewal option.

In most cases, the artist is expected to deliver the first album within the first year of the contract. Even though streaming and downloading have made the concept of an "album" outdated, it is still used in recording contracts to define the artist's obligations, and in marketing to promote the artist's latest releases. To meet the delivery requirement for each album, the contract will typically require the artist to record at least 10 individual songs, totaling at least 50 minutes of playing time (with variations depending on the genre). The contract will permit the label to review each album that the artist delivers to determine whether it is commercially marketable, and to accept or reject the album.

If the label exercises all of its renewal options, the artist's total obligation under the contract is typically 7 albums within 7 years. Under the laws of most states, 7 years is the maximum enforceable term for personal services contracts.

During the term of the agreement, the artist will have an exclusive obligation to make recordings *only* for that record label. The record label imposes this exclusivity requirement in order to ensure that its recording does not have to compete with recordings that the same artist makes for a different label.

When the artist is a band or musical group, the exclusivity requirement will apply to each its members. This means that the individual members cannot record solo projects, and may even need the record label's consent to work as side musicians on another artist's recording project. If the record label consents, it may insist on receiving a credit on the other recording (e.g., "Artist Annie appears courtesy of Big Label Records").

Even after the contract terminates, the contract may specify a period of time during which the artist is not allowed to record for any other label.

§ 10.3 ARTIST COMMITMENT AND CREATIVE CONTROL

The contract will specify the number of albums the recording artist is required to deliver during the contract term. Typically, this will be one album for each contract period (meaning one album for the initial period, then one for each renewal term so long as the label exercises the renewal options). The contract should specify the minimum number of songs for each album, and the minimum total running time. (Ten songs and 50 minutes are typical.) In some contracts, the delivery commitment for each period will be not an entire album but a specific number of individual masters or an EP consisting of three or more individual masters. Failure to meet delivery deadlines may lead to financial penalties or contract termination.

The contract will establish certain qualitative criteria for each master. For example, it may require the songs to be previously unrecorded by the artist, to conform to a certain style or genre, to meet a minimum standard of technical quality, and—more vaguely—to be "commercially" satisfactory.

The contract may specifically address other elements of creative control—for example, selecting a producer, which songs (and how many) to include, what lyrics are acceptable, and which recording studio to use, as well as marketing strategies, release schedule, and cover art. All of these are negotiable.

The contract should also address the parties' respective rights if the label decides not to release a recording, or fails to release it within a specified time frame. Does the artist have the right to reclaim the master, and if so, is the label entitled to any compensation? Can the artist terminate the contract?

In addition to delivering recordings, artists may also be obligated to participate in various activities, such as personal appearances and interviews, that are designed to promote their albums. The contract should be specific about the nature of these commitments. The label should pay the expenses for these activities, and the contract should indicate whether these are recoupable against artist royalties. If the contract includes a touring obligation, the artist should insist on a commensurate level of tour support.

§ 10.4 ARTIST COMPENSATION

A. ADVANCE

In a standard recording contract, the label will pay the artist an advance that is recoupable against any future royalties the label would otherwise owe the artist. Artists should recognize that the advance is essentially a loan, which the artist must pay back to the label out of his or her royalties. If the royalties are insufficient to enable full recoupment, the artist will not have to repay the remaining balance. In some cases, however, the recording contract calls for the advance for one album to be cross-collateralized with royalties due from other albums; this means that an unrecouped advance from one album can be recouped out of the royalties generated by a more successful album.

The size of the advance is negotiable, and can range from less than $100,000 (for newer artists) to $1 million or more (for the most successful artists). Out of the advance, the artist must pay the recording costs of the first record, including studio rental, fees for the producer, engineers, and session musicians, and the cost of renting and maintaining instruments and equipment, as well as other costs such as fees for the artist's manager and lawyers. The artist may be able to negotiate additional advances for the subsequent recordings required under the contract.

In addition to recouping recording costs, the contract may also permit the label to recover additional costs against the artist's royalties, such as distribution and promotion costs, tour support (if any), and the cost of making music videos. The larger the recoupable costs, the longer it will take the artist to begin receiving royalty payments. If the record is not successful, it might not recoup, and artist might receive no royalties at all.

Before signing a recording contract, artists should pay special attention to the provisions that delineate the royalty streams against which the advance and other expenses paid by the label will be recouped. The artist's advance should be recoupable only against future royalties payable by the record label. If the artist is also a songwriter whose publisher is affiliated with the record label, the label may try to include a provision allowing recoupment against publishing royalties. Also, the advance should not be recoupable against the artist's share of the § 114 statutory royalty for noninteractive streaming that is collected and distributed directly to the artist by SoundExchange (see Chapter 7).

The artist should also take note of how much control each party exercises over the recording costs and other costs associated with the release. Will the label pay the recording costs directly, or will it advance the funds to the artist and require the artist to pay the recording costs? Who decides which recording studio will be rented? (Will it be a studio owned by the label? If so, then the label is paying the studio rental costs to itself.) Who determines the recording budget, and which party is responsible for recording costs that go over-budget? If the recording comes in under-budget, does the artist get to keep the difference? Are marketing costs recoupable, or does the label absorb all of these costs?

Some artists may negotiate a larger advance in exchange for a lower royalty rate. The opposite is possible as well: A successful artist that can afford to pay recording costs out of pocket may arrange to receive no advance at all, but a much higher royalty percentage.

B. ROYALTIES

The contract should specify the various types of royalties that the label will pay to the artist, how those royalties will be calculated, and when they will be paid. The label should also commit to sharing information with the artist, through periodic accounting statements, so that the artist can determine whether the royalties have been calculated correctly.

For each type of royalty, the specific pool of revenue that is the source of the royalty is called the royalty *base*. The percentage of the royalty base that is the artist's share is the royalty *rate*. Therefore, the amount of each type of royalty that is payable to the artist is determined by multiplying the base by the corresponding rate.

The label should pay the artist royalties from multiple revenue streams, including sales of physical records and downloads, master recording licenses, interactive streaming royalties, and merchandise related to the recording. In some contracts, the same rate applies to all royalty streams. In others, there will be different rates for different royalty sources. For example, under Eminem's 1998 recording contract he was entitled to a 50% royalty on licensing revenues and a 12–20% royalty on record sales. In a dispute over the proper characterization of permanent downloads and ringtone sales, Eminem prevailed, persuading a court that these should be treated as licensing revenues subject to the higher royalty rate. *See* F.B.T. Productions LLC v. Aftermath Records, 621 F.3d 958 (9th Cir. 2010).

Similar lawsuits followed. Today, to avoid such disputes, contracts that apply different rates to different revenue streams should define each revenue stream clearly. Some uncertainty may persist; because new media and modes of exploitation may arise in the future, it may be impossible to categorize all possible revenue streams in advance.

1. Record Sales

Although the concept of record sales dates back to the days when consumers bought actual physical records, the term will be defined more broadly in today's recording contracts. It will certainly include sales of digital downloads as well as physical media. In some contracts, the term may also encompass revenues from interactive streaming. Alternatively, the contract may use different terminology to describe streaming revenues. Regardless of terminology, the artist's compensation should include a specified percentage of each of these revenue sources. However, the royalty base will be defined differently for each revenue stream, and the royalty rate may differ as well.

The royalty rate for both physical record sales and downloads is typically 10–20%. Sometimes, the royalty rate will start low but increase as revenues reach agreed-upon benchmarks. For downloads, the royalty base is the revenue that the label actually receives from the download service. For the sale of physical records, however, the royalty calculation is more complex. It begins with the record's "royalty base price," which is typically defined as the published wholesale price minus discounts and sales taxes. The royalty base price is then multiplied by "net sales," which is the number of records distributed to retailers, minus returns.

However, the net sales figure is not a simple as it seems. Although the practice is less common today, some labels may deduct an additional amount for "free goods," which are records shipped to retailers for free as a sales incentive. The contract should limit the number of records deducted as free goods; typically, these should be no more than 15% of albums and 20–30% of singles shipped. (To avoid double-counting that would unfairly reduce the royalty base, any free goods that are returned to the label should be excluded from the returns that are subtracted in calculating net sales.) Net sales also do not include any promotional records that the label gives away to radio stations, critics, and the media.

Multiplying the net sales figure by the royalty base price yields the sales royalty base, which is then multiplied by the royalty rate to determine the artist's total royalty from physical record sales.

2. Streaming

The royalty rate for on-demand ("interactive") digital streaming is typically 15–20% for new artists, but may be as high as 50% for the most popular artists. In most cases, the same rate applies to both audio streaming and streaming of music videos.

In contrast, record labels typically do not pay artists royalties for noninteractive (radio-style) digital streaming. This is because, under 17 U.S.C. § 114, the artists featured on a recording receive their statutory share of noninteractive royalties directly from SoundExchange. (See Chapter 7.)

3. Master Use Licenses

Record labels may license their master recordings for incorporation into other audio or audiovisual works, such as motion pictures, television shows, commercials, video games, compilations and movie soundtrack albums, or for other uses, such as ringtones. There are no standard forms for master use licenses (also called "master recording" or sometimes "synch" licenses, but not to be confused with synch licenses for musical works), so they are all customized for each specific use. Recording contracts typically give artists 50% of the label's master licensing revenues.

4. Tour Support

Touring is extremely expensive. Therefore, many artists will seek tour support from their labels. Labels that provide this support do so in the expectation that the tour will promote record sales.

Tour support may range from modest (e.g., promotional materials) to full-scale (hotel, transportation, equipment rental, per diems for the band, and salaries for tech crew and a road manager). The more support the label provides, the more likely it is to want control over decisions related to the tour (e.g., tour dates, opening acts, and the size and type of venues). Any amounts the label spends for the tour will be recoupable against the artist's royalties.

Major labels are more likely to provide substantial tour support than independent labels. They are especially likely to provide support for bands that are releasing their first recording, because those bands may be well known in some regions but need national exposure in order to sell more recordings.

The amount and nature of tour support, and the extent of each party's authority to make decisions related to the tour, should be spelled out in the recording contract.

§ 10.5 CONTROLLED COMPOSITIONS

Record labels must pay mechanical royalties to the owners of musical compositions (songwriters and/or music publishers) for the right to make recordings of the copyrighted musical works. (See Chapter 5.) The standard mechanical royalty rate is typically the same as the compulsory mechanical royalty rate under 17 U.S.C. § 115: For each physical record or individual download, the current royalty is 12.4 cents per musical work for recordings up to 5 minutes in length, or 2.38 cents per minute of playing time for recordings over 5 minutes.

In the past, it was common for recording contracts to include a "controlled composition" clause. Under this clause, if the recording artist (or the producer) is also one of the writers of a song that will be included on the album, the record label will pay a reduced royalty for any songs that the songwriter has written or co-written, or which the songwriter owns or controls. The reduced royalty is typically 75% of the otherwise applicable mechanical royalty.

Today, however, most controlled composition clauses cannot be enforced with respect to mechanical royalties arising from digital downloads and streaming. The Digital Performance Right in Sound Recordings Act (DPRA) of 1995 provides that, for recording contracts entered into after June 22, 1995, the compulsory mechanical rate overrides any lower rate imposed by the recording contract. 17 U.S.C. § 115(c)(2)(A). Therefore, controlled composition clauses can be enforced only with respect to physical record sales and recordings created under older recording contracts.

Despite this change in the law, some record labels still include controlled composition clauses in their contracts. There is a risk that the label could attempt to enforce such clauses by recouping the difference against the artist's share of other income streams. To eliminate any uncertainty, artists should negotiate to remove these outdated provisions before signing. Overall, their use is declining, and at least one major label, BMG, has dispensed with them altogether.

§ 10.6 360 DEALS

A record label might ask an artist to sign a "360" deal. While these arrangements are common, they are also complex, and an artist should not sign such a contract without consulting an experienced music attorney who can explain the contract terms.

Labels began turning to 360 deals when their revenues from record sales declined. In a 360 deal, the label becomes entitled to a share of several revenue streams that would, in the past, have belonged to the artist alone. These include income from touring, merchandise, television appearances, sponsorships, and other ancillary income. If the artist is also a songwriter, the label may seek a share of the artist's publishing revenues. It may even control the artist's social media accounts.

In some 360 deals, the label will spend significant sums to promote the artist and subsidize the artist's touring, merchandising, and marketing expenses in addition to paying the usual recording costs.

Some sources report that the use of 360 deals by record labels is declining, as artists negotiating newer contracts have increasingly been able to whittle them down to a lesser "multi-rights" arrangement. However, some artists have entered multi-rights deals with concert promoters such as Live Nation. In these deals, the promoter receives a share of the artist's touring revenue, including tour-related merchandise and sponsorships, in exchange for significant tour support.

§ 10.7 OWNERSHIP OF MASTERS

Typically, the recording contract will give the label copyright ownership of each recording that the artist delivers under the agreement. The sound recording copyright is referred to as the "master."

In addition to language assigning the copyright in the masters, the contract will also describe these recordings as "works made for hire" authored by the record label. However, for recordings created after 1977 this language may be ineffective under federal copyright law. (See Chapter 3.) This is why the contract will include a copyright assignment as a back-up.

If the recording is a work made for hire, then the record label will own the masters for the entire copyright term, even after the recording contract expires. If the contract merely assigns the copyright, then the record label will still own the masters after the contract expires, but its ownership might end when the assignment is eligible for termination, as discussed below.

However, some artists are able to negotiate more favorable terms. For example, the artist may own the masters and grant the label only the right to exploit their copyright for a specified term of years in a particular territory (e.g., the United States). Alternatively, the contract might call for ownership of the masters to revert automatically to the artist after a specified term.

Some artists have been able to buy their masters back from their label, although in many cases this can be prohibitively expensive. However, Prince regained control of his masters from Warner Bros. in 2014, reportedly in exchange for recording two new albums.

Prominent artists who own their masters include Jay-Z and Rihanna. Independent artists—those not signed to a major label—are more likely to own their masters; examples include Chance the Rapper and Frank Ocean.

Artists can also regain the copyright to their masters by exercising their termination rights under § 203 of the Copyright Act. 17 U.S.C. § 203. However, this must be done within a particular window of time. For recording contracts, this window opens up 35 years from the recording's release, or 40 years from the date of the contract, whichever term ends earlier. Because the process is technical, and requires significant advance planning, artists will need the help of an attorney to effect a valid termination. Although labels can attempt to resist termination by pointing to the "work made for hire" clause in the recording contract, the courts have not yet ruled on the validity of these clauses. (For artists who created sound recordings between February 15, 1972 and December 31, 1977, termination rights are governed by § 304 instead. Earlier recordings have no termination rights at all.) For more on termination rights, see § 3.10 above.

As noted earlier, most recording contracts do not obligate the label to release each album that an artist delivers. If a label is unwilling or unable (perhaps for financial reasons) to release a recording, what rights does the artist have? Since the artist may want to explore other options for releasing the recording, the contract should also address who owns the masters under these circumstances. Even if the artist has the right to reclaim them, the label may be entitled to reimbursement for the recording costs.

§ 10.8 RE-RECORDING PROHIBITIONS

Artists who are unable to regain ownership of their masters in a timely manner may wish to re-record their music after the expiration of their recording contract, creating new masters. This does not infringe the label's sound recording copyright, even if the new masters sound very similar to the old ones, because federal copyright law expressly permits the creation of soundalike recordings. 17 U.S.C. § 114(b). Note, however, that if the artist is not also the songwriter, he or she will need mechanical licenses for the underlying musical works in order to make the new recordings. This is not a major obstacle, because the new masters will qualify for the compulsory mechanical license under § 115.

However, recording contracts typically prohibit the artist from re-recording the same songs for a specified term of years after the contract's expiration. This provision protects the record label's investment in the master recordings in a way that federal copyright law does not.

If an artist is unable to repurchase his or her masters, and does not want to wait 35 years to effect a copyright termination (and deal with the legal uncertainties surrounding such termination), he or she may find that recording new masters after the re-recording prohibition expires is an attractive option. The artist's career may still be going strong (which would be a riskier proposition if the artist were to wait 35 years to reclaim the original masters through termination under copyright law), making it potentially worthwhile to create new masters. However, the new masters will involve new recording costs, and will be competing with the old masters, making the artist's return on investment uncertain.

The poster child for re-recording—Taylor Swift—was particularly well positioned to take advantage of this option. As soon as the re-recording prohibition in her previous contract with Big Machine Records expired, she recorded "Taylor's Version" of her hit albums. She had no trouble persuading her fiercely loyal fan base to purchase and stream "Taylor's Version" rather than the Big Machine recordings.

The success of Swift's re-recording strategy has reportedly led major record labels to lengthen the term of the re-recording prohibition in their new contracts. While in the past the term was typically 2 to 7 years (depending partly on whether it was measured from the original release date or the date of contract expiration), new contracts reportedly have extended the term to 10–15 years, or even longer in some cases.

§ 10.9 ACCOUNTINGS AND AUDITS

Contracts usually require labels to pay artists their royalties on a semi-annual basis, usually within 90 days after the end of each semi-annual period. Each royalty payment should be accompanied by an accounting statement showing how the royalties were calculated. In addition, it is important that the contract give the artist the right to audit the label's books and records periodically in order to verify that the royalties were determined correctly. The auditor should be an independent accountant with no ties to the record label. The contract should indicate when and where the audits can take place, and should require good faith cooperation by the label.

Audit rights are so important, in fact, that California has enacted them into law. Under California law, recording artists have the unwaivable right to audit the record label's books and records, once per year, using the auditor of their choice, to determine whether they have received all the royalties they are owed. The artist must request the audit within 3 years after the end of the relevant royalty period (as established in the contract). Cal. Civ. Code § 2501.

The contract should also address which party pays for the audits. For example, the audit may be at the artist's expense, unless it reveals a significant underpayment (a term that should be defined in the contract), in which case the label would pay for the audit.

§ 10.10 NAME AND LIKENESS

The record label will need a license to use the artist's name and likeness in connection with marketing the recording. However, there should be clearly defined limits on the scope and duration of this license.

For example, the license can be limited to uses in connection with marketing the artist's own recordings. Alternatively, it could apply more broadly to activities promoting the label itself. The term of the license should be limited to the duration of the recording contract.

Although the contract may give the label a *license*, the artist should retain *ownership* of his or her name and likeness rights. The contract should reserve the artist's right to use those rights in connection with his or her other projects (e.g., live performances, commercials, and film or television roles) even while the recording contract is in force.

§ 10.11 KEY PERSON

If the artist is a band or musical group, there may be some members whose continued presence is crucial to the band's appeal—for example, a charismatic lead singer. The recording contract may include a key person clause (sometimes phrased as a key "member" or even key "man" clause) designating one or more such individuals as indispensable to the continuation of the recording contract. The contract will likely give the record label the option to terminate the deal if the key person leaves the group.

A key person clause may work the other way as well. If the artist wants to work only with a particular person at the record label, then the contract can give the artist the option to terminate the contract if the key person leaves the label.

In either case, the contract should clearly specify the identity of the key person(s) whose departure will trigger the clause. It is especially important to specify the key person(s) in musical groups, in order to prevent the record label from terminating the contract due to the departure of a group member who was not designated as "key."

§ 10.12 TERMINATION

The contract should define the circumstances under which either party has the right to terminate the agreement.

If a party is in breach of the agreement, the contract may allow that party to cure the breach within a specific time frame. If the party fails to cure the breach, the other party will have the option to terminate. For example, if the artist fails to deliver a recording on time, or the label fails to send timely payments or accountings, such breaches may be subject to cure, with termination as the last resort. A significant breach, if uncured, may also be grounds for a breach of contract suit, with the breaching party liable for damages. *See, e.g.*, Cal. Labor Code § 2855.

Other breaches may not be subject to cure. For example, the contract may include some version of a "morals" clause, under which certain conduct by the artist will give the label the immediate option to terminate, in order to avoid damage to the label's reputation.

If an artist breaches the contract by failing to deliver the agreed-upon recordings, the record label may, in addition to suing for damages, be able to get an injunction preventing the artist from recording for another label for the remainder of the contract term.

See MCA Records, Inc. v. Newton-John, 90 Cal. App.3d 18, 153 Cal. Rptr. 153 (Cal. App. 1979); Cal. Civ. Code § 3423.

If the label files for bankruptcy, the artist should have the option to terminate and move on to a different label or distributor. (A bankruptcy by the *artist* can also enable the artist to terminate the contract, although the final decision is up to the bankruptcy courts.)

A record label can also terminate its relationship with an artist simply by declining to pick up its option to renew. This means that the artist has been dropped from the label.

If a label decides to drop an artist while it still holds unreleased tracks, the contract typically does not require the label to return ownership of those masters to the artist. This obviously presents a problem for the artist, who will want to release those tracks. The artist may be able to negotiate the return of those masters, in exchange for a lump sum payment or a royalty share. Alternatively, the artist may negotiate for a waiver of the re-recording restriction for those particular tracks, enabling the artist to record new masters of the same songs (under a new mechanical license), either independently or under a contract with a different label.

CHAPTER 11
CONTRACTS WITH MINORS

§ 11.1 RIGHT TO DISAFFIRM

Young artists play an important role in the music industry, both as performers and as songwriters. (Taylor Swift signed her first publishing deal at age 14, and released her first single at age 16.) Like other artists, they enter into a variety of contracts—with record labels, publishers, tour promoters, and/or managers.

However, contracts with songwriters and performers under the age of majority present a unique problem: Generally speaking, minors lack the legal capacity to enter a binding contract. Therefore, they are free to disaffirm their contracts (other than contracts for "necessities" such as food and clothing). They can disaffirm while they are still minors, or within a reasonable time after attaining the age of majority (age 18 in most states). A recording artist who is a minor can therefore walk away from a recording contact and sign with a different label. A minor's disaffirmance can also deprive a publisher or record label of the valuable intellectual property rights that it acquired from the minor—e.g., the right to publish a song the minor has written or to distribute a sound recording on which the minor has performed.

For example, the members of the band New Edition signed recording contracts with Streetwise Records when they were only 14 years old. Less than a year later, after releasing their hit debut *Candy Girl* through Streetwise, they disaffirmed those contracts and signed with a different label. Although their contracts with Streetwise had given the latter ownership of the band's name (a trademark), as a result of the disaffirmance Streetwise lost these rights, and the band was able to continue performing and recording as New Edition. *See* Bell v. Streetwise Records, Ltd., 640 F.Supp. 575 (D. Mass. 1986). (There is no indication that the band tried to prevent further distribution of *Candy Girl.*)

§ 11.2 LIMITATIONS ON RIGHT

Despite the general rule permitting disaffirmance, there are variations in state laws. In Georgia, for example, a minor cannot disaffirm a contract connected with any profession, trade, or business that the minor is practicing with the permission of a parent or guardian. Ga. Code § 13–3–21.

Several states have enacted laws making minors' contracts in the entertainment industry enforceable if they satisfy certain criteria, including approval by a court. These states, and several others, also require that a portion of the minor's earnings be set aside in a trust for the sole benefit of the minor, accessible when he or she reaches the age of majority.

California's statute applies to a minor's contract to render "artistic or creative services," explicitly including services as a songwriter, musician, or singer. It also applies to contracts in which a minor sells or licenses copyrights or the right to use the minor's name, voice, likeness, recording, performance or life story incidents. (In contrast, the statute does not mention trademarks.) Cal. Fam. Code § 6750. The law requires the employer or other contracting party to put 15 percent of the minor's earnings into a trust account that complies with specific statutory requirements. *Id.* §§ 6752–53. Upon court approval, the minor can no longer disaffirm the contract. The California law does not apply to a contract in which the minor retains *someone else*'s services, such as the services of a manager; thus, a minor can disaffirm his or her contract with a manager. However, a separate statute prevents a minor from disaffirming a court-approved contract with a licensed talent agency. Cal. Lab. Code § 1700.37.

Nevada's statute is similar to California's, without the additional provision covering talent agencies. Also, the requirement of a trust account for the minor applies only with respect to contracts that have received court approval. NRS §§ 609.400–550.

New York, too, has adopted a statute to prevent disaffirmance. Like California, New York allows enforcement of a minor's contract if the contract has received court approval. However, while the New York statute applies to contracts to perform services as a musician, vocalist, or "other performing artist," it is narrower than California's law in that it does not encompass songwriters' agreements or transfers of intellectual property rights. In one respect, New York's law is broader than the California's: It also applies to contracts in which another party has agreed to perform services *for* the minor in connection with the minor's work as a performer—for example, a management contract. Thus, if a minor's agreement with a manager is court-approved, then the minor cannot disaffirm the agreement. N.Y. CLS Art & Cult. Affrs. § 35.03.

Like California, New York requires 15 percent of a minor entertainer's earnings to be placed in a trust. This requirement applies to both performers and songwriters. N.Y. EPTL § 7–7.1.

In Tennessee, the Protection of Minor Performers Act prevents minors from disaffirming court-approved contracts. TN Code §§ 50–5–201–50–5–222. It applies to minors who provide "artistic or creative services," including musicians, vocalists, and songwriters. If the court approves the minor's contract, it must require that 15% of the minor's earnings be set aside in a trust. (As in Nevada, Tennessee's trust requirement applies only to court-approved contracts.) However, the statute does not cover a minor's contract employing a non-entertainer, such as a manager. Also, the statute is ambiguous on at least one point: It does not expressly state that it applies to sales or licenses of intellectual property rights that are separate from a contract for personal services; thus, while it clearly applies to a minor's agreement to provide songwriting *services*, it is not clear whether it applies to a minor's sale or license of copyright in songs that he or she has already written.

The purpose of placing a portion of a minor's earnings into a trust is to ensure that at least some portion of those earnings will be safeguarded until the child reaches the age of majority or becomes legally emancipated. Without this arrangement, there is a risk that the child, the parents, or the legal guardian could spend all of the child's earnings before the child is old enough to take financial responsibility. These trusts are sometimes called Coogan Trust Accounts, named after the 1920s child actor Jackie Coogan, whose earnings were squandered by his parents and manager. (As an adult, his most famous role was Uncle Fester in television's *The Addams Family*.) In addition to California, New York, Nevada, and Tennessee, a variety of laws requiring trust accounts for minors in the entertainment industry have been enacted in Illinois, Kansas, Louisiana, New Mexico, North Carolina, and Pennsylvania.

§ 11.3 PARENTAL GUARANTEES

If a state does not have a court approval procedure, or if the state provides one but the contracting parties do not use it, there is typically a greater risk that an underage artist will disaffirm a contract. One way to reduce the risk is to require the minor's parents or legal guardian to sign a personal guarantee that the minor will fulfill his or her contractual obligations. If the minor fails to perform, the parents will be liable for damages. This can increase the pressure on the minor to comply with the contract. Courts in California have enforced such guarantees. *See, e.g.*, Berg v. Traylor, 148 Cal.App.4th 809 (2007); Adams v. Tabor-Smith, 2002 WL 31082390 (Cal. App. Sept. 17, 2002) (unpub.); Raden v. Laurie, 120 Cal.App.2d 778 (1953). In New York, however, a parental guarantee is unenforceable if the minor's contract could have been submitted for court approval. N.Y. Gen. Oblig. Law § 3–107. This gives the party entering a contract with a minor a strong incentive to use the court approval process, with its accompanying protections for the minor.

§ 11.4 WORKING CONDITIONS

In addition to laws addressing disaffirmance and requiring trust accounts, state laws may also address working conditions (including educational requirements) for children working in the entertainment industry. Child entertainers are not protected by the federal Fair Labor Standards Act, and most states exclude child entertainers from their otherwise-applicable child labor laws. However, some states (such as California and New York) have separately enacted rigorous protections for child entertainers. Others, such as Tennessee, provide no protections at all. *See, e.g.,* TN Code § 50–5–107.

INDEX

References are to Pages

ACCRUAL OF CAUSE OF ACTION
Copyright infringement, 133

ADVANCES
Publishing, this index
Recording Contracts, this index

AMERICAN FEDERATION OF MUSICIANS
Generally, 27–29

ANTITRUST
Performing rights organizations. Performance Rights in Musical Works, this index

ARTIFICIAL INTELLIGENCE
Copyright infringement, 104–105
Name, Likeness, and Voice Protections, this index

ASSIGNMENTS
Copyrights, this index
Right of publicity, 261–262
Songwriter agreements with publisher, 147–148, 152–154

ATTORNEY'S FEES
Copyright infringement, award to prevailing party, 134

AUDIO HOME RECORDING ACT
Generally, 127–128

AUDIOVISUAL RECORDINGS
Copyright Law, this index

AUDITS
Royalties, this index

BOOKING AGENTS
Generally, 13–14

BOOTLEGGING
Live performances, federal anti-bootlegging statute, 273–274

BUSINESS ISSUES
Generally, 7–31
Booking agents, 13–14
Choice of entity
Generally, 20–25
Corporations, 21–22
Limited liability companies, 20–22, 280
Loan-outs, 20–23, 280
Sole proprietorships, 22
Corporations, 21–22
Distributors, this index
Independent contractor *vs.* common law employee status, 26–27
Inducement letters, 23–25
Insurance, 30–31
Labor Organizations, this index
Limited liability companies, 20–22, 280
Loan-outs, 20–23, 280
Managers, this index
Musical groups, special considerations, 25–26
Producers, this index
Publishers, 17
Sole proprietorships, 22
Union representation, eligibility for, 26–27

CHILDREN
Minors, Contracts With, this index

COMMON LAW
Perpetual common law copyrights, 65
Trademarks, this index

CONTRACTS AND AGREEMENTS
Generally, 2
Distributors, 19–20
Managers, agreements with. Managers, this index
Minors, this index
Producers and production companies, contracts with, 15–16
Publishing agreements. Publishing, this index

Recording Contracts, this index

CONTRIBUTORY LIABILITY
Copyright infringement. Copyright law, this index

COPYRIGHT LAW
Generally, 33–139
Assignments
Generally, 56–59
Jointly authored works, 56
Licenses compared, 60
Payments, 56
Recordation, 57
Signed writing requirement, 56
Songwriter agreements with publisher, 147–148, 152–154
Termination rights, 71–72
Works made for hire compared, 57–59
Attachment of protection as work is fixed in tangible form, 42
Audio Home Recording Act, 127–128
Audiovisual recordings
Generally, 39–40
Fixation requirement for copyright, 43
Mechanical licenses, 162
Commencement of copyright protection
Generally, 41–43
Audiovisual recordings, 43
Automatic attachment as work is fixed in tangible form, 42
Initial fixation, 43
Computerized tools, use of, 36
Contributory liability. Infringement, below
Copyright Act of 1976, 33
Copyright Claims Board, 134
Creative choices, human creators, and AI, 36
De minimis copying. Infringement, below
Deposit copy, submission of, 46–47
Digital platforms
Generally, 128–132
Digital Millenium Copyright Act
Generally, 129–132
Knowledge requirement, 131–132
Notice and takedown regime, 131–132

Right and ability to control infringing activity, 132
Safe harbor provisions, 130–132
Liability for infringement, 129
Duration of copyright
Generally, 62–71
Foreign works, 69–70
Post-1978 works
Generally, 62–64
Works made for hire, 63
Works not made for hire, 63
Pre-1929 works, 66
Pre-1978 works
Generally, 64–68
Copyrights not yet expired, 66–67
Current status of older works, determining, 64
Perpetual common law copyrights, 65
Public distribution, works not intended for, 65
Renewal option, 67
Special rules, 67–68
When copyright attached, 65–66
Sound recordings, 68–69
Termination rights, below
Works created but not federally copyrighted as of January 1, 1978, 70–71
Exceptions and limitations to exclusive rights of owners
Generally, 111–128
Agricultural fairs, 124
Audio Home Recording Act, 127–128
Digital downloads and resales, first sale, 112–113
Dramatic *vs.* nondramatic musical works, 123
Fair use, below
First sale, below
Jukeboxes, 122
Music streaming, first sale, 112–113
Musical works, limitations specific to
Generally, 122–127
Agricultural fairs, 124
Compulsory mechanical license, 122
Dramatic *vs.* nondramatic musical works, 123
Jukeboxes, 122

Nonprofit public performances, 124
Nonprofit veterans' and fraternal organizations, 124
Public performance rights, 122–123
Public place, transmissions received in, 125–127
Religious services, 123–124
Teaching activities, 123
Vending establishments, 125
Nonprofit public performances, 124
Nonprofit veterans' and fraternal organizations, 124
Orphan works, 121
Public performance rights, 122–123
Public place, transmissions received in, 125–127
Religious services, 123–124
Sound recordings, limitations specific to, 121
Special relevance exception, first sale, 112
Teaching activities, 123
Vending establishments, 125
Exclusive rights of owners
Generally, 82–87
Copies or phonorecords, 85
Derivative works incorporating pre-existing sound recordings, 87
Exceptions and limitations
Generally, 85, 111–128
Exceptions and limitations, above
Fair use, below
First sale, below
Public performance rights
Generally, 83–85
Exceptions and limitations, 122–123
Sound recordings, 83–85
Right to reproduce sound recordings and other works, 86
Soundalike recordings, 86–87, 101
Extraterritorial reach of federal law, none, 111
Fair use
Generally, 113–120
Affirmative defense, 114
Commercial use, 115–116
Creativity of copyrighted work, 117–118
List of factors to be considered, 115

Market for copyrighted work, substitution effect, 119–120
Nature of copyrighted work, 117–118
Parodies, 118
Portion used, amount and substantiality, 117–118
Public interest, categories deemed to serve, 114–115
Purpose and character of use
Generally, 115–117
Commercial use, 115–116
Television commercials, 116
Transformative nature of use, 116–117
Federal statutes
Generally, 33
No extraterritorial reach, 111
Sound recordings, 40–41
First sale
Generally, 112–113
Digital downloads and resales, 112–113
Mechanical licenses, 163
Music streaming, 112–113
Special relevance exception, 112
Fixing of work in tangible form, 37
Foreign law, ownership under, 81
Foreign works
Duration of copyright, 69–70
Termination of rights, 76
Independent contractors. Works made for hire, below
Infringement
Generally, 88–111
Access plus sufficient similarity, 92
Accrual of claim, 133
Artificial intelligence, generative
Generally, 104–105
Abuse, potential for, 105
Licensing agreements, 105
Training and output phases, 104
Attorney's fee award to prevailing party, 134
Contributory liability
Generally, 106–109
Digital platforms, 129
Knowing facilitation or inducement, 107

Second Circuit standard, 106–107
Staple article of commerce doctrine, 107–109
Copying
Generally, 90
Access plus sufficient similarity, 92
Copyrightable expression requirement, 89, 92
De minimis copying, below in this group
Proving, 91–92
Subconscious copying, 99
Unoriginal components or copyrightable expression, 93–96
Copyright Claims Board, 134
Copyrightable expression or unoriginal components, 93–96
Criminal charges for willful infringements, 134
Damages, actual or statutory, 133–134
De minimis copying
Generally, 99–104
Corollary to substantial similarity test, 99
Imitating sound recording, 100–101
Sampling, 100–104
Defined, 88
Delay in bringing suit, 133
Digital Millenium Copyright Act. Digital platforms, above
Direct or indirect, 88
Elements of liability
Generally, 88–98
Copying, above in this group
Strict liability, 88–89
Substantial similarity, below in this group
Expert opinion, 94
Federal jurisdiction, 133
Flea market selling infringing copies, 110
Imitating sound recording, 100–101
Injunctive relief, 133
Knowing facilitation or inducement, 107
Ninth Circuit approach, 98
Online services, vicarious liability, 110
Parallel independent creation, 90
Political campaigns, 137–139
Proceedings and remedies, 133–134
Sampling, 100–103

Second Circuit approach, 98
Secondary liability
Generally, 88, 106–111
Contributory liability, above in this group
Vicarious liability, below in this group
Staple article of commerce doctrine, 107–109
Strict liability, 88–89
Subconscious copying, 99
Substantial similarity of copyrightable expression
Generally, 89, 92
Ninth and Second Circuit approaches, 98
Unoriginal components distinguished, 93–96
Vicarious liability
Generally, 109–111
Digital platforms, 129
Flea market selling infringing copies, 110
Online services, 110
Second Circuit rule, 109
Venue operators, 109–110
Injunctive relief, 133
Jointly authored works
Assignments, 56
Licenses, 61–62
Ownership of copyright, 48–50
Termination rights, 77
Jukeboxes, 122
Length. Duration of copyright, above
Licenses
Generally, 59–62
Artificial intelligence systems, 105
Assignments compared, 60
Exclusive or non-exclusive, 60–62
Implied licenses, 61
Jointly authored works, 61–62
Multiple parties, overlapping non-exclusive licenses, 61
Payment for, 60
Political campaigns, below
Recordation, 61
Revenue, major sources. Publishing, this index
Signed writing, 61

Sound recordings, 59–60
Termination rights, 71–72
Types of licenses, 59–60
Mechanical license, compulsory
See also Mechanical Licenses, this index
Musical works, limitations specific to, 122
Termination rights, 75
Music and sound recordings
Generally, 37–41
See also Performance Rights, this index
Audiovisual recordings, 39–40
Composition and recording as separate works, 37–39
Definition of sound recording, 161–162
Duration of copyright for sound recordings, 68–69
Exceptions and limitations, above
Federal protection of sound recordings, 40–41
Imitating sound recording, 100–101
Licenses for sound recordings, 59–60
Performance Rights, this index
Political campaigns, use in, 135–139
Production libraries, sound recordings created for, 53
Right to reproduce sound recordings and other works, 86
Works made for hire doctrine
Generally, 51–52
Applicability to sound recordings, 53–56
Assignments compared, 57–59
Music videos. Digital platforms, above
Nonprofit public performances, 124
Nonprofit veterans' and fraternal organizations, 124
Notice and registration
Generally, 44–48
Benefits of registration
Generally, 44–47
Monetizing copyright, 45
Prerequisite to suing infringers, 44–45
Prima facie evidence of copyright's validity, 45
Statutory damages, right to recover, 45
Transactions involving copyright, ability to record, 45–46
Deposit copy, submission of, 46–47, 96
Format of copyright notice, 44

Forms for registration, 47
Online completion of registration process, 46
Optional but recommended, 44
Preregistration, 47–48
Novelty distinguished from originality, 35–36
Original works of authorship, 34–35
Originality defined, 35
Orphan works, 121
Ownership of copyright
Generally, 48–50
Author as original owner, 48
Changes in ownership, recording, 47
Creative contributors, 49
Exceptions and limitations, above
Exclusive rights of owners, above
Fair use, above
Foreign law, ownership under, 81
Joint works, 48–50
Production libraries, 52–53
Works made for hire, below
Parodies
Fair use, 118
Market for copyrighted work, effect on, 119–120
Performance rights. Public performance rights, below
Political campaigns, use of music and sound recordings
Generally, 135–139
Ads, use in, 137
Blanket licenses, 136
Infringement, liability for, 137–139
Internet use, 137
License requirement, 135
Public performances, 136
Sound records, use of, 137
Synchronization licenses, 137
Post-1977 grants. Termination rights, below
Post-1978 works. Duration of copyright, above
Pre-1929 works, duration of copyright, 66
Pre-1978 works and grants
Duration of copyright, above
Termination rights, below

Production libraries, 52–53
Protected works, 34–37
Public performance rights
Generally, 83–85
Exceptions and limitations, 122–123
Sound recordings, 83–85
Public place, transmissions received in, 125–127
Recordation of documents
Assignments, 57
Licenses, 61
Registration. Notice and registration, above
Religious services, 123–124
Securing copyright protection, 41–43
Sheet music, submission of, 96
Sound recordings. Music and sound recordings, above
Soundalike recordings, 86–87, 101
Substantial similarity. Infringement, above
Teaching activities, 123
Termination rights
Generally, 71–80
Blanket compulsory mechanical licenses, 75
Deceased authors, rights of surviving family members, 75
Derivative works exception, 73–75
Foreign copyrights, 76
Gap grants, 80
Nonwaivable nature of right, 71–72
Post-1977 grants
Generally, 76
Joint works, 77
Second chance provisions, 77
Surviving family members, rights of, 77
Pre-1978 grants
Generally, 77–79
Effective date of termination, 79
Extended renewal term, 77–78
Second chance rationale, 79
Surviving family members, rights of, 78
Timing, reason for, 77
Right to terminate, 71–72
Second chance, 77, 79

Signed written notice, 76
Statutory provisions, 72
Surviving family members, rights of, 77, 78
Works made for hire, 73
Vending establishments, 125
Vicarious liability. Infringement, above
Websites hosting user-provided content. Digital platforms, above
Works made for hire
Generally, 50–56
Allocation of ownership in contract, 59
Assignments compared, 57–59
Duration of copyright, 63
Independent contractors
Generally, 50–51
Motion pictures or collective works, contributions to, 51
Requirements for work made for hire, 51
Musical works, 51–52
Ownership of copyright, 53
Scope of employment, creation within, 50
Sound recordings, 53–56
Termination rights, 73

CORPORATIONS
Business issues, 21–22

COVER RECORDINGS
Mechanical licenses, 164, 166

CRIMINAL OFFENSES
Copyright infringement, willful, 134

CYBERSQUATTING
Name, likeness, and voice protections, 276–277
Trademarks, unauthorized use, 252–253

DAMAGES
Copyright infringement, actual or statutory damages, 133–134

DIGITAL MILLENIUM COPYRIGHT ACT
Copyright, this index

DIGITAL PLATFORMS
Copyright Law, this index

Streaming Services, this index

DISTRIBUTORS
Generally, 17–20
Contracts, 19–20
Hybrid business model, 19
Independent distributors, 18–19
Major labels, 18
Open platform category, 19

DOMAIN NAMES
Cybersquatting, this index

ELECTRICAL TRANSCRIPTION LICENSES
Revenue source, 145–146

EPHEMERAL RECORDINGS
Performance Rights in Sound Recordings, this index

FAIR USE
Copyright Law, this index

FEDERAL JURISDICTION
Copyright infringement, 133

FIRST AMENDMENT
Name, Likeness, and Voice Protections, this index
Trademarks, this index

FIRST SALE
Copyright Law, this index

FOREIGN COUNTRIES
International subpublishing, 159
Trademarks, this index

FOREIGN LAW
Ownership of copyright, 81

INDEPENDENT CONTRACTORS
Common law employee status compared, 26–27
Copyright law, works made for hire, 50–51

INDUCEMENT LETTERS
Business issues, 23–25

INFRINGEMENT
Copyright, this index
Trademarks, this index

INJUNCTIVE RELIEF
Copyright infringements, 133

INSURANCE
Business issues, 30–31

INTERNET
Campaign ads, use of musical work, 136–137
Digital platforms. Copyright Law, this index
Streaming Music, this index

JOINTLY AUTHORED WORKS
Copyright, this index

JURISDICTION
Copyright infringement, exclusive federal jurisdiction, 133

KEY PERSON
Agreements with managers, keyman clause, 9
Recording contracts, 298–299

LABOR ORGANIZATIONS
Generally, 26–29
American Federation of Musicians, 27–29
Eligibility for union representation, 26–27

LICENSES
Copyright Law, this index
Fractional licensing, 193
Mechanical Licenses, this index
Revenue, major sources. Publishing, this index
Trademarks, licensing and merchandise, 256

LIKENESS
Name, Likeness, and Voice Protections, this index

LIMITED LIABILITY COMPANIES
Business issues, 20–21
Recording contracts, 280

LOAN-OUTS
Business issues, 20–23
Recording contracts, 280

MANAGERS
Generally, 7–13
Agreements with
Generally, 8–9
Handshake deals, 11–12
Keyman clause, 9
Post-term commissions, 11
Review by attorney, 11
Business managers, 12–13
Compensation, 10–11
Handshake deals, 11–12
Personal manager
Business manager compared, 12
Role of, 7–9
Post-term commissions, 11

MASTER RECORDINGS
Mechanical licenses, 162
Recording contracts, ownership of masters, 292–295

MECHANICAL LICENSES
Generally, 161–183
Audiovisual works, 162
Audit rights, Mechanical Licensing Collective, 180
Blanket licenses. Mechanical Licensing Collective, below
Changes in arrangement of licensed work, 167
Code numbers, internationally recognized, 180
Compulsory licenses
Generally, 164–183
Blanket licenses. Mechanical Licensing Collective, below
Congressional intent, 166
Cover recordings, 164, 166
Digital distribution only, 165
Dramatic and nondramatic musical works, 164–165
Mechanical Licensing Collective, below
MMA procedure, 172–173
Physical vs digital formats, 165, 169–173

Procedures, below
Section 115 licenses, 165
Substantive rules, below
Congressional intent, 166
Consent to first sound recording, 163
Copyright Law, this index
Cover recordings, 164, 166
Data usage reports, 179–180
Digital deliveries. Physical formats *vs.* digital deliveries, below
Digital distribution only, 165
Dramatic and nondramatic musical works, 164–165
Historical background, 161
Master recordings, 162
Mechanical Licensing Collective
Generally, 174–183
Administration of, 174
Administrative assessment, 182
Audit rights, 180
Blanket compulsory licenses
Administration of, 174
Collection of fees, 177
Digital music services, 175
Nondramatic musical works, 176
Royalty rates, 176–177
Sound recordings, separate license required, 176
Board of directors, voting and nonvoting members, 181
Code numbers, internationally recognized, 180
Collection of fees, 177
Data usage reports, 179–181
Default by licensee, 182
Digital music services, 175
Dispute resolution mechanism, 180–181
Enforcement actions, 182–183
Fees, determination and collection, 177, 180
Grounds for rejecting notice of license, 175
Musical Works Database, 177–178
Nondramatic musical works, 176
Notice of license, 174–175
Royalty rates, 176–177
Sound recordings, separate license required, 176

Unmatched and unclaimed royalties, 178–179
Voluntary licenses, administration of, 174, 181
Music Modernization Act of 2018, substantive and procedural rules, 167–169, 170–173
Musical Works Database, 177–178
Negotiated licenses, 163
Pass-through licenses, 163
Physical formats *vs.* digital deliveries
Generally, 165
Procedure, 170–173
Substantive rules, 167–168
Primary purpose, licensee's, 167
Procedures
Generally, 169–173
Digital deliveries, 170–173
Physical formats, 169–170, 175–176
Statutory process, bypassing, 170
Revenue source, 143
Royalties, unmatched and unclaimed, 178–179
Royalty rates, 168–169, 176–177
Sound recordings
Defined, 161–162
Separate license required, 176
Spotify strategy for lower payouts, 169
Streaming music, interactive and non-interactive, 162–163, 171
Substantive rules
Generally, 166–169
Changes in arrangement of licensed work, 167
Music Modernization Act of 2018, 167–169
Physical formats *vs.* digital deliveries, 167–168
Primary purpose, licensee's, 167
Royalty rates, 168–169
Termination rights, 75
Voluntary licenses, 163

MERCHANDISE
Trademarks, licensing and merchandise, 256

MINORS, CONTRACTS WITH
Generally, 301–306
Entertainment industry
Court approval of contract, 302–304
Minor's contract with manager or talent agency, 303
Set aside of earnings in trust, 302–305
Lack of capacity to contract, 301
Parental guarantees, 305–306
Right to disaffirm
Generally, 301–302
Limitations on right, 302–305
Working conditions, 306

MORALS CLAUSE
Recording contracts, 299

MUSICAL GROUPS
Business issues, special considerations, 25–26
Jointly authored works. Copyright Law, this index
Names. Trademarks, this index

MUSICAL WORKS DATABASE
Generally, 177–178

NAME, LIKENESS, AND VOICE PROTECTIONS
Generally, 257–277
Actual voice *vs.* vocal imitations, 260
Artificial intelligence
Generally, 258, 269–272
Digital voice replicas, unauthorized use, 270–272
Remedies for statutory violations, 272
Standing to bring suit, 272
Voice manufactured by, 260, 269
Assignments. Licenses and assignments, below
Bootlegging live performances, federal protection, 273–274
Commercial speech, 263–264
Cybersquatting
Names of living individuals, protection of, 276
Unauthorized use of trademark in domain name, 252–253, 276–277
Elvis impersonators, 264–265

First Amendment considerations
Generally, 263–269
Commercial speech, 263
Elvis impersonators, 264–265
News broadcasts, 265–266
Partially commercial speech, 263–264
Statutory exceptions for specific activities, 264
Transformative use test and comparable approaches, 266–269
Licenses and assignments
Generally, 261–262
Assignments to be avoided, 262
Written agreement, recommended contents, 257
Live performances, federal anti-bootlegging statute, 273–274
News broadcasts, First Amendment considerations, 265–266
Partially commercial speech, 263–264
Postmortem rights, privacy and publicity, 260–261
Privacy and publicity, rights of
Generally, 259–261
Actual voice *vs.* vocal imitations, 260
Artificial intelligence, voice manufactured by, 260
Postmortem rights
Generally, 260–261
Limitations, 261
States recognizing or not recognizing, 261
Scope of protection, 259–260
State laws, 241, 259–260
Publicity. Privacy and publicity, rights of, above
Recording contracts, scope and duration of license, 297–298
Stage names, 233, 274–276
Statutory exceptions for specific activities, 264
Trademark and unfair competition laws
Generally, 274–276
See also Trademarks, this index
Multiple theories, suing infringers under, 275
Publicity claims *vs.* false endorsement claims, tests for assessing, 275–276
Scope of protection, 275
Stage names, 233, 274–276
Video games, use of athletes' identities, 275–276
Transformative use test and comparable approaches, 266–269

Unauthorized appropriation, impact of, 257–258
Unfair competition. Trademark and unfair competition laws, above
Video games, use of athletes' identities, 275–276

NOTICE
Copyright Law, this index
Mechanical license, notice of, 174–175
Trademarks, notice of pending registration, 229–230

OWNERSHIP
Copyright Law, this index
Master recordings, 292–295
Trademarks, ownership of band name, 237

PARENT AND CHILD
Contracts with minors, parental guarantees, 305–306

PARODIES
Fair use, 118
Market for copyrighted work, effect on, 119–120
Trademarks, criticism, commentary, or parody, 241–243

PERFORMANCE RIGHTS IN MUSICAL WORKS
Generally, 185–201
See also Performance Rights in Sound Recordings, this index
Allocation of blanket license fees, 193–194
Antitrust consent decree. Performing rights organizations, below
Copyright Law, this index
Dramatic public performances, 186–187
Foreign public performance royalties, 200–201
Fractional licensing, 193
Grand performances, 187–188
Licenses as revenue source, 142–143
Nondramatic public performances
Generally, 188
Royalties, 156–157
Performing rights organizations
Generally, 188–201
Allocation of blanket license fees, 193–194

Antitrust consent decree (ASCAP and BMI)
Generally, 190, 193, 194–200
DOJ, continuing oversight, 198
Organizations not bound by decree, 199–200
Public performance, determining what constitutes, 197–198
Reasonableness of licensing fees, 196–197
State laws, enforceability, 200
Choosing a PRO, 191
Fees charged to blanket licensees, 190, 193–194
Foreign public performance royalties, 200–201
Fractional licensing, 193
Membership, 189
Public database, searchable, 191–192
Remitting fees to songwriters and publishers, 192
Role of, 189–190
Public database, searchable, 191–192
Public performance, what constitutes, 185–186, 197–198
Remitting fees to songwriters and publishers, 192
State laws, enforceability, 200

PERFORMANCE RIGHTS IN SOUND RECORDINGS
Generally, 203–220
De minimis payments, avoiding, 218
Digital audio transmissions, limitation to, 203
Distribution Fund and subfunds, 217–219
Ephemeral recordings
Generally, 219–220
Server copies, 219
Statutory license, 219
Statutory royalties, 219–220
EU Court of Justice ruling, 204
Featured artists choosing to share royalties, 216–217
Interactive streaming licenses
Generally, 211–213
Audit rights, exercise of, 212
Contract negotiations, 212
Exclusive licenses, 211
Interactive streaming service defined, 207
Sharing royalties with artists, 212
Usage data reporting, 212–213

Voluntary negotiation, 211
No general public performance right, 203–204
Noninteractive streaming licenses
Generally, 213–219
De minimis payments, avoiding, 218
Distribution Fund and subfunds, 217–219
Featured artists choosing to share royalties, 216–217
Letters of Direction, shared royalties, 216–217
Qualifying as noninteractive service, 209–210
Radio-style experience, 208–209
Rate-setting proceedings, 213
Searchable public database, 215
SoundExchange
Generally, 214–215
Administrative costs, 216
Collection and distribution of statutory royalties, 215
Distribution Fund and subfunds, 217–219
Letters of Direction, shared royalties, 216–217
Monthly payments by licensees, 215
Searchable public database, maintenance of, 215
Statutory license, use of, 213
Statutory royalties, allocation of, 213–214
Time limit, claims for distribution from Omissions Fund, 219
Unclaimed royalties, 216
SoundExchange. Noninteractive streaming licenses, below
Streaming of sound recordings
Generally, 205–207
Categories of digital audio transmissions, 206
Distinguishing interactive and noninteractive services
Generally, 207–211
Interactive streaming service defined, 207
Noninteractive streaming, radio-style experience, 208–209
Qualifying as noninteractive service, 209–210
Sound recording performance complement, 210
Exempt digital audio transmissions, 206
Interactive streaming licenses, above
Non-exempt digital audio transmissions, interactive and noninteractive services, 206–207
Noninteractive streaming licenses, above
Section 106 license requirements, 205–206

Sound recording performance complement, 210

PERFORMING RIGHTS ORGANIZATIONS
Performance Rights in Musical Works, this index

PRIVACY RIGHTS
Name, Likeness, and Voice Protections, this index

PRODUCERS
Generally, 14–17
Beat makers, 16–17, 101–102
Contracts with, 15–16
Upfront fee and royalties, 15–16

PUBLIC PERFORMANCES
Performance Rights, this index

PUBLICITY, RIGHT OF
Name, Likeness, and Voice Protections, this index

PUBLISHING
Generally, 17, 141–160
Advances
Publisher, advances received from licensees, 154
Recoupable against future royalties, 149, 155–156
Agreements with publishers
Generally, 147–149, 152–159
Attorney, review by, 152
Compensation. Royalties, below
Grant of copyright, 152–154
Key provisions, 152
Reversionary rights, 153–154
Term of agreement, 153
Assignment of copyright to publisher, 147–148, 152–154
Audits of royalties, 155
Co-publishing arrangements, 148–149, 151
Compensation. Royalties, below
Cross-collateralization, 156
Defined, 141
Electrical transcription licenses as revenue source, 145–146
Exploitation rights, restrictions on, 159
Full service publishers, 147–149

Independent publishers, 147
International subpublishing, 159
Licensing revenue, major sources
Generally, 142–146
Electrical transcription licenses, 145–146
Mechanical licenses, 143
Other sources, 146
Public performance licenses, 142–143
Synchronization licenses, 144–145
Major music publishers, 147–149
Mechanical licenses as revenue source, 143
Nondramatic public performance royalties, 156–157
Print publication royalties, 157–158
Public performance licenses as revenue source, 142–143
Revenue. Licensing revenue, major sources, above
Reversionary rights, 153–154
Revisions to work, publisher's right, 158
Royalties
Generally, 154–158
Advances recoupable against future royalties, 149, 155–156
Agreements, recommended provisions, 155–156
Audits, 155
Co-publishing arrangements, 148–149, 151
Cross-collateralization, 156
Nondramatic public performance royalties, 156–157
Nonrefundable, 155
Other royalties, 158
Print publication royalties, 157–158
Self-publishing songwriters, 151
Self-publishing
Generally, 149–152
Advantages and disadvantages, 149
Payment of royalties, 151
Publishing administrators, 149–150
Separate publishing entity, establishing, 150–151
Songwriter agreements. Agreements with publishers, above
Songwriter's options
Self-publishing, above
Traditional publishers, 146–149
Synchronization licenses as revenue source, 144–145

RECORDATION OF DOCUMENTS
Copyright assignments and licenses, 57, 61

RECORDING CONTRACTS
Generally, 279–300
360 deals, 291–292
Accounting and audits, 296–297
Advances
Generally, 283–285
Cross-collateralization, 284
Future royalties, recoupable against, 283
Recoupable costs and fees, 284–285
Size of advance as negotiable, 284
Artist commitment and creative control
Generally, 282–283
Decision not to release recording, rights of parties, 282, 294–295
Delivery requirements, 282
Promotional activities, 283
Qualitative criteria for masters, 282
Touring obligation, 283
Bankruptcy, label filing for, 300
Breach of contract, 299–300
Buying masters back from label, 293
Compensation of artist
Generally, 283–290
Advances, above
Royalties, below
Controlled composition clauses, 290–291
Costs and fees, recoupable, 284–285
Creative control. Artist commitment and creative control, above
Cross-collateralization, 284
Curing breach of contract, 299
Decision not to release recording, rights of parties, 282, 294–295
Delivery requirements for albums
Generally, 281, 282
Failure to deliver, 299–300
Dropping artist from label, 300
Exclusivity requirement, 281

Individual band members, applicability of exclusivity requirement, 281
Key person clause, 298–299
Loanout or LLC, use of, 280
Main concerns, 279
Master use licenses, royalties, 289
Masters, ownership of
Generally, 292–295
Buying back from label, 293
Failure to release recording, 294–295
Regaining copyright by exercising termination rights, 294
Works made for hire, 293
Masters, qualitative criteria, 282
Morals clause, 299
Multi-rights arrangements, 292
Name and likeness, scope and duration of license, 297–298
Negotiating, 279–280
Non-release of recording, rights of parties, 282, 294–295
Promotional activities, 283
Qualitative criteria for masters, 282
Record sales. Royalties, below
Renewal options
Generally, 280–281
Declining to pick up, 300
Re-recording prohibitions, 295–296
Royalties
Generally, 286–290
Information sharing, 286
Master use licenses, 289
Multiple revenue streams, 286–287
Record sales
Generally, 287–288
Free goods, 288
Net sales, 288
Revenue streams included, 287
Royalty rate, 287–288
Royalty base, 286
Royalty rate, 286
Streaming, 288–289
Tour support, 289–290

Streaming, royalty rates, 288–289
Term of contract, 280–281
Termination of contract, 299–300
Tour support, 289–290
Touring obligation, 283
Works made for hire, ownership of masters, 293

REVISIONS
Publisher's right to revise work, 158

ROYALTIES
Advances recoupable against future royalties, 149, 155–156, 283–285
Assignments, payment for, 56
Audits
Generally, 155
Interactive streaming licenses, 212
Mechanical Licensing Collective, 180
Publisher's records, 155
Recording contracts, 296–297
Blanket mechanical licenses, 176–177
Foreign public performance royalties, 200–201
Licenses, payment for, 60
Music Modernization Act of 2018, 168–169
Nondramatic public performance royalties, 156–157
Other royalties, 158
Performance Rights in Sound Recordings, this index
Print publication royalties, 157–158
Producers, upfront fee and royalties, 15–16
Publishing, this index
Recording Contracts, this index
Self-publishing songwriters, 151
Songwriter agreements. Publishing, this index
Unmatched and unclaimed, 178–179, 216

SOUNDEXCHANGE
Ephemeral recordings, collection and distribution of statutory royalties, 219–220
Noninteractive streaming licenses. Performance Rights in Sound Recordings, this index

STAGE NAMES
Trademarks, 233, 274–276

STREAMING SERVICES
First sale, 112–113
Mechanical licenses, 162–163, 170–173
Sound recordings. Performance Rights in Sound Recordings, this index

SYNCHRONIZATION LICENSES
Political campaigns, use of music and sound recordings, 137
Revenue source, 144–145

TRADEMARKS
  Generally, 221–256
Common law protection
    Generally, 226–228
  Elements of creative works, 226–227
  Infringement claims, 227–228, 239
  Territorial scope, 227
Copyright and trademark, protection by both, 224
Creative works, claims against
    Generally, 241–252
  Criticism, commentary, or parody, 241–243
  Defenses, 244–245
  Dilution claims, 242–244
  False designation of origin, 244
  First Amendment protection
      Generally, 248–252
    Artist-friendly alternative tests, 251–252
    Content of creative works, 250–251
    Criticism, commentary, or parody, 241–243
    Infringer's own goods, use of trademark as source indicator, 248
    Most restrictive approach, 251
    Rogers test, 248–251
    Titles of creative works, 248–249
  Infringer's own goods, use of trademark as source indicator, 248

No likelihood of confusion
Generally, 245–247
Factors considered, 245
Music distinguished from movies and television shows, 247
Trademark used too prominently or pervasively, 246–247
Prominent or pervasive use of trademark, 246–247
Titles of creative works, 248–249
Cybersquatting, unauthorized use of domain name
Generally, 252–253, 276–277
Arbitration as alternative remedy, 253
Bad faith intent to profit, factors to consider, 252–253
Defined, 222–226
Dilution. Infringement and dilution claims, below
Domain names. Cybersquatting, above
Element of larger creative work, 224
Establishing trademark rights
Generally, 226–238
Common law protection, above
Federal registration, below
Foreign countries, protection in, below
Federal registration
Generally, 228–234
Advantages of registering, 228
Applications
Generally, 229–230
Intent to use application, 231
Opposition, 230–231
Eligibility for principal register, 230
Intent to use application, 231
Legal requirements, 230
Name or likeness of living person, consent requirement, 230
Notice of pending registration, 229–230
Opposition to application, 230–231
Rebuttable presumption of validity, 231
Registration bars, 230
Two or more using similar trademarks, 231–233
First Amendment protection. Creative works, claims against, above

Foreign countries, protection in
Generally, 234–236
Differences with U.S. registration, 234–235
Infringement in another country, 235–236
Lanham Act, inapplicability to overseas conduct, 235–236
Infringement and dilution claims
Generally, 239–241
Common law marks, 227
Dilution claims, 240, 242–244
Likelihood of confusion
Appreciable number of ordinarily prudent consumers, 240
Common law marks, 227–228, 239
Factors considered, 225–226, 239
Lanham Act
Generally, 221
False designation provisions, 244
Infringing conduct overseas, inapplicability, 235–236
Licensing and merchandise, 256
Likelihood of confusion
Creative works, claims against, above
Infringement and dilution claims, above
Merchandise, 256
Name or likeness of living person, consent requirement, 230
Names of musical groups
Generally, 236–238
Boy bands, 238
Change in membership, 236–237
Contracts or absence of, 237–238
Ownership of name in band as whole, 237
Unauthorized use of band's name. Truth in Music Act, below
Principal register, 228, 230
Qualifying as trademark, 223–224
Registration. Federal registration, above
Secondary meaning, 224, 227
Selecting name, 221, 233–234
Source identifier, 222–223
Stage names, 233, 274–276
Stage persona, 225

Truth in music laws
Generally, 254–256
Exceptions to statutory prohibition, 255–256
False or misleading association, 255
No private right of action, 256
Unauthorized use
Creative works, claims against, above
Cybersquatting, above
Infringement and dilution claims, above
What is a trademark, 222–226

TRUST ACCOUNTS
Earnings of minor, 302–305

TRUTH IN MUSIC LAWS
Trademarks, this index

UNIONS
Labor Organizations, this index

VIDEO GAMES
Use of athletes' identities, 275–276

VOICE
Name, Likeness, and Voice Protections, this index

WORKING CONDITIONS
Minors, contracts with, 306

WORKS MADE FOR HIRE
Copyright Law, this index
Recording contracts, 293